District Gazetteers of India Series 83

CENTRAL PROVINCES DISTRICT GAZETTEERS

SAUGOR

(DESCRIPTIVE)

District Gazetteers of India Series 83

CENTRAL PROVINCES DISTRICT GAZETTEERS

SAUGOR

(DESCRIPTIVE)

R. V. RUSSELL

30 Volumes (In 33 Bindings)

(20th, Vol. A)

GYAN

Published by

Gyan Publishing House
5, Ansari Road
Daryaganj, New Delhi-110002
Phone: 011-47034999, 9811692060
E-mail: books@gyanbooks.com

Distribution Network
gyanbooks.com
India, USA, Canada, UK, Australia, France

ISBN: 978-93-6208-539-9 (Set) 30 Volumes (In 33 Bindings)
978-93-6208-026-4 (PB)

First Published, 1905

2nd Impression 2024

Printed at: Gyan Press, Delhi.

CENTRAL PROVINCES DISTRICT GAZETTEERS (20th, Vol. A)
Author: R. V. RUSSELL

LIST OF VOLUMES

S. NO.	ISBN NO.	VOLUME	TITLE	AUTHOR	PRICE	PAGES
			ASSAM DISTRICT GAZETTEERS			
1	9788121285926	1st	Cachar	B. C. Allen	600	300
2	9788121285919	2nd	Sylhet	B. C. Allen	750	378
3	9788121285902	3rd	Goalpara	B. C. Allen	400	203
4	9788121285896	4th	Kamrup	B. C. Allen	675	344
5	9788121285889	5th	Darrang	B. C. Allen	725	364
6	9788121285872	6th	Nowgong	B. C. Allen	560	280
7	9788121285865	7th	Sibsagar	B. C. Allen	675	343
8	9788121285858	8th	Lakhimpur	B. C. Allen	690	347
9	9788121285841	9th	Naga Hills and Manipur	B. C. Allen	580	294
10	9788121285834	10th	The Khasi And Jaintia Hills, The Garo Hills And The Lushai Hills	B. C. Allen	675	363
11	9788121285827	11th	The Sadiya and Balipara Frontier Tract	B. C. Allen	375	190
			BENGAL DISTRICT GAZETTEERS			
12	9788121218672	1st	Angul	L. S. S. O'Malley	340	168
13	9788121259637	2nd	Bakarganj	J. C. JACK	970	194
14	9788121218696	3rd	Balasore	L. S. S. O'Malley	450	228
15	9788121259590	4th	Bankura	L. S. S. O'Malley	1000	199
16	9788121218375	5th	Bhagalpur	J. Byrne	390	194
17	9788121218290	6th	Birbhum	L. S. S. O'Malley	300	150
18	9788121259651	7th	Eastern Bengal and Assam - Bogra	J. N. Gupta	940	188
19	9788121218351	8th	Burdwan	J. C. K. Peterson	450	227
20	9788121259538	9th	Calcutta District Gazetteer - Statistics, 1901 - 02		340	68
21	9788121218313	10th	Champaran	L. S. S. O'Malley	410	205
22	9788121259613	11th	Eastern Bengal District Gazetters - Chittagong	L. S. S. O'Malley	1080	216
23	9788121259552	12th	Chota Nagpur Tributary		130	26
24	9788121259415	13th	The Cooch Behar Gazette: Statistics		1460	292
25	9788121218412	14th	Cuttack	L. S. S. O'Malley	490	248
26	9788121261357	15th	Eastern Bengal District Gazetteers Dacca	B. C. Allen	400	207
27	9788121218436	16th	Darbhanga	L. S. S. O'Malley	360	180
28	9789362089335	17th	Darjeeling	L. S. S. O'Malley	500	248
29	9788121259453	18th	Eastern Bengal District Gazetteers - Dinajpur	F. W. Strong	890	178
30	9788121259392	19th	Faridpur	L. S. S. O'Malley	700	140
31	9788121218474	20th	Gaya	L. S. S. O'Malley	540	270
32	9788121214032	21st	Bihar and Orissa District Gazetteer: Hazaribagh	E. Lister	715	234
33	9788121218337	22nd	Hooghly	L. S. S. O'Malley	680	340
34	9788121218191	23rd	Bengal District Gazetteer Howrah	L. S. S. O'Malley	390	199
35	9788121259293	24th	Eastern Bengal and Assam - Jalpaiguri	John F. Gruning	890	178
36	9788121259279	25th	Jessore	L. S. S. O'Malley	960	192
37	9788121259231	26th	Khulna	L. S. S. O'Malley	1100	220
38	9788121259217	27th	Malda	G. E. Lambourn	670	134
39	9788121267854	28th	Manbhum	H. Coupland	600	313
40	9788121218498	29th	Midnapore	L. S. S. O'Malley	500	252
41	9788121218597	30th	Monghyr	L. S. S. O'Malley	560	280
42	9788121259156	31st	Murshidabad	L. S. S. O'Malley	1250	250
43	9788121259576	32nd	Bengal District Gazetteers - Muzaffarpur	L. S. S. O'Malley	940	188
44	9788121259132	33rd	Mymensingh	F. A. Sachse	960	192
45	9788121259118	34th	Nadia	J. H. E. Garrett	1070	214
46	9788121259095	35th	Eastern Bengal and Assam - Noakhali	J. E. Webster	580	115
47	9788121218450	36th	Feudatory States of Orissa	L. E. B. Cobdenramsay	790	395
48	9788121259071	37th	Pabna	L. S. S. O'Malley	710	142
49	9788121218511	38th	Palamau	L. S. S. O'Malley	380	190
50	9788121218634	39th	Patna	L. S. S. O'Malley	500	250
51	9788121218535	40th	Puri	L. S. S. O'Malley	650	328
52	9788121218757	41st	Purnea	L. S. S. O'Malley	440	220
53	9788121258937	42nd	Rajshahi	L. S. S. O'Malley	1080	216
54	9788121256681	43rd	Bihar and Orissa District Gazetteers: Ranchi	M. G. Hallett	1350	278
55	9788121258913	44th	Eastern Bengal and assam - Rangpur	J. A. Vas	890	178
56	9788121218559	45th	Sambalpur	L. S. S. O'Malley	480	242
57	9788121214056	46th	Santal Parganas	L. S. S. O'Malley	940	308
58	9788121218610	47th	Saran	L. S. S. O'Malley	380	190
59	9788121218658	48th	Shahabad	L. S. S. O'Malley	380	190
60	9788121256704	49th	The Gazetteer of Sikhim	H. H. Risley	960	481
61	9788121218573	50th	Singhbhum, Saraikela And Kharsawan	L. S. S. O'Malley	560	280
62	9788121259439	51st	Eastern Bengal District Gazetteers - Tippera	J. E. Webster	730	146
63	9788121259033	52nd	24 Parganas	L. S. S. O'Malley	1420	284

S. NO.	ISBN NO.	VOLUME	TITLE	AUTHOR	PRICE	PAGES
			CENTRAL PROVINCES DISTRICT GAZETTEERS			
64	9789362081728	1st, Vol. A	Akola (Descriptive)	A. E. Nelson, C. Brown	870	436
65	9789362085481	2nd, Vol. A	Amraoti (Descriptive)	S. V. Fitzgerald, A. E. Nelson	1050	524
66	9789362089267	3rd,Vol. A	Balaghat (Descriptive)	R. V. RUSSELL	430	216
67	9789362083494	4th, Vol. A	Betul (Descriptive)	R. V. RUSSELL	610	306
68	9789362085146	5th, Vol. A	Bhandara (Descriptive)	R. V. RUSSELL	580	292
69	9789362088390	6th, Vol. A	Bilaspur (Descriptive)	R. V. RUSSELL	870	434
70	9789362086044	7th, Vol. A	Buldana (Descriptive)	A. E. Nelson	1090	543
71	9789362089014	8th, Vol. B	Chanda (Descriptive)	R. V. RUSSELL	470	234
72	9789362086938	9th	Chhattisgarch Feudatory State	E. A. De Brett	880	440
73	9789362082961	10th	Chhindwara (Descriptive)	R. V. RUSSELL	550	274
74	9789362089342	11th, Vol. A & B	Damoh (Descriptive and Statistical Tables 1891-1901)	R. V. RUSSELL	830	414
75	9789362081230	12th, Vol. A	Durg (Descriptive)	A. E. Nelson	460	232
76	9789362086037	13th, Vol. A	Hoshangabad (Descriptive)	R. V. RUSSELL	860	430
77	9789362086792	14th, Vol. A	Jubbulpore (Descriptive)	A. E. Nelson	950	474
78	9789362089663	15th, Vol. A & B	Mandla (Descriptive and Statistical Tables 1891-1901)	R. V. RUSSELL	370	186
79	9789362086419	16th, Vol. A	Nagpur (Descriptive)	R. V. RUSSELL	790	394
80	9789362080646	17th, Vol. A	Narsinghpur (Descriptive)	R. V. RUSSELL	510	257
81	9789362084835	18th, Vol. A	Nimar (Descriptive)	R. V. RUSSELL	600	299
82	9789362087737	19th, Vol. A	Raipur (Descriptive)	A. E. Nelson	790	396
83	9789362080264	20th, Vol. A	Saugor (Descriptive)	R. V. RUSSELL	570	285
84	9789362081117	21st, Vol. A	Seoni (Descriptive)	R. V. RUSSELL	460	232
85	9789362084965	22nd, Vol. A	Wardha (Descriptive)	R. V. RUSSELL	600	302
86	9789362083401	23rd, Vol. A	Yeotmal (Descriptive)	R. V. RUSSELL	550	277
87	9789362080325	24th, Vol. I, Pt. I	Gwalior (Text and Tables)	R. V. RUSSELL	980	489
88	9789362087133	24th, Vol. I, Pt. II	Gwalior (Maps)	R. V. RUSSELL	400	198
89	9789362086341	24th, Vol. I, Pt. III	Gwalior (Village List)	R. V. RUSSELL	810	406
90	9789362085467	24th, Vol. I, Pt. IV	Gwalior (Photos)	R. V. RUSSELL	1400	698
91	9789362087393	25th, Vol. II	Indore (Text and Tables)	C. E. Luard	1050	524
92	9789362084422	26th, Vol. III	Bhopal (Text and Tables)	C. E. Luard	540	272
93	9789362086815	27th, Vol. IV	Rewah (Text and Tables)	C. E. Luard	500	250
94	9789362087584	28th, Vol. V, Pt. A	Western States - Malwa (Text)	C. E. Luard	1520	762
95	9789362087300	29th, Vol. VI, Pt. A	Eastern States - Bundelkhand (Text)	C. E. Luard	930	463
96	9789362082169	30th, Vol. VI, Pt. B	Eastern States - Bundelkhand (Tables)	C. E. Luard	830	417
			GAZETTEER OF THE BOMBAY PRESIDENCY:			
97	9788121283441	1st, Part I	History of Gujarat	Ed.: James M. Campbell	3220	644
98	9788121285582	1st, Part II	History of the Konkan Dakhan and Southern Maratha Country	Ed.: James M. Campbell	4200	840
99	9788121285568	2nd	Gujarat, Surat and Broach	Ed.: James M. Campbell	2990	598
100	9788121285544	3rd	Kaira and Panch Mahals	Ed.: James M. Campbell	1690	339
101	9788121285520	4th	Ahmedabad	Ed.: James M. Campbell	1860	372
102	9788121285506	5th	Cutch, Palanpur, and Mahi Kantha	Ed.: James M. Campbell	2390	478
103	9788121285483	6th	Rewa Kantha, Narukot, Cambay, and Surat States	Ed.: James M. Campbell	1450	290
104	9788121285469	7th	Baroda	Ed.: James M. Campbell	3260	652
105	9788121285445	8th	Kathiawar	Ed.: James M. Campbell	3790	758
106	9788121285421	9th, Part I	Gujarat Population - Hindus	Ed.: James M. Campbell	3170	636
107	9788121285407	9th, Part II	Gujarat Population - Musalmans and Parsis	Ed.: James M. Campbell	1520	304
108	9788121285384	10th	Ratnagiri and Savantvadi	Ed.: James M. Campbell	2500	501
109	9788121285360	11th	Kolaba and Janjira	Ed.: James M. Campbell	2550	513
110	9788121285346	12th	Khandesh	Ed.: James M. Campbell	3190	638
111	9788121285322	13th Part I	Thana	Ed.: James M. Campbell	2050	413
112	9788121285308	13th Part II	Thana	Ed.: James M. Campbell	1770	357
113	9788121285285	14th	Thana - Places of Interest	Ed.: James M. Campbell	3290	659
114	9788121285261	15th Part I	Kanara	Ed.: James M. Campbell	2340	348
115	9788121285247	15th Part II	Kanara	Ed.: James M. Campbell	1740	348
116	9788121285223	16th	Nasik	Ed.: James M. Campbell	3490	698
117	9788121285209	17th	Ahmadnagar	Ed.: James M. Campbell	3860	772
118	9788121285186	18th Part I	Poona	Ed.: James M. Campbell	2930	586
119	9788121285162	18th Part II	Poona	Ed.: James M. Campbell	2680	537
120	9788121285148	18th Part III	Poona	Ed.: James M. Campbell	2500	503
121	9788121285124	19th	Satara	Ed.: James M. Campbell	3450	692
122	9788121285100	20th	Sholapur	Ed.: James M. Campbell	2730	547
123	9788121285087	21st	Gazetteer of the Bomaby Presidency: Belgaum	Ed.: James M. Campbell	2570	514
124	9788121285063	22nd	Dharwar	Ed.: James M. Campbell	4200	841
125	9788121285049	23rd	Gazetteer of the Bombay Presidency:Bijapur	Ed.: James M. Campbell	3550	712
126	9788121285025	24th	Kolhapur	Ed.: James M. Campbell	2250	450

S. NO.	ISBN NO.	VOLUME	TITLE	AUTHOR	PRICE	PAGES
127	9788121285001	25th	Botany	Ed.: James M. Campbell	2040	408
128	9788121284981	26th, Part I	Materials Towards a Statistical Account of the Town and Island of Bombay - History	Ed.: James M. Campbell	2500	504
129	9788121284967	26th, Part II	Materials Towards a Statistical Account of the Town and Island of Bombay - Trade and Fortifications	Ed.: James M. Campbell	2690	538
130	9788121284943	26th, Part III	Materials Towards a Statistical Account of the Town And Island of Bombay - Administration	Ed.: James M. Campbell	2450	702
131	9788121284929	27th	General Index	Ed.:R. E. Enthoven	2190	428
			MADRAS DISTRICT GAZETTEERS			
132	9788121258814	1st	Anantapur	W. Francis	1140	227
133	9788121258555	2nd	Malabar	C. A Innes & F. B Evans	3010	602
134	9788121258791	3rd	Bellary	W. Francis	1890	377
135	9788121258777	4th	Statistical Appendix For Chingleput		280	56
136	9788121258753	5th	Coimbatore	K. N. Krishnaswami Ayyar	3420	628
137	9788121232814	6th	Madras District Gazetteers District Gazetteer Cuddapah	C. F. Brackenbury	1120	285
138	9788121258715	7th	Statistical Appendix For Ganjam		370	73
139	9788121256766	8th, Vol. 1st	Godavari District Gazetteer	F. R. Hemingway	650	320
140	9788121256803	8th, Vol. 2nd	Godavari District Gazetteer	F. R. Hemingway	160	83
141	9788121258678	9th	Statistical Appendix For Kistna		640	127
142	9788121258654	10th	Statistical Appendix For Kurnool		270	54
143	9788121258616	11th	Madura	W. Francis	1900	379
144	9788121258579	12th	Statistical Appendix For Madura		740	148
145	9788121258630	13th	The Nilgiris	W. Francis	2190	437
146	9788121234276	14th	Madras District Gazetteers Gazetteer Of The Nellore District Brought Upto 1938		1150	386
147	9788121258517	15th	North Arcot		590	118
148	9788121258494	16th, Vol. 1, Part I	Salem	F. J. Richards	1710	343
149	9788121258593	16th, Vol. 1, Part II	Salem	F. J. Richards	1800	360
150	9788121258456	17th	South Arcot	W. Francis	2400	480
151	9788121258470	18th	Statistical Appendix For South Canara		400	80
152	9788121258432	19th, Vol. 1st & 2nd	Tanjore: Main Volume and Statistical Appendix		2070	401
153	9788121258395	20th	Tinnevelly	H. R. Pate	2740	547
154	9788121258418	21st	Statistical Appendix For Tinnevelly		320	64
155	9788121258371	22nd, 1st & 2nd	Trichinopoly: Main Volume and Statistical Appendix	F. R. Hemingway	2440	487
156	9788121241953	23rd	Vizagapatam District Gazetteer	W. Francis	760	385
			PUNJAB DISTRICT GAZETTEERS			
157	9788121255943	1st	Ambala District 1883-84		620	124
158	9788121255967	2nd	Amritsar		1180	236
159	9788121255981	3rd	Delhi		1300	260
160	9788121256001	4th	Ferozepore		950	188
161	9788121256025	5th	Faridkot		350	70
162	9788121256049	6th	Gujranwala 1893-94		1270	254
163	9788121256063	7th	Gujrat	C. E. Luard	1140	228
164	9788121256087	8th	Gurdaspur 1891-92		1260	252
165	9788121256100	9th	Gurgaon 1883-4		1020	203
166	9788121256124	10th	Hazara	H. D. Watson	2290	458
167	9788121256148	11th	Hissar district and Lohar State		1840	367
168	9788121256162	12th	Hoshiarpur		1420	283
169	9788121256186	13th	Jhang		1070	213
170	9788121256209	14th	Jhelam		1010	202
171	9788121256223	15th	Jalandhar District 1883-84		540	108
172	9788121256247	16th, Vol. XIV-A	Jullundur District, with maps and Kapurthala		1990	398
173	9788121256261	17th, Pt. I	Kangra (Proper)		1450	290
174	9788121256285	17th, Pt. II	Kangra (Kulu, Lahual, Spiti)		1800	357
175	9788121256308	18th	Karnal		1930	386
176	9788121256322	19th	Kohat		1540	307
177	9788121256346	20th	The Lahore District 1883-84		1220	244
178	9788121256384	21st	Ludhiana and Maler Kotla		1680	335
179	9788121256407	22nd	Lyallpur		735	147
180	9788121256421	23rd	Mianwali		1170	234
181	9788121256445	24th	Montgomery	P. J. Fagan	1590	318
182	9788121258364	25th	Multan (1901-02)	E. D. Maclagan	2400	480
183	9788121258708	26th	The Rohtak District 1883-84		980	196
184	9788121258746	27th, Vol. III A	Dujana State 1904		500	16
185	9788121256483	28th	Shahpur District		1780	356
186	9788121256506	29th	Simla District		800	159

S. NO.	ISBN NO.	VOLUME	TITLE	AUTHOR	PRICE	PAGES
187	9788121256520	30th	The Chamba State		2040	408
188	9788121256544	31st	The Chenab Colony 1904		1550	310
189	9788121256568	32nd	Kalsia State		270	53
190	9788121256582	33rd	Suket and Mandi		770	154
191	9788121256605	34th	Phulkian States, Patiala Jind And Nabha 1904		2070	414
192	9788121256643	35th	Simla Hill States		2220	443
193	9788121256667	36th	Sirmur		920	183
			RAJPUTANA DISTRICT GAZETTEERS			
194	9789362088994	1st, Vol. I-A & B	Ajmer-merwara (Text and Statistics Tables)	C. C. Watson	1230	246
195	9789362080882	2nd. Vol. II-A & B	Mewar Residency (Text and Statistics Tables)	K.D. Erskine	1700	339
196	9789362088444	3rd, Vol. III-A & B	The Western Rajputana States Residency And The Bikaner Agency	K.D. Erskine	3590	718
			UNITED PROVINCES OF AGRA AND OUDH DISTRICT GAZETTEERS			
197	9789362087560	Vol. I	Agra	H. R. Nevill	2260	452
198	9789362082466	Vol. II	Aligarh	H. R. Nevill	1300	260
199	9789362089779	Vol. III	Allahabad	H. R. Nevill	2050	409
200	9789362081346	Vol. IV	Almora	H. G. Walton	1670	333
201	9789362085658	Vol. V	Azamgarh	D. L. Drake Brockman	1750	349
202	9789362080547	Vol. VI	Bahraich	H. R. Nevill	1410	281
203	9789362085214	Vol. VII	Ballia	H. R. Nevill	1750	350
204	9789362084668	Vol. VIII	Banda	D. L. Drake Brockman	1750	349
205	9789362086518	Vol. IX	Bara Banki	H. R. Nevill	1720	344
206	9789362084101	Vol. X	Bareilly	H. R. Nevill	1640	327
207	9789362086631	Vol. XI	Basti	H. R. Nevill	1610	321
208	9789362083814	Vol. XII	Benares	H. R. Nevill	2290	458
209	9789362086105	Vol. XIII	Bijnor	H. R. Nevill	1820	363
210	9789362081674	Vol. XIV	Budaun	H. R. Nevill	1890	378
211	9789362086891	Vol. XV	Bulandshahr	H. R. Nevill	2100	419
212	9789362081520	Vol. XVI	Cawnpore	H. R. Nevill	2210	442
213	9789362088031	Vol. XVII	Dehra Dun	H. G. Walton	1710	342
214	9789362088710	Vol. XVIII	Etah	E. R. Neave	1600	320
215	9789362082992	Vol. XIX	Etawah	D. L. Drake Brockman	1390	277
216	9789362082220	Vol. XX	Farrukhabad	E. R. Neave	1620	324
217	9789362083869	Vol. XXI	Fatehpur	H. R. Nevill	1890	377
218	9789362085962	Vol. XXII	Fyzabad	H. R. Nevill	1700	339
219	9789362087997	Vol. XXIII	Garhwal	H. G. Walton	1270	254
220	9789362089892	Vol. XXIV	Ghazipur	H. R. Nevill	1600	320
221	9789362085436	Vol. XXV	Gonda	H. R. Nevill	1650	330
222	9789362080271	Vol. XXVI	Gorakhpur	H. R. Nevill	1890	378
223	9789362086129	Vol. XXVII	Hamirpur	D. L. Drake Brockman	1390	277
224	9789362087638	Vol. XXVIII	Hardoi	H. R. Nevill	1680	336
225	9789362081636	Vol. XXIX	Jalaun	D. L. Drake Brockman	1180	236
226	9789362084309	Vol. XXX	Jaunpur	H. R. Nevill	1750	350
227	9789362084187	Vol. XXXI	Jhansi	D. L. Drake Brockman	1960	391
228	9789362089168	Vol. XXXII	Kheri	H. R. Nevill	1650	330
229	9789362086778	Vol. XXXIII	Lucknow	H. R. Nevill	1760	352
230	9789362088635	Vol. XXXIV	Mainpuri	H. R. Nevill	1740	348
231	9789362080424	Vol. XXXV	Meerut	H. R. Nevill	2170	434
232	9789362081087	Vol. XXXVI	Mirzapur	D. L. Drake Brockman	2430	486
233	9789362085443	Vol. XXXVII	Moradabad	H. R. Nevill	1900	380
234	9789362082763	Vol. XXXVIII	Muttra	D. L. Drake Brockman	2140	428
235	9789362089915	Vol. XXXIX	Muzaffarnagar	H. R. Nevill	2260	451
236	9789362086143	Vol. XL	Naini Tal	H. R. Nevill	1890	377
237	9789362086761	Vol. XLI	Partabgarh	H. R. Nevill	1560	312
238	9789362081124	Vol. XLII	Pilibhit	H. R. Nevill	1570	314
239	9789362084453	Vol. XLIII	Rai Bareli	H. R. Nevill	1610	322
240	9789362088284	Vol. XLIV	Rampur	H. R. Nevill	1170	234
241	9789362083654	Vol. XLV	Saharanpur	H. R. Nevill	2190	438
242	9789362083142	Vol. XLVI	Shahjahanpur	H. R. Nevill	1510	302
243	9789362083623	Vol. XLVII	Sitapur	H. R. Nevill	1590	317
244	9789362089939	Vol. XLVIII	Sultanpur	H. R. Nevill	1330	266
245	9789362080851	Vol. XLIX	Unnao	H. R. Nevill	1530	305

CENTRAL PROVINCES DISTRICT GAZETTEERS

SAUGOR

DESCRIPTIVE

R. V. RUSSELL

1905

PREFATORY NOTE.

The extant Settlement Reports on the Saugor District are those of Colonel Maclean (1867) and Mr. De Brett (1902). The chapters on Agriculture and Land Revenue Administration in the District Gazetteer consist largely of extracts from Mr. De Brett's report. Mr. Cleveland's tahsīl report on the Saugor tahsil also contains some useful information. Some good notes on departmental and other subjects were furnished by Mr. A. K. Smith. The chapter on Forests is mainly reproduced from a note by Mr. C. Somers Smith, Deputy Conservator. The present writer is much indebted to Major Sutherland, I. M. S., who placed at his disposal a number of manuscript notes on various subjects, principally medical and social, which he had collected with a view to publishing an account of the District himself; on hearing that the District Gazetteer was to be written he gave up his intention and kindly made over his notes to the Gazetteer Superintendent. Major Sutherland has also composed a monograph on certain customs of the people of the Saugor District for the purposes of the Ethnographic Survey, selections from which have been included in the Gazetteer. His contributions are as far as possible acknowledged in the text. The writer is also indebted to Bābu Kāli Prasanna Mukerjī, pleader of Saugor, who has furnished much of the material for notes on the leading castes, and to Mr. Hīra Lāl, Assistant Gazetteer Superintendent, for notes on Archæology and Language, and for information on various other matters relating to the District, with which he has an intimate acquaintance. Pyāre Lāl Misra, a resident of Saugor and a clerk in the Gazetteer office, also contributed some material to the chapters on History and Population.

NAGPUR: R. V. R.

19th July 1905.

SAUGOR DISTRICT GAZETTEER.

CONTENTS.

APPENDIX.

INDEX.

CHAPTER I.—GENERAL DESCRIPTION.

CHAPTER II.—HISTORY AND ARCHÆOLOGY.

Chapter III.—POPULATION.

CHAPTER IV.—AGRICULTURE.

CHAPTER VI.—FORESTS AND MINERALS.

CHAPTER VII.—FAMINE.

CHAPTER VIII.—LAND REVENUE ADMINISTRATION.

CHAPTER IX.—GENERAL ADMINISTRATION.

APPENDIX.—GAZETTEER OF TAHSILS, TOWNS, IMPORTANT VILLAGES, RIVERS AND HILLS.

List showing names of Deputy Commissioners who have held charge of the Saugor District since its constitution, with the dates of their periods of office.

Name of Deputy Commissioner.	Period. From	Period. To	Remarks.
Captain G. F. S. Browne ...	1-8-60	19-9-61	
	1-3-62	31-3-62	
	8-12-62	23-5-63	
Major J. B. Dennys ...	20-9-61	28-2-62	
Captain H. F. Newmarch ...	1-4-62	7-12-62	
Major J. N. H. Maclean ...	24-5-63	27-4-68	
	1-2-71	30-9-72	
	1-2-73	30-9-74	
Major J. C. Wood ...	28-4-68	9-11-69	
Captain H. C E. Ward ...	10-11-69	31-1-71	
	1-12-78	10-11-80	
T. B. Morris, Esq ...	1-10-72	31-1-73	
F. Venning, Esq., I.C.S. ...	1-10-74	31-10-74	
Major J. L. Loch ...	1-11-74	6-7-78	
Major W. L. Novern ...	7-7-78	30-11-78	
Colonel C. H. Plowden ...	11-11-80	30-4-83	
	1-7-83	28-2-86	
D. O. Meiklejohn, Esq , I.C.S.	1-5-83	30-6-83	
Colonel H. M. Repton ...	1-3-86	10-4-88	
Colonel S. Brooke ...	11-4-88	Mar. 1891	
C. R. Cleveland, Esq., I.C.S.	Mar. 91	30-9-91	
	19-5-98	27-7-1900	
Colonel T. W. Hogg ...	1-10-91	16-4-93	
	1-8-93	30-11-96	
Colonel H. Hallett ...	17-4-93	31-7-93	
F. A. T. Phillips, Esq., I.C.S.	1-12-96	18-5-98	
R C. H. Moss King, Esq., I.C.S.	28-7-1900	26-3-01	
E. Batchelor, Esq., I.C.S ...	27-3-01	28-11-01	
R. A. B. Chapman, Esq., I C S.	29-11-01	20-2-03	
	22-6-03	30-10-04	
C. A Clarke, Esq., I C.S. ...	21-2-03	21-6-03	
H. M. Laurie, Esq., I.C.S ...	31-10-04	To date (end of 1904).	

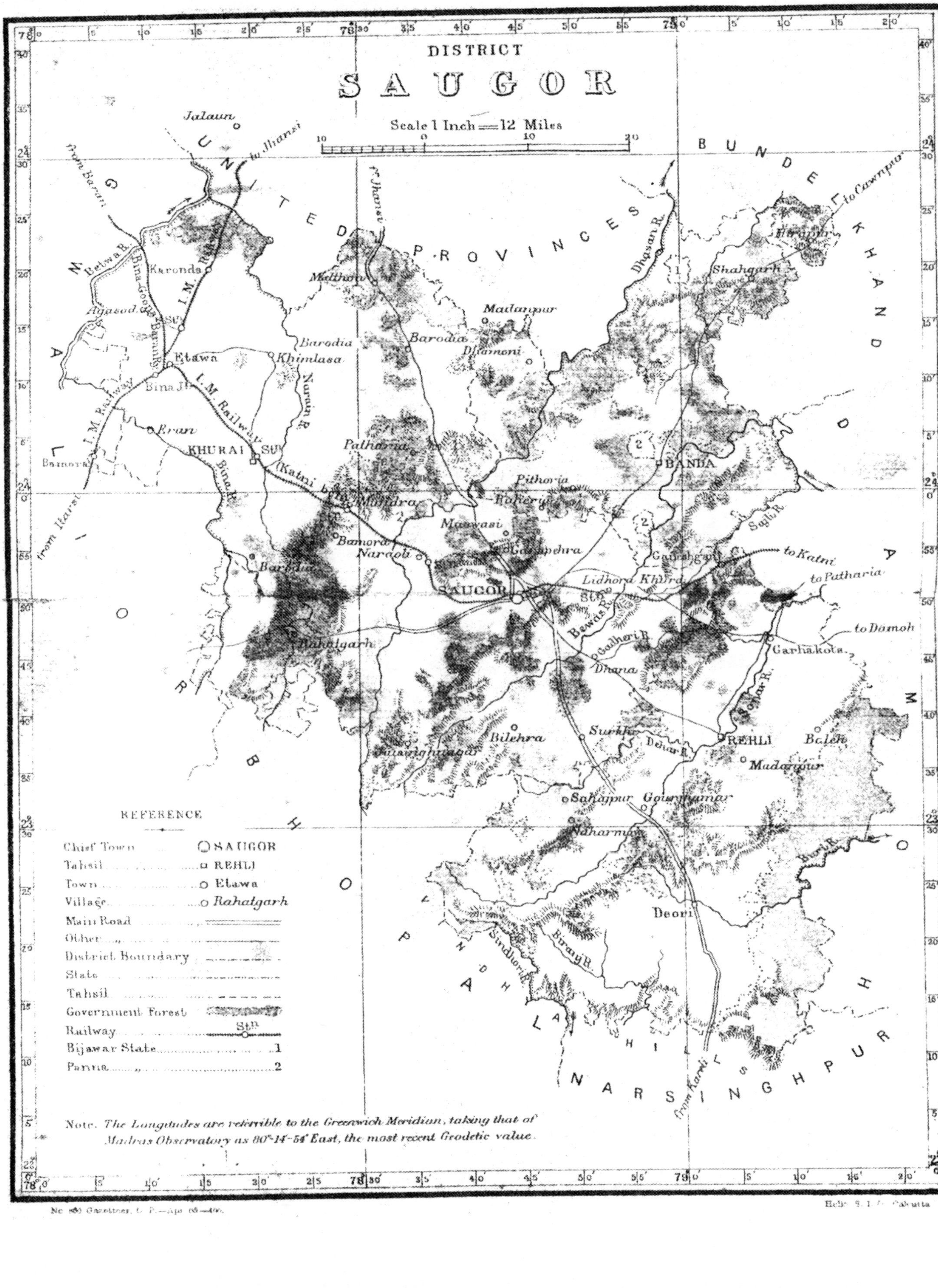

No. 850 Gazetteer, C. P.—Apr. 05—400.

Helio. S. I. O. Calcutta

SAUGOR DISTRICT.

CHAPTER I.

GENERAL DESCRIPTION.

BOUNDARIES AND PHYSICAL FEATURES.

Physical aspects.

1. The Saugor District is situated in the extreme north-west of the Central Provinces between north latitude 23° 5′ and 24° 25′ and east longitude 78° 10′ and 79° 15′. It forms part of the Jubbulpore Division. The name Saugor is derived from *sāgar*, a sea, and was given to the head-quarters town after the large lake round which it has been built. The District forms with Damoh an extension of the great Mālwā plateau and consists of a flat open black-soil tract about 1,000 feet above the level of the Nerbudda valley from which it is separated by the steep escarpment of the Vindhyan hills. It is bounded on the north by the Lalitpur subdivision of the Jhānsi District of the United Provinces, and by the Native States of Bijāwar, Pannā and Charkhāri; on the east by Pannā and the Damoh District; on the south by the Narsinghpur District and the Native State of Bhopāl; and on the west by the Bhopāl and Gwalior States. Saugor has a total area of 3,962 square miles, and is the ninth largest District in the Central Provinces in point of size. It is divided into four tahsīls of which Khurai occupies the north-west, Bandā the north-east, Saugor the centre, and Rehli the south of the District. The District is narrowest at its south-eastern corner and slopes towards the north-east, gradually extending in width until it culminates in the heights overlooking the Bundelkhand plain. Its greatest length from south-east to north-west is about 112 miles,

and its greatest breadth from west to east about 72 miles. The country is generally flat and undulating, with numerous isolated hills. Its most open parts are the plain forming the Khurai tahsīl on the north-west, and another called the 'Havelī' which consists of the Garhākotā, Rehlī and Deorī parganas on the south-east.

Hill-ranges.

2. The principal range of hills is along the north of the District from north of Mālthone through Dhāmoni to Pannā State. It is the dividing range from Bundelkhand, and the country lying below it is called *Ghatia nīche*, while that above it on the Saugor side is called *Ghatia upar*. Another range runs south from Mālthone to Rāhatgarh and separates the Khurai tahsīl, which is generally level, from the rest of the District. East of the Khurai tahsīl the character of the country is very broken, low flat-topped hills rising from the plain in all directions, some covered with trees, others stony and barren. A small range broken at intervals extends from Lidhorā through Bandā and Saugor to Jaisinghnagar, while on the south-east of Saugor there are two small broken ranges, one running from Bherā through Dhāna to Surkhī, and another from Shāhpur through Abchand and Nāharmow to the south-western border. Another range runs south of Rehlí through Baleh and Gourjhāmar. These ranges are all more or less parallel lying from north-east to south-west. Another line of hills extends along the south of the District overlooking the Nerbudda, and proceeds into Narsinghpur.

Elevation.

3. The general elevation of the country varies from 1,300 to 1,900 feet. Only two or three points exceed an elevation of 2,000 feet. The hill above the lake at Saugor is 2,033 feet high and that of Nāharmow 2,240 feet. The Trigonometrical Survey station at Tinsmāl is 2,139 feet in height. The height of the plain country is greatest in the centre and north and decreases to the west, east and south. The line

of the railway ascends from 1,352 feet at Bīna to 1,636 at Nariaolī and 1,700 at Saugor, and then falls to 1,381 feet at Ganeshganj. Towards the south the country falls in elevation from Saugor, Rehlī being 1,296 feet high and Deorī 1,409, while Garhākotā is only 1,229 feet. One mile from Rāhatgarh the elevation is 1,563 feet. Towards the north the country remains higher. Rānīpurā, ten miles from Saugor on the Jhānsi road, is 1,576 feet, and Bāndri twenty miles distant is 1,696 feet. Points taken on the 7th and 15th miles of the Cawnpore road are 1,660 and 1,610 feet high respectively.

Rivers.

4. The principal rivers are the Sonār, the Bewas, the Dhasān, the Bīna and the Betwā. The Sonār rises in the south-western corner of the District and flows through the Rehlī tahsīl, past Gourjhāmar, Rehlī and Garhākotā, after which it passes into Damoh and joins the Ken river in Pannā State. Its principal tributaries are the Dehār which joins it at Rehlī, and the Gadherī at Garhākotā. The Koprā rises in the centre of the Rehlī tahsīl and flows into the Sonār in Damoh. The Bewas enters the District on the south-west from Bhopāl, and flows north-east draining the eastern portion of Saugor and the south-east of Bandā. A little to the north of Bandā it turns eastward through a gorge into the Damoh District, where it falls into the Sonār near Narsinghgarh. The Dhasān also enters the District from Bhopāl territory about five miles west of the Bewas, but takes a more northerly course through the centre of the Saugor and north of the Bandā tahsīls, forming, for the last twenty miles of its length in the District, the boundary between Jhānsi and Saugor. The Bīna rises in Bhopāl and enters the District in the extreme west of the Saugor Tahsil. It flows almost due north past Rāhatgarh and then turns in a westerly direction towards Bhopāl. The river forms the boundary between Pathāri State and Saugor for about twenty-five miles, till it passes Eran, cutting off the Eran pargana from the remainder of the Khurai tahsīl. It then divides

Saugor from Gwalior for a few miles and passes into Gwalior to join the Betwā. The Betwā only flows along the border of the District for thirty miles, separating the northern part of the Khurai tahsil from Gwalior State. It is joined by the Narain river which drains the central portion of the Khurai tahsil.

Drainage and character of rivers.

5. The drainage of the District is north and east, and the streams traversing it carry their waters to the Ganges and Jumna. Only two small streams in the south-west, the Biranj and Sindhor, take their rise in the Deorí pargana of the Rehli tahsil, and fall into the Nerbudda during its course through Narsinghpur. The Sindhor separates Saugor and Bhopāl for the greater part of its course. The Nerbudda itself does not now touch the District. Besides the above rivers small streams and nullahs are found in great numbers owing to the hilly and undulating nature of the country, and unless steps are taken to counteract it, their rapid drainage is most detrimental to the soil, scouring away the finer and more fertile particles, and gradually rendering the surface of the fields uneven. The damage when once started spreads rapidly, and field after field is ruined unless prompt measures are taken to check the violent rush of water across them. Nor do the people derive any advantages in the way of irrigation from the rivers. Some good villages are found along their banks, but for large portions of their length, they are fringed by scrub jungle. Even the good villages cannot profit from the streams, as the banks are usually much cut up by ravines, and are so steep that the expense of raising water from the river-bed to the level of the cultivated fields would be prohibitive. The neighbourhood of a river is also a disadvantage owing to the wild animals which are harboured in its forests and ravines and which prey upon the crops. Crops bordering a river also appear to be more liable to damage from frost than those further removed from water.

6. The boundaries of Saugor interlace slightly with those of the Pannā and Bijāwar States in the Bandā tahsil. One village of Bandā, Burerā, is situated wholly in Bijāwar State. Two villages of Pannā, Papetā and Mad Deorā, lie wholly within the Bandā tahsil, the former adjoining Rurāwan and the latter Hirāpur. Two villages of the Bijāwar State, Semrā and Lohāni, also lie wholly within the Bandā tahsīl, the former adjoining Kishenpur and Dalia, and the latter Indorā and Tigorā.

Interlacing of boundaries.

GEOLOGY.

7. The District is mainly covered by the Deccan trap, but there are two great inliers of Vindhyan sandstone; one runs down from the northern hills to the latitude of Saugor but a little west of it, and broadening out opposite Khurai dies away to the south; the other trends south-west from near Garhākotā to beyond Surkhī, with a length of about twenty miles and a mean width of five. The Vindhyan outcrops belong to the group called the upper Rewā, which is described as a mixture of thick massive strata and false-bedded flags, usually hard and compact and often glazed or semi-vitrified, and yellowish, reddish, or greyish white in colour. The rocks frequently contain beautiful ripple-marks formed by the lapping of water on a sandy shore. To the east and south-east of Saugor the infra-trappean or Lametā limestone is largely developed, attaining a thickness of over a hundred feet in places, but it varies greatly in this respect, being sometimes entirely absent, and the trap then resting directly on the Vindhyās. Garhākotā itself and a narrow strip of country as far south as Rehlī are on limestone. Calcareous intertrappean beds with fossilised shells and plants occur largely near Saugor. These indicate a period when between the successive lava flows the crust cooled sufficiently to permit vegetation to appear on it, the remains of which have been preserved when the surface was again covered by a subsequent flow. Besides small shells some trunks of palm trees, and colossal

Geology.

vertebrate bones, supposed to have belonged to large Pachyderms or possibly to Cetacea, have been found. A nearly continuous outcrop of these beds may be traced for miles from the Saugor parade ground to the foot of the hills to the north of the Indore road, and a similar bed is found to the south of Saugor near Narāyanpur. In the north-eastern forests of the District east of the Dhasān, the rocks belong to the Lower Vindhyans, represented by the Dulchīpur sandstone and conglomerate, while the Bundelkhand gneiss occurs in the Shāhgarh forests.

BOTANY.

Trees.

8. The principal timber tree of the District is teak, but its growth is generally stunted, and specimens beyond three feet in girth are rarely found. Next to teak the most important tree is *sāj* (*Terminalia tomentosa*), which is found more or less over the whole area. It is deciduous, and has a grey to black bark with broad deep longitudinal fissures, and short shallow transverse cracks; on dry hillside forests it is often a stunted tree with grey pubescent large and thick leaves, but in the moister places in valleys and on the plains, it is a large tree with nearly glabrous and rather thin leaves. Its timber is dark-coloured, rather like walnut but rougher and darker. Akin to the sāj is the *kohā* (*Terminalia Arjuna*) easily recognised from sāj by its smooth silvery-grey bark, its narrower grey leaves, and by its preferring the banks of streams. If planted in avenues it has to be watered for six years. *Bījāsāl* (*Pterocarpus Marsupium*) is scattered all over the forests of the District. The *tendū* or ebony (*Diospyros tomentosa*) is common, but its wood is used mainly for the shafts of carts, and not for ornamental furniture. When burnt it gives out showers of sparks. Its fruit is eaten. *Dhau* or *dhaurā* (*Anogeissus latifolia*) is a common tree with a grey bark, and leaves turning red in the cold season. It does not grow to any great height and its timber is used mainly for fuel except in Tigorā forest where large trees of 6 feet in girth

are found. *Haldū* (*Adina cordifolia*), *harua* (*Erythrina suberosa*), *kem* (*Stephegyne parvifolia*), and *tinsā* (*Ougenia dalbergioides*) are less common timber trees, while *lendia* (*Lagerstrœmia parviflora*) is fairly frequent. This last gives a small timber used for fuel. *Sāleh* (*Boswellia serrata*) and *kullū* (*Sterculia urens*), the former with a yellow or greenish-yellow and the latter with a light-coloured smooth bark, are characteristic of the dry sandstone hills. *Jamrāsi* (*Elæodendron Roxburghii*), *ghont* (*Zizyphus xylopyra*), *aonlā* (*Phyllanthus Emblica*), and *gunjā* (*Odina Wodier*) are smaller trees found commonly all over the forests. The ghont is the principal lac-bearing tree of the District. The fruit of the aonlā is pickled and is also used as a tonic. The *achār* (*Buchanania latifolia*), whose fruit called *chironjī* is eaten as a sweetmeat, is common in all forests. The sandalwood (*Santalum album*) is found near Jalandhar and Chheolā Ramgarhā, but the tree is small and contains little heart-wood, and the *beherā* or satinwood (*Chloroxylon Swietenia*), grows in the south-east of the District. *Palās* or *chheolā* (*Butea frondosa*) is abundant in the hills and plains, and its bright scarlet flowers with black sepals appearing in the hot weather months add greatly to the scenery. Its roots are used for making cordage, and its leaves for leaf-plates, while the flowers give the dye used at the Holī festival. The palās tree is also one of the most suitable for the cultivation of lac, the insect being propagated by tying small pieces of the stick-lac off a bearing tree, on a branch of the one on which it is intended to grow. *Kumi* or *Kumhī* (*Careya arborea*) is common in ravines and valleys. It is a big tree conspicuous for its large leaves which turn red in the cold season and has a small yellowish flower. *Sihāru* or *harsinghār* (*Nyctanthes Arbor-tristis*) is a small tree growing to 10 or 12 feet with a crooked stem and forming the undergrowth of teak forests. It has fragrant flowers with yellow tubes and white petals which are often used for garlands. Bamboos grow on most of the hill-slopes.

Shrubs.

9. Among shrubs and creepers the following may be mentioned. *Karondā (Carissa Carandas)* is a common shrub in ravines growing up to about 5 feet. It has a very small white flower with a strong and sweet scent, and a small berry, which is very good in tarts and preserves. Tigers are said to haunt karondā jungle. It is also cultivated in gardens and is then called 'rai-karondā.' *Makoi (Zizyphus Oenoplia)* is a straggling shrub covered with small and strong thorns, difficult to cut, and is used for fencing.

Trees of the open country.

10. *Babūl (Acacia arabica)* is the commonest tree in the open country and is most planted in avenues. *Reunjhā (Acacia leucophlœa)*, distinguished from babūl by its light-coloured bark, is fairly common, and *khair (Acacia Catechu)* grows both in the forests and open country, forming a large part of the crop in the dryer forests. *Kanjī* or *karanj (Pongamia glabra)*, which is almost an evergreen tree, is planted in avenues. *Kachnār (Bauhinia variegata)* is found both in the forests and in avenues. It flowers in the hot season, when devoid of leaves, and the large white flowers with usually four purple and one white or variegated petal cover the branches. *Mahuā (Bassia latifolia)* is common both in the forests and open country, especially in the north-east. The usual fruit-bearing and sacred trees grow round the villages as the mango, *ber* or wild plum, tamarind, *nīm (Melia indica)* which is evergreen, *bel (Aegle Marmelos)*, pīpal and banyan. *Jāmun (Eugenia Jambolana)* is sometimes planted in avenues, as is also *shīsham (Dalbergia latifolia)*. Custard-apple trees (*Anona squamosa*) grow in the enclosures of the old forts at Rāhatgarh, Dhāmoni and Garhpahrā.

Grasses.

11. The principal grazing grasses are *kel (Andropogon annulatus)* and *musyāl (Iseilema Wightii)*. Kel is a straight grass with a thin ear. Musyāl has a bearded ear and is much esteemed. These grasses grow mixed and are largely

used as fodder. They are now pressed and exported. *Ukrī* (*Saccharum officinarum*) grows in swamps and damp places. Cattle do not usually eat it unless the ground is dry. *Ganer* or *gunaiyā* (*Anthistiria scandens*) is a very tall grass with spikelets in bunches which turn to a bright reddish colour after flowering. It is mainly used for thatching. *Senā* is another grass described locally as thin and drying up quickly and not eaten by cattle when they can get anything else. It is probably *Pollinia argentea*, an excellent fodder grass when young, but afterwards becoming coarse. *Dūb* (*Cynodon Dactylon*), which is the best fodder grass of all, grows on the boundaries of fallow fields and in gardens. It requires a stiff soil and a certain amount of moisture. It is sometimes sold in Saugor in bundles called *kāndis*. *Rūsa* grass (*Andropogon Schœnanthus*) grows largely in the forests, but the oil is not extracted in Saugor. *Kāns* (*Saccharum spontaneum*) invades black-soil fallow land very rapidly and cannot be eradicated by the country plough. Much land became covered with *kāns* during the famines, and embankments have been undertaken by the Irrigation Department as a means of reclaiming it. *Sarkā* or *sonthā* is described locally as a long thin grass growing with kāns. It is probably *Saccharum ciliare* and is employed in Northern India for thatching, and for the manufacture of matting, rope and paper, and also as a fodder grass when quite young. In Saugor the Kuchbandhias are said to use it for making mats to hold vessels. The commonest grass in the forests is *Andropogon contortus* the well-known spear-grass.

WILD ANIMALS, ETC.

Wild animals.

12. The forests of the District are fairly well stocked with game. The following notes are taken from information kindly furnished by Major Sutherland, I. M. S., and Dr. Quinn, Civil Surgeons of Saugor and Damoh, respectively. Neither the

wild buffalo nor the bison are found in Saugor. Forsyth mentions in the 'Highlands of Central India' that a lion was shot in the District in 1851, but they have of course long been extinct. The tiger (*Felis tigris*) called locally *nāhar* is fairly common. It is very destructive to cattle, less so to game, and except when wounded scarcely ever to man. Man-eating tigers are scarcely known. Tigers are found on the hills and rocky ravines in wet weather. They select particular haunts, and when one is shot another after a brief interval takes its place. They are not very large in Saugor. The leopard or panther (*Felis pardus*), called locally *tendua*, is found in large numbers all over the District. It causes great destruction to cattle, being in this respect a greater pest than the tiger. The leopard cat (*Felis Bengalensis*), Hind. *cheetā billī*, has been seen in Damoh and probably also exists in Saugor. The length of its head and body is 24 to 26 inches and of its tail 11 to 13 inches. The jungle cat (*Felis chaus*), Hind. *junglī billī*, is very common and very destructive to pea-fowl, partridges and hares. The Indian lynx (*Felis caracal*) is very rare, frequenting scrub jungle. The Indian desert cat (*Felis ornata*) probably also exists though it is rare. The striped hyæna (*Hyæna striata*) is found in all parts of the District. The wolf (*Canis pallipes*) is very rare and hence is not destructive. The wild dog (*Cyon Dukhunensis*) is found in the forests and is very destructive to game. It has little or no fear of man. Jackals and foxes are very common. The common otter (*Lutra vulgaris*) is found in all parts of the District in rivers and streams, and sometimes also in tanks. It lives in burrows with several entrances just above the water, and usually one underneath. The Indian sloth bear (*Ursus labiatus*), Hind. *rīchh* or *adameād*, is found all over the District. It lives in caves in the hot and wet weather, and when it has young. In the cold season it lives in grass and bushes. When the mahuā is in fruit bears can easily be shot in the morning on their way home from the groves. When wounded the bear charges fearlessly. The young are easily tamed but are a nuisance. This animal dies hard, and Dr. Quinn relates that he has put as many as four ·577 express bullets into the body of one without bringing it down.

Deer and antelope.

13. The District has most of the deer of the Province, but not the *bārāsinghā* or swamp-deer. Sāmbhar and *cheetal* or spotted deer are fairly plentiful, and good heads are obtained. The nilgai is found in all parts of the District. Herds of black-buck are common in the open country, and the best heads shot in the Province have probably been obtained in Saugor. Heads of 24 inches are by no means rare, and it is believed that specimens of 26 and 27 inches have been obtained as against 28¾ inches recorded as having been shot in Jaipur.[1] Its numbers have greatly decreased of late years and good heads are now not common. The four-horned antelope (*Tetracerus quadricornis*) is fairly common, and the *chinkāra* or Indian gazelle is numerous in all parts of the District. The ribfaced or barking deer (*Cervulus muntjac*) is rare.

Land game birds and shore birds.

14. Among land game birds may be mentioned the painted sand-grouse, which is rare and usually found in couples on open ground; while the common or rock sand-grouse is found in large numbers all over the District in the season. They may be seen late in the evening near water, where they drink before retiring for the night. They probably do not breed locally. The common pea-fowl is found in all parts of the District. This bird is not considered sacred locally, and is destroyed both by Hindus and Muhammadans. It is easily tamed. The red spur-fowl is found in jungles all over the District, but is not common and is very shy. The painted partridge is found in all parts of the District, but is not common. It can always be recognised by its peculiar call. This bird is very fond of perching

[1] The Indian Shikar Field Book by W. S. Burke.

on the *palās* tree. Its flesh is good. The grey or spurred partridge is found everywhere. It is easily tamed and can frequently be seen in the possession of natives. Its flesh is dry and tasteless and it is a foul feeder. Major Sutherland mentions the black partridge (*Francolinus vulgaris*) in his list of game-birds. [1]This bird is stated to reside in those parts of the Peninsula where the painted partridge is absent, and not to occur in Rājputāna, but it is certainly present in Saugor. The jungle quail (*Perdicula Asiatica*) is found in all parts of the District. The large grey quail (*Coturnix communis*) and rain quail (*Coturnix coromandelica*) are rare. The button quail (*Turnix Dussumierii*) is common. These birds rise only once and have a single note. The large stone plover (*Esacus recurvirostris*), the stone plover or bastard florican (*Œdicnemus crepitans*), the spurwinged plover (*Hoplopterus ventralis*), the Eastern golden plover (*Charadrius longipes*), the little winged plover (*Ægialitis minutus*), the *titehrī* or red-wattled lapwing (*Sarcogrammus Indicus*), the Indian courser (*Cursorius coromandelicus*), the redshank (*Totanus calidris*), and greenshank (*Totanus glottis*), the green and blue-rock pigeon and the rufous, spotted, little brown, Indian ring and red doves are other birds identified by Major Sutherland. The great Indian bustard has been seen in Damoh, and probably also therefore exists in Saugor. The *sāras* crane (*Grus antigone*) is very common in all parts of the District, and is usually met with in pairs. It is easily tamed. The common crane (*Grus communis*) is very rare and the demoiselle crane (*Anthropoides Virgo*) does not appear to visit the District.

Ducks.

15. The District is not a good one for snipe and duck shooting owing to the paucity of tanks. The grey lag and barheaded geese are seen but rarely, while the comb duck or black-backed goose (Hind. *nuktā*) is very common and indigenous. This bird is seen only in small flocks, and is rather partial to pools

[1] Burke's Indian Shikar Field Book.

and very slow in its flight. Major Sutherland's list includes the pink-headed duck (*Rhodonessa caryophyllacea*) which is not commonly supposed to visit the Central Provinces. The Brahmini duck, though indigenous, is said to be found here only in the season, usually in pairs and on the rivers. The shoveller is rare. Other varieties of immigrant duck are the mallard and grey duck or gadwall, which are fairly common and the pintail and wigeon, the red-crested pochard, a cousin of the canvas-back of America, the red-headed and white-eyed pochards, the tufted or golden-eye, all of which are rare, and the smew or white-headed merganser which is very rare. The common teal and blue-winged or garganey teal are very common in the season, and the bronze-capped teal is stated by Dr. Quinn to be common in Damoh. The whistling and cotton teal are indigenous. Mahseer of small size are found in the rivers and *murrel* (*Ophiocephalus striatus and gachua*) in the tanks.

RAINFALL AND CLIMATE.

Rainfall.

16 Rainfall[1] is registered at the four tahsil towns, Saugor, Khurai, Rehli and Bandā. The average annual falls at each station are as follows:—Saugor, 48 inches; Khurai, 47; Rehlī, 46; and Bandā, 40. The smaller amount recorded at Bandā may be due to the fact that the rainfall diminishes towards the north. The highest annual total ever registered at Saugor was 120 inches in 1858, the year after the Mutiny. The minimum fall registered was 17 inches at Rehlī in 1892-93, while Bandā received a little over 17 inches in 1883-84. In Saugor the rainfall has exceeded 50 inches in 16 out of 32 years. As a rule about 7 inches are received in June, 16 inches in July, 12 inches in August, 7 to 8 inches in September and something over an

---

[1] The statistics of rainfall and temperature are taken from the Indian Meteorological Memoirs, Vol. 17.

inch in October. The average during the seven dry months is 2½ inches. The rains have seldom failed seriously until within recent years, and injury to the crops has more frequently been caused by excess than by deficiency of rainfall. Storms of hail which seriously damage the standing crops are of very frequent occurrence, but they usually extend only over a small area. The Saugor tahsil seems to be less liable to hailstorms than the rest of the District. Owing to the hilly nature of the country thunder-storms are frequent, but dust-storms are not nearly so common as further north.

Temperature and climate.

17. The temperature of Saugor and the District generally is very moderate in proportion to the latitude. An observatory was established in 1870 at an elevation of 1,769 feet, and was removed to another site with an elevation of 1807 feet in 1896. The average monthly minimum and maximum temperatures are 52° and 77° in January, 78·5° and 105° in May, and 74° and 83·5° in July. The highest temperature recorded was 114·4° on 11th June 1897, and the lowest 39·1° on 9th February 1893. Although the lowest temperature is thus 7° above freezing point, slight frosts occur during the cold weather and cause damage to the crops on low-lying land near rivers, which have apparently the effect of producing a substantially lower temperature in their vicinity. The climate is generally pleasant and salubrious. The temperature on grass may be 12° or more lower than that of the air.

CHAPTER II.

HISTORY AND ARCHÆOLOGY.

HISTORY.

The Gupta inscriptions.

18. The earliest historical record in the Saugor District consists of four inscriptions[1] of the early Gupta period which have been discovered at Eran near Khurai. The Gupta kings were a Hindu Brahmanical dynasty reigning in Northern India with their capital at Patnā, their era commencing from A. D. 319. One inscription gives the name of Samudragupta on a stone which has now been removed to Calcutta Samudragupta was the king who revived the great horse sacrifice or *Ashwamedha* which had long been in abeyance this fact demonstrates his importance, as the horse had first to be taken through all surrounding countries followed by an army, and all kings who opposed its entry on their territories must be conquered, while if they allowed it they were held to accept the position of feudatories. Another inscription on a stone column 47 feet high standing at Eran gives the name of Budhgupta and is dated of the Gupta era 165, corresponding to 484-85 A. D. A third inscription on the chest of a huge boar about 11 feet high also *in situ* mentions the name of Toramāna who belonged to the Hūnas, a foreign race of Indo-Scythians, who came from the Punjab and overthrew the Guptas, Toramāna's date being about the end of the fifth century. A fourth inscription on a small stone pillar, afterwards converted into a *lingam*, stands under some tall trees near the left bank of the Bīna, about half a mile to the south-east of Eran. It is a posthumous inscription of a chieftain Goparājā who came to Eran with the powerful king Bhānugupta in 191 or

---

1 Fleet's Gupta Inscriptions. Text pp. 18—28, 88—93 and 158—161.

510 A. D. and was killed there in a great battle, his wife burning herself on his funeral pyre. This is perhaps the oldest record of a *satī* immolation in India. These inscriptions show that Eran was a province of the Gupta kings, its classical name being Erakaina,[1] and a place of considerable importance at this early period.

Jajhotī.

19. At a subsequent period Saugor was included in Jajhotī,[2] the classical name of Bundelkhand, which formed the kingdom of the Chandel Rājputs of Khajurahā and Mahobā. The earliest mention of Jajhotī is by Hiuen Tsiang, the Chinese pilgrim, in A.D. 641 The Chandel Rājputs traced their descent from Chandramā, the god of the moon, who embraced Hemavatī, the beautiful daughter of Hemrāj, the family priest of a king of Benāres. The kingdom of the Chandels extended from the Dhasān river on the west to the Vindhyā mountains on the east, and from the Jumna on the north to the sources of the Ken river on the south. The first Chandel king whose date is known reigned in 800 A.D., and before him there may have been a dynasty of Jijhotia Brāhmans who derive their name from Jajhotī. Hiuen Tsiang speaks of a Brāhman king in Jajhotī at the time of his visit. Besides inscriptions the Chandels have left a number of fine temples, none of which, however, are found in Saugor. By Madanpur[3] just across the border in Lalitpur Sub-division of Jhānsi District is an inscription recording the defeat of Parmāl Deo, a Chandel prince, by Prithwī Rāj, the famous Chauhān king of Delhi, at Orai in 1182 A.D. Chand who was the court poet of Prithwī Rāj describes the exploits of the Chandels, and especially of the two Banāphar heroes Alhā and Udal, who were the generals of the Chandel king. Alhā and Udal are popular heroes of folklore, and their 52 battles are celebrated in songs still well known to the people.

---

1 Cunningham's Archæological Reports, Vol. X, pp. 76—90.

2 Cunningham's Ancient Geography of India, pp. 481—485, and Archæological Reports, Vol. XXI, pp. 77, *et seq.*

3 Cunningham's Archæological Reports, Vol XXI. p. 171.

On his defeat Alhā retired to the forests round Maihar and Orchhā, where like Frederick Barbarossa he is still said to dwell, and nightly to kindle a lamp in the temple of Devī on a hill in the forest. The Chandels were subsequently defeated by the Muhammadans in 1203 A.D., and their dynasty declined in importance from this time. But Durgāvati, the famous queen of the Garhā-Mandlā dynasty, is believed to have been a Chandel princess.

The Ahīrs.

20. According to tradition Saugor was subsequently governed by a race of Ahīrs or herdsmen, whose headquarters were at Garhpahrā or old Saugor a place seven miles north of the present city. Some landowners called the Faulādia Ahirs still exist, who are supposed to be the descendants of the former dominant race. In about 1023 A.D. the Ahirs were subverted by Rājā Nihāl Shā of Jālaun who took possession of Saugor and the surrounding country with about 330 villages.

Settlement of Saugor by the Dāngis.

21. The first settlement on the present site of Saugor was made in 1660 by Udan Shā, a descendant of Nihāl Shā, who built a small fort on the site of the present one, and founded a village close to it called Parkotā which is now part of the town. His grandson Pirthipat, a Dāngi Rājput, is the first ruler of whom any thing is known. He was a man of weak intellect and is well remembered in popular tradition. He is said to have amused himself by shooting arrows at the moon from the terrace of his high palace at Garhpahrā, and his licentious habits have been commemorated in local sayings according to which he enforced the 'droit de seigneur,' compelling every bride to pass her wedding-night with him.

The Bundelās of Pannā.

22. The incapacity of the king of Garhpabrā coming to the knowledge of Chhatar Sāl, the well-known Rājā of Pannā, he sent his sons Hirde Sā and Jagat Rai to take possession of Garhpahrā

and the adjoining country. Pirthīpat made no resistance. but gave up the whole of his dominions with the exception of a small settlement at Parkotā on which he was permitted to remain unmolested. On the annexation of Saugor by the Marāthās, Pirthīpat was given Bilehrā with twelve villages for his maintenance, and his descendants still live there with a revenue-free grant of five villages.[1] In 1733 Muhammad Khān Bangash, the governor of Allahābād, on behalf of the Mughal Empire was appointed Sūbahdār of Mālwā. He shortly afterwards entered Bundelkhand and invaded the territories of Chhatar Sāl. The latter solicited assistance from Bājī Rao Peshwā of Poona which was readily afforded. The Peshwā moved expeditiously into Bundelkhand, surrounded Muhammad Khān Bangash, and forced him to take refuge in the fort of Jītgarh, near Kālinjar in Bānda District. where he was reduced to the greatest distress until rescued by a band of Afghāns headed by his son. Bundelkhand, however, was completely evacuated by the Imperial troops, and Chhatar Sāl was so pleased with the aid afforded by his new ally that he conferred on him a fort and district in the neighbourhood of Jhānsi yielding a revenue of two and a quarter lakhs of rupees, adopted him as his son, and on his death, which happened very soon after, bestowed on him a third of his possessions, or an equal share with his own sons Jagat Rai and Hirde Sā, the former of whom was styled Rājā of Kālpee and the latter of Bundelkhand.

The Marāthās.

23. In the following year (1734) the government of Mālwā was made over to Bājī Rao with the tacit consent of the Emperor.[2] He entered into a close alliance with Jagat Rai and Hirde Sā for the purpose of mutual protection and support against the Muhammadans, the Bundelkhand princes agreeing 'to accompany Bājī Rao in all his expeditions to Hindustān, and in

[1] Colonel Maclean's Settlement Report, pp. 7—8.

[2] Grant Duff's History of the Marathas, Ed. 1878, i.p.p. 438-439.

'the case of his being engaged in a war in the Deccan to 'defend Bundelkhand for at least two months, and if at the 'end of that time the Marāthās should not be advancing to 'their assistance, to make the best terms they could as a 'means of temporary safety but to break them the moment 'they were joined by their Hindu allies.' Bājī Rao's share of the territories of Chhatar Sāl was fixed to yield an annual revenue of five lakhs of rupees.[1]

History of other portions of the District.

24. The country which had been in the possession of the Dāngi dynasty and had been wrested from them by Chhatar Sāl seems to have comprised the tracts surrounding Saugor, Rehlī, and Garhākotā. Other portions of the District were held by different rulers, but of their history little remains. An inscription in the fort of Rāhatgarh, dated 1255 A.D., shows that at that period it was occupied by the Pramaras or Ponwārs of Dhār. Parts of the District were held by Gond chiefs and became subject to the authority of Sangrām Sā, the famous king of the Garhā-Mandlā line (died A.D. 1530). Thus in the history of Mandlā it is mentioned that Narendra Sā, who died in 1731, ceded to the Mughal Emperor the territories of Dhāmoni, Garhākotā and Shāhgarh in order to obtain his recognition. The southern part of Saugor, also belonging to the Mandlā dynasty, was ceded to Chhatar Sāl, about the same time as the latter conquered Pirthīpat. The northern portion, including the Khurai and Khimlāsa tracts, had been reduced to subjection by the Mughals, and in 1695 Aurangzeb granted Khurai, Garholā, and Eran to a Dāngi chief. Dhāmoni in the north of the District was held by the Muhammadans, and was the site of a large fort and cantonment. Although the historian of Mandlā mentions Dhāmoni as having been ceded to the Emperor in 1736, it is elsewhere[2] stated that it became an integral part of the Delhi empire in 1619, and was the residence of five successive

---

1 Grant Duff, Ed. 1878, i.p. 471. | 2 C.P. Gazetteer, 1st Ed., p. 407.

governors appointed from Delhi, the last of whom was subverted by Chhatar Sāī.[1] It is probable that Dhāmoni was taken by the Mughals in 1634 A.D. from Jujhār Singh, the Bundelā prince of Orchhā, and its subsequent cession by Mandlā, if it occurred, can only have been in the nature of a legal confirmation of an already existing fact. Dhāmoni was conquered from the Mughals by Chhatar Sāl and became part of his dominions.

Govind Rao Pandit.

25. On his departure from Saugor the Peshwā appointed one Govind Rao Bundelā to govern the territories which had accrued to him. Govind Rao, of whom several stories are still current, had been, it is said, originally the Peshwā's cook. One day when travelling, Bājī Rao, who was a Kokanasth Brāhman, was observing a fast, and therefore made no halt for his midday meal. Govind Rao, his cook, who was a Karhāda Brāhman, did not observe this fast, and therefore begged Bājī Rao for ten minutes' leave to enable him to take some food. On this being granted Govind Rao went to the bank of a river and finding a corpse being burnt proceeded to cook his food on the funeral pyre. Bājī Rao who had observed him remarked that a man who could do this could do anything, and from that time commenced rapidly to advance him in position. Govind Rao, surnamed Bundelā, as the governor of Bundelkhand, proved an able administrator, and between 1735 and 1760 reduced to subjection the outlying tracts of Saugor, and the adjoining District of Damoh. He first fixed his headquarters at Rāngir, a small village near Rehlī, but subsequently built the present fort of Saugor on the site of an old one erected by the Dāngis and greatly improved and beautified the town, which rapidly increased in importance under his administration, and became the capital of the surrounding country. Govind Rao was killed before Pānīpat in 1760, being cut off with a small

[1] Elliot's History, Vol. vii, p. 49.

force while engaged in a raid on the supplies of the Afghān army.[1] It is said that he was so fat that he was unable to mount his horse without assistance, and was thus prevented from escaping. As a reward for his good service the Peshwā granted Saugor and the surrounding territories free of revenue to his family.

His successors.

26. Govind Rao was succeeded by his son Bālāji Rao who was again succeeded by his son Raghunāth Rao, commonly known as Abba Sāhib. In 1799 Saugor was plundered by Amīr Khān Pindāri, then in the pay of Jeswant Rao Holkar. An account given in Malcolm's 'Memoir of Central India'[2] states that 'A scene of promiscuous and un-'restrained pillage continued for the whole period (almost a 'month), that the army remained near this unfortunate city. 'Saugor had been taken by storm after being defended for 'some days, and was set on fire on the day of the storm, 'and the flames continued to rage in one quarter or another 'of the town for the whole period. Only about four or five 'hundred of the garrison and inhabitants were killed, but all 'were ruined; for no property was spared, and the last 'days were employed in dragging the tanks and wells to 'obtain what had been cast into them for the purpose of 'temporary concealment. Every species of insult and 'torture were inflicted upon the male and female inhabitants 'of Saugor. The Afghān soldiers, when they caught a 'Brāhman or Hindu of high caste, used to feel his head, and 'examine the skin with great care, to discover by its soft-'ness and delicacy, whether he had been leading a luxurious 'life or one of labour, and according to the result of this 'inspection they liberated their prisoner or proceeded to 'extremities with him.' Amīr Khān was driven off by the approach of an army of the Rājā of Nāgpur to whom the Saugor ruler had applied for assistance. Another sack of

[1] Grant Duff, i. p. 611.

[2] Ed. 1824, i.p. 207.

Saugor by Amīr Khān is mentioned in the historical section of Colonel Maclean's Settlement Report, but no details of it are available. Meanwhile in 1781 the last king of the Gond Garhā-Mandlā line had been deposed, and the districts of Mandlā and Jubbulpore were brought under the domination of the Saugor rulers. They were held, however, only for 18 years during which time Mandlā was ruined and depopulated by the extortion and tyranny of Vināyak Rao, an official sent from Saugor to govern it. In 1798 Jubbulpore and Mandlā were ceded by the Peshwā to Raghuji II of Nāgpur, who also obtained possession of Dhāmoni from a subordinate chief. Raghunāth Rao or Abba Sāhib died in 1802, without heirs and his wives Rādha Bai and Rukmā Bai carried on the government assisted by their agent Vināyak Rao. In 1814 Sindhia marched from Gwalior and plundered Saugor, making Vināyak Rao prisoner and releasing him on a payment of Rs. 75,000.

Garhākotā.

27. During this period Garhākotā and Shāhgarh had been governed by the descendants of Hirde Sā, the son of Chhatar Sāl. In 1810 the Nāgpur troops invested Garhākotā, and killed the chief Mardan Singh. His son, Arjun Singh, begged assistance from Sindhia, promising to cede a half of his territories as the price of his delivery from the Nāgpur troops Sindhia acceded to these terms and despatched an army under the command of Colonel Jean Baptiste. The latter defeated and put to flight the Nāgpur troops, and according to stipulation retained possession of Mālthone and Garhākotā, leaving to Arjun Singh the country of Shāhgarh with other territory. Baptiste remained at Garhākotā for some time as governor of the fort and the existing village of Karnelgarh is named after him. Arjun Singh retired to Shāhgarh, and though he managed some nine years afterwards to seize Garhākotā by a stratagem, he was ejected by a British force. His descendants, as will be seen, rebelled

in the Mutiny of 1857. The Rāhatgarh pargana had been in the possession of the Bhopāl rulers until 1807 when it was also taken by Sindhia after a siege of seven months.

Annexation of Saugor.

28. In 1818, on the deposition of the Peshwā by Lord Hastings, his possessions in Saugor and Damoh passed to the British. Pensions aggregating two and a half lakhs of rupees were settled on the widows Rādha Bai and Rukmā Bai, Vināyak Rao and other officers. The descendant of Vināyak Rao is an Honorary Magistrate at Saugor and enjoys a pension The widows had adopted a son Balwant Rao who was sent to live at Jubbulpore with the title of Rājā of Saugor. He adopted his daughter's son Raghunāth Rao who is still (1904) living and enjoys a pension of Rs. 5,000 a year.

Annexation of other parts of the District.

29. The outlying portions of the District came into possession of the British in various ways. The Dhāmoni pargana of the Bandā tahsīl was ceded to us in 1818 by Appa Sāhib Bhonsla. The parganas of Rāhatgarh in the Saugor tahsīl, and Garhākotā, Deorī, Gourjhāmar and Nāharmow in the Rehlī tahsīl, collectively known as the Panch Mahāls, were originally made over to us by Sindhia in 1820-1825 for management. Our possession was confirmed in 1844 and sovereignty was acquired in 1861. The Kanjia pargana of the Khurai tahsīl was acquired from Sindhia by an exchange of territory in 1860.[1] The Shāhgarh pargana was confiscated after the Mutiny. The Bherā pargana of the Bandā tahsīl was acquired by transfer from the Bundelkhand States in 1818, and a small territory in the north-east corner of the tahsīl round the village of Hīrāpur was similarly transferred from the Bundelā State of Charkhāri after the Mutiny. Seven villages were also acquired from the Pannā State. After its cession, Saugor formed part of the Saugor and Nerbudda territories and was placed under

---

[1] Aitchison's Treaties, Vol. IV, p. 81

an Agent to the Governor-General at Jubbulpore, while on the constitution of the North-Western Provinces in 1835, the Saugor and Nerbudda territories were added to the new Province.

The Bundelā Rising.

30. In March 1842 occurred what is known as the Bundelā rising. Jawāhir Singh, Bundelā of Mauzā Chandrāpur near Jhiknī, and Madhkur Shā and Ganeshjū of Narhut on the *ghāts* in the north of the District, went into open rebellion on account of having been served with decrees from the civil courts at Saugor. They killed several of the police and burned and plundered the towns of Khimlāsa, Khurai, Nariaolī, Dhāmoni and Binaikā. Delan Shā, a Gond chief of Narsinghpur, also rose and plundered Deorī and the surrounding territory and the Chānwarpātha tract of Narsinghpur. The rebellion lasted for about a year, when Madhkur Shā and Ganeshjū were arrested in the Bānpur State, the former being hanged and the latter transported. The remaining leaders gave themselves up and were pardoned. The whole District suffered immensely from this outbreak, and the land revenue was realised with difficulty for several years.

Madhkur Shā.

31. Madhkur Shā has become a hero of folklore among the people. It is related that it was not on account of the civil court decrees that he revolted but because of the tyranny of a chief constable. Madhkur Shā had engaged a Bernī or dancing-girl at the Holī, when the chief constable of the adjoining police-station, who also wanted a Bernī but could not get one, sent and forcibly carried off the girl engaged by Madhkur Shā from his house. Madhkur Shā could not brook this insult and went out and slaughtered all the police. Subsequently when he was in hiding he could not be caught until his own sister, whose house he visited at night, betrayed him to the troops. Even when they wanted to arrest him as he was sleeping in the house,

for some time no one dared lay hands on him, as all were awed by the glow on his face, until finally a number of men seized him together. His body was burnt behind the Saugor jail, and a *chabūtra* or shrine was raised to him, which is still worshipped and maintained by the residents of Gopālganj quarter. People are said to be cured of fever by making vows at the shrine.

Daulat Singh.

32. At about the same period flourished another notorious Bundelā dacoit, Daulat Singh of Dongrā in Lalitpur, whose *penchant* was to cut off the noses of both sexes, and occasionally the breasts of women, with the exception of such as addressed him as 'brother' whom he released. Several stories are told of him, and a nullah about a mile south of Mālthone on the Saugor-Jhānsi road is still called Naktā Nullah because there Daulat Singh sat and carried on his nefarious occupation. He was caught and hanged at Jhānsi.

Changes of administration.

33. In consequence of the supposed discredit thrown on the British Administration by the Bundelā disturbances, Lord Ellenborough broke up the administration of the Saugor and Nerbudda territories, and reorganised it under an Agent to the Governor-General with an entirely new body of officers. The arrangement was not found to work well however, and the territories were again attached to the North-Western Provinces in 1852 with which they were administered until the formation of the Central Provinces in 1861.

The Mutiny.

34. [1]In June 1857 when the Sepoy Mutiny commenced, the regiments stationed at Saugor were the 31st Native Infantry commanded by Major Hampden, the 42nd commanded by Colonel Dalzell, with the 3rd Irregular Cavalry and a few European gunners. The station was commanded by Brigadier Sage. On the

[1] The description of occurrences during the Mutiny is taken from a narrative submitted by Major Erskine, Commissioner of Jubbulpore, to the Secretary to Govt., North-Western Provinces, No. 368-A., dated 10th August 1858.

8th June the news reached Saugor of the death of Captain Gordon, Deputy Commissioner of Jhānsi, while opposing the mutineers, and of the murder of all the Europeans in the station by the Rānī of Jhānsi. At the same time it was heard that the Rājā of Bānpur had assembled troops at Lalitpur, and surrounded the Deputy Commissioner of Chanderī, and that the Rājā of Shāhgarh whose principality lay north-west of Saugor and Damoh was raising troops and making preparations for war. A small force was despatched towards Chanderī under Major Gaussen of the 42nd. On the 14th June it transpired that some men of the 42nd were endeavouring to prevent the detachment from proceeding on its march. They were seized, tried and sentenced to six months' imprisonment by native court-martial, and sent under police guard to Hoshangābād jail. Meanwhile the roads of the cāntonment were patrolled night and day by the 3rd Cavalry to prevent the rest of the 42nd from attempting a rescue, while on the 27th June the European officers and artillerymen and the residents of the station moved into the fort by order of the Brigadier, taking all the arms they could collect, and the treasure from the District office. The detachment intended for Chanderī reached Mālthone, and more than once the European officers who accompanied it were informed that the sepoys were counselling their murder. On its arrival it found that the passes to the north were held by the Rājā of Bānpur's troops, and it therefore halted to protect the northern frontier of the District, and received a reinforcement of 400 men from Saugor. Major Gaussen then proceeded to attack the fort of Bālā Bahut on the southern border of Chanderī, which he took with the loss of a few men and an officer, Ensign Wadham, whose tomb is in the Dāk Bungalow compound at Mālthone.

The Lalitpur prisoners.

35. The detachment then returned to Saugor where news was received that the five officers and three ladies at Lalitpur were alive,

and were being kept in confinement by the Rājā of Bānpur. He shortly afterwards sent them to Tehrī which place they reached after many trials and hardships through the good offices of Muhammad Ali Khān, Mukhtār of the Rājā of Bānpur. At Tehrī they were kindly treated through the good offices of the Rājā of Orchhā's tutor, and again befriended by Muhammad Alī Khān and his servant, both of whom afterwards received substantial rewards. The Tehrī authorities at the request of the officers sent them towards Saugor, but on the way they were seized and imprisoned by the rebel Rājā of Shāhgarh, who after keeping them in a most wretched condition for three months, allowing them only an anna a day each for subsistence, sent them into Saugor.

Mutiny of the garrison.

36. On the morning of the 1st July the portion of the 3rd Cavalry remaining at Saugor, excepting some of the native officers and about fifty troopers, broke out into open mutiny and went to the mosque, and sharpened their swords. At the same time Sheikh Ramzān, the senior Sūbahdār of the 42nd, raised the Muhammadan flag and called for followers by beat of drum. He was joined by the whole of the 42nd present in the station, a few of the 31st, and the mutineers of the 3rd Cavalry, and on the same day the troops and bad characters of the town plundered the houses in cantonments, though they did not set fire to them, and also seized about Rs. 9,500 in copper and small silver coin which could not be removed from the treasury for want of time and carriage. Sheikh Ramzān took command in cantonments with the title of General. The mutineers next seized the large saluting gun on the Artillery Hill, which had been left there when the rest of the guns were taken into the fort, and brought it down to the Quarter-Guard of the 42nd, which they made their headquarters. The 31st Regiment with the exception of 45 men had kept aloof from the mutineers, and now requested permission to attack them, which the Brigadier

allowed, but did not permit the European officers to accompany them. They were, however, supported by a strong body of Customs chaprāsis who had been armed with muskets under the leadership of Captain Pinkney and Lieutenant Hamilton, the Assistant Commissioner. The mutineers fired a round shot into the 31st, and a desultory musketry-fire was kept up all day, but with little damage to either side. Next morning, however, the mutineers decamped towards Shāhgarh taking with them some carriages belonging to the officers, but abandoning them on the road.

The Rājās of Bānpur and Shāhgarh.

37. The Rājās of Bānpur and Shāhgarh now sent emissaries to all the petty chiefs in the Saugor and Nerbudda territories inciting them to join in the rebellion. Many rose in Saugor and Damoh, and a few in Jubbulpore, Mandlā and Narsinghpur, but Hoshangābād and Seonī remained tranquil. About the 9th July the tahsils and station-houses of Khurai and Binaikā were attacked, the former by the Rājā of Bānpur and the latter by the Shāhgarh troops. The tahsildār of Khurai and most of the police at both places joined the insurgents. Major Gaussen arrived at Saugor on the 12th, but most of his troops had deserted, and on his departure the Rājā of Bānpur had taken possession of the north of the District. A company of the 31st with two European officers and Lieutenant Hamilton was now despatched towards Binaikā, and on the 21st July were attacked near there by the Shāhgarh rebels who were repulsed with the loss of a gun. As the rebels were subsequently reinforced the detachment returned to Saugor. The Nawāb of Amāpāni in Bhopāl now took possession of the fort of Rāhatgarh, driving out such of the police as he could not induce to join him. The Shāhgarh troops occupied Garhākotā, and the Rājā of Bānpur with about 1,300 men moved down from the north and took up a strong position at Nariaolī, 12 miles from Saugor, from which place on

the 25th July his forces advanced to the cantonment and fired on the artillery barracks. They decamped when the troops moved out against them.

Condition of the District.

38. Practically the whole District was now in the hands of one or other of the rebel leaders, and the mālguzārs, many of whom were well disposed, were forced to join and assist them with men and food, or were plundered and often tortured. No mails were received in Saugor for weeks, with the exception of occasional notes brought by highly-paid runners, several of whom were caught, and mutilated or killed. On the 17th September the Nariaolī rebels again advanced to the Rāhatgarh gate of the town and fired a few shots, and next day a detachment of the 42nd under Colonel Dalzell and 200 Customs chaprāsis under European Officers were sent out to attack them. The attack, however, failed and Colonel Dalzell was killed, and Lieutenant Prior, the Executive Engineer, wounded. About this time the Lalitpur party arrived in Saugor. On the 2nd October a detachment was sent against the rebels on the Narsinghpur road who were dispersed. The detachment then patrolled the road and postal communication with Narsinghpur was reestablished. A party of 100 men under Lieutenant Dickens was subsequently sent against Rehlī, but before their arrival it had been recovered by a landowner named Girdhāri Naik, who held it until the troops arrived, and assisted them in repelling an attack made by the mutineers of the 52nd Regiment from Jubbulpore. The Narsinghpur road had now been cleared by the Deputy Commissioners of the two Districts who marched along it, and supplies began to come in, while prices fell 30 per cent. in the Saugor bazar. On the 15th December a party was sent to attack the rebels at Bhāpel, about eight miles west of Saugor, but was repulsed with the loss of seven killed, including a European gunner, and four wounded.

The Central India Field Force.

39. By the end of December, order was being restored and most of the troops and officers were moving about the District. On the 25th January 1858 the Deputy Commissioner received authentic information that Sir Hugh Rose's force might be expected at Saugor by the end of the month, and next day the troops arrived at Rāhatgarh, the fort being immediately attacked and evacuated by the rebels on the 29th. On the 31st a large body of rebels under the Bānpur Rājā moved to Barodia and Jhila against Sir Hugh Rose, but were attacked and dispersed by him with the loss of 100 killed and many wounded, the British loss being one killed and six or seven wounded. On the 3rd February the force under Sir H. Rose arrived at Saugor, and those officers and ladies who were still residing in the fort returned to their houses. On the 9th Sir Hugh Rose moved on to Garhākotā, arriving there on the 10th, when he was fired on from the fort. The fire was returned and preparations made for a siege, but on the night of the 11th the enemy evacuated the fort and fled towards Shāhgarh. They were overtaken by a column under the command of Captain Hare of the Hyderābād Contingent, and about a hundred cut up. Sir Hugh Rose then returned to Saugor, and the Bānpur rebels on hearing this at once fled from Nariaolī and Khurai enabling the police to reoccupy these posts. The Field Force marched towards the north on the 27th February, and four days afterwards Mālthone and the Madanpur pass were secured and the Shāhgarh and Bānpur rebels with the mutineers of the 52nd defeated with great slaughter, after which Sir Hugh Rose proceeded towards Jhānsi.

Restoration of order.

40. Tranquillity was now rapidly restored throughout the District, but the northern portions and especially the Eran pargana long retained traces of the ravages to which they had been subjected Saugor is perhaps a solitary instance

of a station and city being held almost intact, while the whole surrounding country was in the possession of the rebels. The prestige of the fort had always been very great among the people, and subsequently stood higher than ever. Viewing the operations as a whole, and considering the inferior quality of the rebel forces opposed to him, it seems necessary to conclude that the Officer Commanding the garrison might have displayed more enterprise, but it must be remembered that the only regular troops he had were natives of whose fidelity he was very doubtful, while in the event of a serious disaster he had no ground for hoping that a British force could be despatched to assist him, at a time when every available man was needed for the vitally important struggle proceeding in Northern India. Bakhat Balī, the rebel Rājā of Shāhgarh, gave himself up and was sent as a state prisoner to Lahore, his estate being confiscated and divided between Saugor and Lalitpur. A similar fate befell the Bānpur Rājā. Delan Shā, the Gond chief who had participated in the outbreak of 1842, again rebelled and was seized and hanged by the Deputy Commissioner of Narsinghpur. Many landholders and others gave assistance to the British and were suitably rewarded. Among them may be mentioned the late Rai Bahādur Thākur Maharāj Singh and his grandfather, Kanhyā Lāl Tiwāri of Dhāna, Girdhāri Naik of Rehlī, and Indrajīt, Jemādār of Saugor, whose services are described in the notices of their respective families.

ARCHÆOLOGY.

41. Remains of archæological interest are described in the articles on the places in which they are found. The most important are those of Eran, the inscriptions at which have been already noticed. There are numerous old forts, the largest being that at Rāhatgarh, built by Sultān Muhammad Khān

[1]Archæology.

[1] See also under the various place-headings in the *Gazetteer*.

of Bhopāl. Next in importance is the fort of Dhāmoni, now in ruins, which was the local headquarters of a Mughal governor. Garhākotā has also a fort, occupying a strong position at the junction of the Sonār and Gadherī rivers, while about two miles north of the town on the borders of the *Ramnā* forest stand the ruins of what appears to have been a large summer palace built by Rājā Mardan Singh. The most remarkable part of these remains is a lofty tower still in tolerable preservation, which is about 100 feet high, and contains six stories with a winding stone staircase the whole way up. The District is full of old forts and little mud fortresses or *garhīs*, the relics of the troublous times through which it has passed, built by the Ahīrs, Gonds and Marāthās. About twenty-seven still exist either wholly or partly in ruins, the most important, other than those already mentioned, being at Garhpahrā, Deorī, Rehlī, Khuraī and Khimlāsa. Ruins of temples built of stone without mortar in the medieval Brahmanic style exist at Eran, Pithoria, Bāmora, and Garholī. Inside the fort at Khimlāsa is a Muhammadan tomb the walls of which are of beautifully perforated screen-work.

CHAPTER III.

POPULATION.

STATISTICS OF POPULATION.

Statistics of area and population, density, towns and villages.

42. The area and population of the District in 1901 were 4,007 square miles and 471,046 persons respectively. Since the census 11 villages containing 1,567 persons and a strip of Government forest in the extreme south abutting on the Nerbudda, have been transferred to the Narsinghpur District, for better adjustment of boundaries, and the revised figures of area and population are 3,962 square miles and 469,479 persons. Both in area and population Saugor approximates fairly closely to the averages for a District in the Central Provinces, being in both respects a little above the average. The area and population of the four tahsils are shown in the marginal statement.

Tahsīl.	Area.	Population.
Saugor ...	1,064	166,399
Rehlī ...	1,254	136,463
Khurai ...	940	93,788
Bandā ...	704	72,829

Rehlī is the largest tahsīl in area, and Saugor in population; while Bandā is the smallest in both respects. The total density of population is 118 persons and the density for the rural area 101 persons. Saugor is now the most thickly populated tahsīl with 156 persons per square mile or 117 excluding towns, while Khurai is the most sparsely populated with a total density of 100 persons. Rehlī and Bandā have 109 and 103 persons respectively per square mile. The most thickly populated part of the open country is Garhākotā Station-house area with 214 persons to the square mile, and next to this Etāwa with 163 persons; Khimlāsa with 106 and Barodia with 94 being the most sparsely populated. The District contains five towns, and 1,935 inhabited villages according to the census returns. The village lists show 2,164 towns and villages, of which 347 are uninhabited and only 1,817 inhabited. Some uninhabited villages must apparently have been shown as inhabited in the census lists. Seven forest and six ryotwāri villages are included in the above total. The average population to a village in the rural area is 208 persons or 42 houses as against 265 persons for all British Districts. The figures of population of the towns in 1901 were Saugor 42,330, Garhākotā 8,508, Etāwa 6.418, Khurai 6,012, and Deorī 4,980. The total urban population was 68,248 persons or 15 per cent. of that of the District. Besides the towns five other villages, *viz.*, Rehlī (3,665), Rāhatgarh (3,554), Jaisinghnagar (2,131), Shāhpur (2,434), and Gourjhāmar (2,264), contain more than 2,000 persons, while there are 35 with more than 1,000 persons. 712 villages contain less than 100 persons or 20 houses, while 1,282 or 66 per cent. contain under 200 persons, this proportion being the highest in the Province with the exception of Mandlā and Chānda.

Names of villages.

43. Among the names of villages which have meanings, the following may be mentioned:—*Bānsa*, the village of bamboos; *Barkhedā*, of the banyan trees; *Bamorī*, of the *babūl* trees; *Berkhedī*, of the wild plum trees; *Kanerā*, from the *kaner* tree (*Nerium odorum*); *Majhgawān*, the central village; *Marhia*, from *marhi*, a small temple; *Masānia*, from *masān*, a cremation ground (under Hindu rule *masān* was also a place where capital sentences were carried out); *Patharia*, a stony hill; *Rāngir*, from *rān*, jungle; *Rāhatgarh*, a pleasure house or country house; *Sainkhedā*, the village of the *fakīrs*; *Semrā* or *Simaria*, from the *semar* or cotton tree (*Bombax malabaricum*); *Mohlī*, from the *māhul* creeper (*Bauhinia vahlii*); and *Barodia*, perhaps from *burā deh*, a large village, or *bar-bandh*, the banyan tree on the tank.

Variation in population.

44. A census of the District has now been taken on five occasions. In 1866 the population was 498,642 persons. At the second census in 1872 an increase of 29,083 persons or 5·8 per cent.

was disclosed, the population being 527,725. It was considered that there had been some immigration from Damoh where the famine of 1868-69 had been somewhat severe. In 1881 the population was 564,950 persons, showing an increase of 7 per cent. on 1872. This increase was the lowest in the Province. The year 1878 had been very unhealthy with a death rate of 56 per mille. The natural increment for the decade was only 2·83 per cent., and it was estimated that about 20,000 of the famine refugees from Gwalior and other States in 1877-78 had remained in the District. At the census 11,000 persons were shown as having been born in Gwalior, 25,000 in Bundelkhand, and 24,000 in the North-Western Provinces. At the next census in 1891 the population was 591,743 persons, showing an increase of nearly 27,000 persons or rather under 5 per cent. on 1881, as against 9·6 for British Districts as a whole. The last years of the decade had been unhealthy with a high death rate. It was considered that there had been some emigration to Central India. The increase was highest in the Khurai tahsīl, 7·9 per cent., and lowest in the Rehlī tahsīl, 1·3 per cent. In 1901 the population was 471,046 persons, having decreased by 120,697 persons or 20·4 per cent. since 1891. The District was one of those most severely affected by famine and scarcity throughout the decade,[1] the number of deaths being in excess of the births in 1894, 1895, 1896, 1897 and 1900, or in five out of the ten years. The decrease was 26 per cent. in the Khurai tahsīl, 24 per cent. in the rural area of Saugor tahsīl, 19 per cent. in Rehlī, and 17 per cent in Bandā. The areas dependent mainly on autumn crops suffered less severely than the wheat-growing tracts. The excess of deaths over births during the decade was 85,000 persons, while the census disclosed a decrease of population 35,000 in excess of that deduced from vital statistics. This difference was small in comparison with that of some of the other badly affected Districts.

[1] See Chapter VII.—Famine.

Births and Deaths.

45. Between 1881 and 1891 the birth rate averaged 43·7 per mille and was the highest in the Province, and the death rate was 38·4 or the second highest. The only conclusion which it appears possible to draw from these figures is that the registration of vital statistics was somewhat more accurate in Saugor than elsewhere. During the decade ending 1901 the annual death rate was 44·7 per mille, which was higher than any District except Nimār ; while the birth rate was 30·3 or the lowest in the Province, these figures sufficiently indicating the severe trials through which the people have passed.

Diseases.

46. Major Sutherland writes on diseases : 'The effects 'of the meteorological conditions on the 'health of the people are direct and in- 'direct. When the high temperature and extreme dryness 'of the hot weather suddenly give place to the lower temper- 'ature and excessive humidity of the rainy season, the people 'are prone to congestion of the abdominal organs resulting in 'bowel diseases. This is more especially evident in years 'of distress when their stomachs have been weakened by 'privation, the result being that the death rate rises with a 'bound as soon as the rains have set in. Later when the 'anopheles mosquitoes have had time to breed in the pools, 'there is a marked increase in the number of fever cases. 'As in the case of bowel diseases the mortality from fever is 'always excessive in years of distress. In the cold weather 'the people tend to crowd together in tightly closed apart- 'ments, and ill-adapted as their clothing is to the sudden 'and excessive variations of temperature, they are subject to 'diseases of the respiratory passages. In the hot weather, 'owing to the pollution of the water-supply, inflammatory 'diarrhœa is prevalent, changing to cholera if the germ should 'happen to be imported. The dust which lies so thickly 'everywhere in the hot weather, and rises in clouds as men 'and cattle pass along the roads, is a fruitful cause of eye

'disorders. The second part of the year is the most un-'healthy, and particularly the months of August, September 'and October.'

Cholera.

47. Epidemics of cholera are comparatively infrequent as compared with other parts of the Province. Severe epidemics occurred in 1869, 1876, 1889, 1896, 1897, and 1900. In four at least of these years, distress or famine was prevalent. The highest number of deaths was recorded in 1869, amounting to 9,376 and being equivalent to an annual rate of 19 per mille. Cholera has not been absent for more than three years at a time since 1874. Major Sutherland considers the mortality to be at the rate of about 50 per cent. of the cases.

Small-pox.

48. There is always a certain amount of small-pox, and in each of twenty-three years between 1870 to 1902 more than a hundred deaths have resulted from this disease. The worst epidemic was in 1875 when 4,447 deaths occurred or at the rate of 8·4 per mille of population. In 1884 there were 718 deaths and in 1895, 476. As a rule the mortality does not exceed two to three hundred a year. Major Sutherland says: 'Undoubtedly a good many, probably 'at least 6 per cent. of deaths reported from small-pox, may 'be attributed to chicken-pox or chicken-pox and malaria.'

Fever.

49. Deaths from fever generally exceed half the total mortality reported, while the highest figures have been recorded in the famine years. The average annual mortality during 1881—1890, was 22·4, and during 1891—1900, 30·7 per mille. Major Sutherland states: 'The parasites principally met 'with are those of tropical fever and benign tertian. 'Quotidian parasites I have not seen, and those of quartan fever 'are rare. Now and then one comes across a case, generally 'among Europeans, where malaria is not the cause of the 'infection. These cases last for days and weeks, but are

'certainly not due to typhoid infection, nor are they obscure 'cases of Mediterranean fever, judging from the results of 'agglutinative experiments. What they are I do not know, 'nor, so far as I have had access to the literature of the 'subject, have they ever been differentiated.' Guinea-worm is rare and most of the cases met with are imported from Damoh, where this disease is common.

Lathyrism.

50. A considerable number of cases of incurable paralysis have resulted from the consumption of *tiurā* (*Lathyrus sativus*) during the famines. This disease has appeared on previous occasions, being noticed by Sleeman in 'Rambles and Recollections' in the early part of the nineteenth century.

Leprosy, blindness, etc.

51. Compared with the Province as a whole, leprosy is very rare in Saugor, and has always been so, though during the last decade (1891—1901) lepers, having specially weak lives and often being unable to support themselves, would have been liable to succumb more rapidly to privation than others. The principal form of the disease met with is the tubercular, in Major Sutherland's experience. Blindness, on the other hand, is very prevalent. the figures being 17 males and 23 females in 10,000 of each sex, as against the Provincial figures of 13 and 18 respectively. The tendency to the seclusion of women, and to passing much time indoors in a smoky atmosphere on account of the coldness of the climate, may perhaps be assigned as reasons for the prevalence of blindness. The proportions of insane and deaf-mutes do not vary greatly from the Provincial average.

Plague.

52. A few cases of plague occurred for the first time in 1903, and its appearance was accompanied by the usual panic and the circulation of wild stories to the effect that it was spread by the Government and that inoculation and disinfection by potassium permanganate were the means by which people were infected with the disease.

Language—Bundelī.

53. The language of the District is the Bundelkhandī or Bundelī dialect of Western Hindi, which is spoken by 97 per cent. of the population. Bundelī differs from Urdū in some points of inflection. In Bundelī the long *a* of the terminations of substantives and adjectives is turned into *o* as *ghoro* for *ghorā*, *Etao achchho gaon hai*, Etāwa is a good village. The change is also made in the participial form of verbs as *khao* for *khāya*. Another tendency is to leave out the aspirate if it is not the initial letter of a word; thus *pahilā* (first) would be *pailo*, *pahar* (3 hours), *pair*, and so on. The *ko* of the oblique case is also changed to *e* as *tum bazāre gaye hate* for *tum bazār ko gaye the*. If the root of a verb ends in long *a* it is changed into *ai* to form the verbal noun as *khaibo* for *khāna*. In the future the termination *ga* is not used in Bundelī, but the Gujarāti termination *shai* altered into *hai* is used, as *u karhai* for *wah karegā*. The past tense of the substantive verb *thā*, *the* is changed to *hato*, *hate* and the long *a* in the termination of the participle is shortened, as for instance *wah jāta thā* would become *u jāt hato*. In Bundelī as in Urdū the particle *ne* always follows the nominative to transitive verbs in the past tenses, and in this respect it differs from Western Hindī. Bundelī has a small literature dating from the time of Chhatar Sāl of Pannā, and his immediate predecessors and successors of the early part of the eighteenth century. One of the leading poets of Hindī literature (Padmākar) was born in Saugor, and his poems, which are very popular, are largely tinctured with Bundelī.

Other languages.

54. Marāthi is spoken by a few thousand persons, the form of the language being the standard Marāthī of Poona, and not the Nāgpur dialect. This is an interesting historical survival of the fact that Saugor was governed direct from Poona by emissaries of the Peshwā, and did not come under the Bhonsla dynasty. The Marāthās now also speak Bundelī, and their Marāthī is much mixed with Hindī words. The same remark applies to

the Khedāwāl Brāhmans, whose Gujarāti is greatly corrupted by the local speech. Muhammadans in the towns talk Urdū, and in the interior Bundelī. The Gonds have almost entirely abandoned their own language and adopted the District vernacular.

Occupations.

55. The District has no mining or factory industries. The proportion of the population supported by pasture and agriculture is 65 per cent. as against an average of 72 per cent. for British Districts. This low proportion is to be explained by the fact that Saugor, like the other Northern Districts, has a large number of persons engaged in personal service, and also that the village artisans and servants are more numerous than in other parts of the Province. Social life in the interior is somewhat more developed and agriculturists get work done for them by the hereditary village servants which elsewhere they do for themselves. The proportion of personal servants, 4·3 per cent., is the third highest in the Province, being exceeded only by Narsinghpur and Hoshangābād. The servants are principally barbers, water-carriers, washermen and cooks. The number of persons engaged in preparing and selling articles of food and drink is also large. The principal classes among these are sellers of milk and ghī, and butchers. *Ghī* or melted butter is one of the most important products of the District, and an extensive cattle-slaughtering industry has grown up in recent years; flesh is also more commonly eaten in the Northern Districts than in the south and east. A considerable number of persons are engaged in selling areca-nut and betel-leaf. The cotton industry, on the other hand, is very weak in Saugor, only four Districts having a smaller number of spinners and weavers. The leather industry is numerically the strongest in the Province, though Damoh in proportion to its population has a larger number of leather-workers. The industry has, however, grievously declined since 1891. Shoes are universally worn in Saugor and Damoh, and the Saugor or Bundelkhandī shoe is a much

more elaborate and highly-finished article than that of other Districts. The pottery industry is numerically the third strongest in the Province, though it also has largely declined in the last decade. Earthen pots are commonly used by all classes, for purposes for which metal ones are substituted elsewhere. The number of leaf-plate makers is also large. One hundred and five persons are shown as medical practitioners without diploma, this number being exceeded only in Wardhā, Nāgpur and Sambalpur. The native doctors still enjoy a large measure of confidence from the people in Saugor. The number of midwives is also unusually large.

RELIGION.

Statistics.

56. The figures of religion show that Hindus constitute 87 per cent. of the population, Animists 4 per cent, Muhammadans 5 per cent, and Jains 3 per cent. The proportion of professed Animists is low in Saugor as compared with other Districts, the forest tribes being found in small numbers and having generally attained to some degree of civilisation. There is nothing noticeable about the local Hindus, their religion being of the same rural and Animistic type as in the rest of the Province.

Village gods.

57. There are a number of village gods to whom practically all classes of the population pay reverence, and the principal of whom are the following:—Khermāta is the goddess of the earth or the village, and is sometimes treated as a local incarnation of Devī, this being no doubt the work of Brāhman priests. She has a small hut and an image of Devī either black or red. She is worshipped by a priest called Pandā, who may be of any caste except the impure castes. When an epidemic of cholera breaks out, the Pandā performs the following ceremony to avert it. He takes a kid, and a small pig or chicken, and some cloth, cakes. glass bangles, vermilion, an earthen lamp, and some country liquor, which is sprinkled all along the way from

where he starts to where he stops. He proceeds in this manner to the boundary of the village, at a place where there are cross-roads and leaves all the things there. Sometimes the animals are sacrificed and eaten. While the Pandā is doing this, every one collects the sweepings of his house in a winnowing fan and throws it outside the village boundary, at the same time ringing a bell continuously. The Pandā must perform his ceremony at night and, if possible, on the day of the new moon. He is accompanied by a few other low-caste persons called Gunias. A Gunia is a person who can be possessed by a spirit in the temple of Khermāta. When possessed he shakes his head up and down violently, and foams at the mouth, and sometimes hangs his head on the ground. Another favourite godling is Hardaul who was the brother of Jujhār Singh, Rājā of Orchhā, and was suspected by Jujhār Singh of loving his wife, and poisoned in consequence by his orders. Hardaul is chiefly honoured at weddings and in the month of Baisākh (April—May), when women visit his shrine, and after cooking and eating their food at it, worship him and go home. Hardaul has a platform and sometimes a hut with an image of a man on horseback carrying a spear in his hand. The shrine is decorated with a flag and is always outside the village. Two days before the arrival of a wedding procession, the women of the family worship Hardaul, and invite him to the wedding. Hanumān is a favourite deity, and his shrine, consisting of a slab with an image of a monkey in half relief and coloured in red vermilion, is seen everywhere. Dūlha Deo is another godling whose shrine is in every village. He was a young bridegroom who was carried off by a tiger on his way to his wedding, or according to another account was turned into a stone pillar by a flash of lightning. Before the starting of a wedding procession, the members go to Dūlha Deo and offer a pair of shoes, and a miniature post and marriage crown. On their return they offer a cocoanut. Dūlha Deo has a stone and platform to the east of the village, or occasionally an image of a man on horseback like Hardaul. Mirohia is the god of the field boundary. There is no sign of him, but every tenant, when he begins sowing and cutting the crops, offers a little curd and rice and a cocoanut, laying them on the boundary of the field and saying the name of Mirohia Deo. It is believed among agriculturists that if this godling is neglected, he will flatten the corn by a wind or cause the cart to break on its way to the threshing-floor. Ghatoia is located on the crossing of a river or nullah, in the shape of a round stone on a platform. A cocoanut and flowers are offered to him. A bride going to her husband's house for the first time must on no account neglect to worship Ghatoia, or she will infallibly fall ill. Pregnant women should also bow before his shrine whenever they see it, or they are likely to suffer from miscarriage. Nāg Deo or the cobra is worshipped on Nāg Panchamī. If there is a shrine all the people go there, and offer betel-leaf mixed with milk and boiled wheat. If there is no shrine they go to a snake hole or *bāmi* and worship him there, or make an image of a cobra on the wall with ghī or cowdung and worship that. To see a snake on Nāg Panchamī is regarded as a good omen, and on that day many Nāths carry about snakes in their baskets from door to door, and the people worship them, and give a pice or two to the Nāth. Gond Bāba is found in many villages. He is not any particular Gond but may be any Gond who has met with a violent death. He is represented simply by a heap of stones with a large one at the top. Mangat Deo is a hero who is celebrated in songs and worshipped. He was a Bundelā, and lived in Chanderī in Gwalior State, where his house is said still to exist. On one occasion the king of Delhi was halting at Chanderī on a march, and the tents of his army surrounded the tank. This was at the time of the *bhujaria* festival, and the women of the town could not get to the tank to throw in their pots of grain-stalks. So Mangat Deo put himself at their head and made a way through the tents so that the women could go to the tank, but was killed while doing so. Hence he has been deified and worshipped.

Primitive ceremonies. The commencement of cultivation.

58. The following are some special ceremonies observed at festivals. *Aktī*, or the 3rd day of the light fortnight of Baisākh (April—May) is the beginning of the agricultural year. On this day the lambardār of the village takes a new *bakhar* or surface plough and a pair of bullocks and goes to the fields accompanied by the tenants. The *pandit* or Brāhman priest sprinkles some water over the share of the *bakhar*, and covers it with cowdung and turmeric. Some grains of til, mūng, urad, juār and other crops are then placed on the *bakhar* together with a rupee, and the lambardār worships it. The lambardār then puts his arms round the share and takes up the rupee with the grain and earth. The grain is sprinkled over the field, which is ploughed with the *bakhar*. Each man then tries to pick up a clod with some grain in it, and, taking it home, places it in his threshing-floor. All the tenants subsequently assemble at the mālguzār's house and betel-leaf is distributed, the women receiving *ghungrī* or boiled wheat and gram. Each tenant also ploughs a little in his own holding, it being necessary to drive an odd number of furrows. This ceremony is called 'haraitā lenā.' On the 11th day of Asārh[1] Sudi (second or light fortnight) the gods are believed to go to sleep. Food is offered to them on this day. They awake again on the 11th day of Kārtik[2] Sudī and are fed and worshipped.

Tīja.

59. The 'Tīja' festival takes place on the 3rd day of Bhādon[3] Sudī. Married women fast for the whole twenty-four hours without drinking or eating. They pass the night singing songs of praise to Mahādeo and Pārvati, and next morning bathe early, and take their food after worshipping Mahādeo. This is supposed to save them from widowhood.

---

[1] June—July. | [2] October—November. | [3] August—September.

The Jawāras.

60. The sowing of the 'jawāras' takes place during the first nine days of the months of Kunwār and Chait.[1] On the first day a small room in the house is cleaned and white-washed. Some earth is then brought from the fields and mixed with manure in a basket. A male member of the family sows wheat in the basket, bathing before he does so. The basket is placed in the room prepared for it, which is called the *diwāla* or temple, and the same man attends on it throughout the nine days, fasting all day and eating only milk and fruit at night. A lamp is kept continually burning in the room, and fed with *ghī* instead of oil, the wick being ignited by a flint, and not with fire kindled in the ordinary way, as this is blown by the mouth and therefore considered impure. During the period of nine days, called the *naorātra*, the plants are watered, and long stalks spring up. On the 8th day the *hom* ceremony is performed, and the *gunias* or devotees are possessed by Devī. On the evening of the 9th day the women putting on their best clothes walk out of the houses with the pots of grain on their heads singing songs in praise of Devī. The men accompany them beating drums and cymbals. The devotees pierce their cheeks with long iron needles, and walk in the procession. High-caste women, who cannot go themselves, hire the barber's or waterman's wife to go for them. The pots are taken to a tank and thrown in, the stalks of grain being kept and distributed as a mark of amity. The wheat which is sown in Kunwār gives a forecast of the spring crops. A plant is pulled out, and the return of the crop will be the same number of times the seed as it has roots. The woman who gets to the tank first counts the number of plants in her pot, and this gives the price of wheat in rupees per mānī.[2] Sometimes marks of red rust appear on the plants, and this shows that the crop will suffer from rust. The

[1] Corresponding roughly to September and March.
[2] A measure of 400 lbs.

ceremony performed in Chait is said to be a sort of harvest thanksgiving. On the 9th day of the Kunwār ceremony another celebration called 'Jhinjhia' or 'Nortā' takes place in large villages. A number of young unmarried girls take earthen pots and, making holes in them and placing lamps inside, carry them on their heads through the village singing and dancing. They receive presents from the villagers, with which they hold a feast. At this a small platform is erected, and two earthen dolls, male and female, are placed on it ; rice and flowers are offered to them and their marriage is celebrated.

Other festivals.

61. The *aonlā* tree (*Phyllanthus Emblica*) is regarded as sacred and is worshipped on the 9th day of Kārtik[1] Sudī (light fortnight). Members of the higher castes go and take their food under the tree and feed Brāhmans under it. If a man has cheated somebody out of some property, and goes and takes his food under the aonlā tree he is freed from his sin. Feeding under the aonlā tree on this day is believed to be a means of going to heaven. Cattle are worshipped at Diwāli (15th Kārtik Badī). Their horns are coloured and patches of green dye are daubed on their bodies, and bunches of the fibrous roots of the *palās* tree (*Butea frondosa*) are tied to their horns. This is the one day of the year on which all cattle are given salt, and also a feed of grain and pulse. The Ahīrs dress up, and go round singing and dancing to the houses of the persons whose cattle they graze, where they are given a present.

The Holī.

62. The Holī festival falls on Phāgun[2] Sudī 15th, and is the end of the Hindu year. A large bonfire is made and worshipped, and obscene songs are sung. The fire from the bonfire burnt at the Holī is taken home, and in some houses kept alight the whole year. In the centre of

[1] October—November.

[2] February—March.

the bonfire a post is planted with a flag, and the direction in which it falls is taken as an omen. East and west are lucky directions, south unlucky, and north neutral. If the flag burns and floats up into the air, a severe famine is indicated. At the Holī festival it is a favourite amusement to have a performance of the village dancing-girls or Bernis. This is called 'Rāee'. The girls dance for the whole night, being recuperated by constant supplies of liquor. Another amusement among the low castes is as follows:—A long slippery pole is placed in the ground, and a bag of *gur* (sugar) and a rupee are tied to the top of it. The women stand round the pole with long bamboos in their hands, to defend it, while the men try to climb the pole, and are beaten by the women. They hold sticks tied in the shape of a cross-bar in their hands to defend themselves. The man who first manages to climb the pole takes the rupee, while the sugar is distributed among the people.

Kabīrpanthīs.

63. Only two sects of Hindus need be mentioned, the Kabīrpanthīs and Bām-Mārgis. Some 6,000 persons return themselves as Kabīrpanthīs[1], mainly Korīs who profess Kabīrpanthīsm because Kabīr, the founder of the sect, was a weaver. Their religion is purely nominal however, and they follow none of the tenets of the sect, neither as a rule burying their dead nor abstaining from liquor, and both worshipping idols and observing caste distinctions. Some, however, bury the dead, and while carrying them to the burying place beat drums as a sign of rejoicing that the soul has been freed from the commission of sins. The Bām-Mārgis are a secret sect whose ritual is distinguished by its obscenity. Some adherents of the sect are believed to reside in the District.

Muhammadans.

64. Muhammadans number some 23,000 persons, of whom 13,000 live in towns. A number of the Muhammadans are Bahnās or cot-

[1] See the Census Reports of 1891 and 1901 for a description of the Kabīrpanthī sect.

ton-carders, whose beliefs and practices are mainly Hindu. The largest numbers of Muhammadans live in Saugor and Garhākotā. They hold about 100 villages in the District, but the only important landlord is the mālguzār of Hirankhedā whose management and treatment of his tenants leaves much to be desired. Recently Azīmullā Khān, a wealthy resident of Saugor, has purchased a number of villages. Saugor contains a number of *fakīrs* or Muhammadan beggars who are very importunate. They have customary dues at births and marriages, and take contributions from fruit-sellers and others in the bazar. They beg from the townspeople at the Rakshābandhan and Holī festivals.

Jains.

65. Saugor is the stronghold of the Jain religion in the Central Provinces and contains some 15,000 Jains or a third of the whole number in the Province. The Jains are either Swetāmbarīs, or Digambarīs. The Digambarīs do not clothe their idols and apply saffron to their feet, while the Swetāmbarīs clothe them, and put saffron on their foreheads. Pārasnāth, one of the 24 Tīrthankars or saints is the chief object of adoration. Jains are nearly always Baniās by caste. Jain temples are generally built outside the village or town, probably because when Hindu kings were in power they were not allowed to build within its precincts. A Hindu should not enter a Jain temple or even build his house within its shadow. The Jain temples and idols are richly decorated, and permanently endowed, gifts to a temple being a mode of expiating sin. The idols are generally in the sitting posture of contemplation and are made of brass, stone, and occasionally of silver and gold. Any Jain who is learned in the sacred books can be a Bhaiji or priest of a temple, the office being honorary, and he being at liberty at the same time to carry on his own profession. He recites from the religious books in the temple. The offerings, which consist of vegetables and fruits are taken by the Hindu Māli, who is employed as a menial servant to clean the temple,

and he retails them in the bazar. Every Jain must perform *darshan* or the contemplation of his idol before taking his food, and if there is no temple in his own village he must walk to another one. Their tenderness of animal life is notorious, but at present they are inclined to resort to subterfuge in order to evade the inconvenience entailed on them by their rules. Thus a Jain may not eat between sunset and sunrise in order to avoid swallowing insects, but now they sometimes place a lamp under a sieve so that the shafts of light may resemble the sun's rays and eat by the light of that. They may not eat fresh roots such as potatoes, as they contain insects, but must have them dried. Ginger also must be eaten dried. Neither Jains nor other Baniās smoke or drink liquor. They chew tobacco and betel-leaf. They do not shave in token of mourning, nor give a feast on the occasion of a death, nor pour libations to the dead. Marriage is little more than a civil contract, and at a marriage they often send presents of flour, vegetables, and ghī to their friends rather than invite them to their houses.

The *Rath* festival.

66 The great ceremony of the Jains is the *rath* or chariot festival for the following description of which I am indebted to Mr. Hīra Lāl. 'A *pandal* or tent is constructed of masonry pillars with coloured cloths spread over them, and 'in this the idols of the hosts and all the guests are 'placed. When the ceremony is performed they are taken 'out and placed on *raths* or wooden cars, sometimes as 'much as five stories high, and each drawn by two elephants. 'The procession of cars moves seven times round the tent, 'at a slow pace, surrounded by all the people. For the performance of this ceremony honorary and hereditary titles are 'conferred. Those who do it once receive the distinction of ''Singhai', for carrying it out twice they become 'Sawai-'Singhai', and on a third occasion 'Seth'. In the Khurai 'ceremony one of the participators was already a 'Seth', 'and, in recognition of his unwonted profusion, a new title

'was created and he became 'Shrimant Seth'. If, however, 'the procession does not go off successfully and the car breaks 'or the elephants refuse to move, the title becomes derisive 'and is either 'Lūle Singhai' (the lame one) or 'Adku 'Singhai' (the stumbler)'.

Christians, Europeans and Eurasians.

67. The number of Christians in 1901 was nearly 1,400, of whom 500 were Europeans, 100 Eurasians, and nearly 800 Native Christians. The Europeans consist mainly of the European troops, the civil officers and missionaries, and a considerable colony of railway servants at Bīna. Saugor is in the Anglican diocese of Nāgpur and is the headquarters of a chaplain who also visits the surrounding stations. It is contained in the Roman Catholic Diocese of Allahābād and has a chaplain and a Loretto convent, which is now provisionally closed, besides the Mission mentioned below.

Native Christians.

68. The number of Native Christians nearly trebled between 1891 and 1901. About half of them are Roman Catholics and most of the remainder Lutherans. Three Missions are working in the District, two supported by the Roman Catholic and Swedish Lutheran Churches and the third by the body known as The Disciples of Christ. The Roman Catholic Mission at Shyāmpurā was founded in 1875. The Mission owns this village, which is just to the north of Saugor, and parts of two others. It maintains orphanages for native boys and girls with nearly 200 inmates. The boys are taught farming, carpentry and smith's work, and the girls sewing and house-work. The staff consists of a priest and several nuns. The Swedish Lutheran Mission has its headquarters at Saugor and Khurai with out-stations at Garhākotā and Khimlāsa. The staff comprises several European and native Missionaries, and the Mission supports boys' and girls' schools with nearly 200 pupils, an orphanage at Saugor, a small school at Khurai, and a village farm at Bagthari where some of the orphans are taught farming. The Mission of the Disciples of

Christ was started at Bīna and Etāwa in 1894. It maintains two day-schools in the bazar between Etāwa and the railway station with an attendance of about 100 children, and a charitable dispensary. The staff comprises a European Superintendent and female zenana missionaries. The Mission belongs to no recognised sect, but teaches the Christian religion and holds services for the English-speaking residents of Bīna.

CASTE.

Principal castes.

69. The population has been recruited mainly by immigration from North-Western India through Bundelkhand. The people are generally more spirited and more free and independent in bearing than those of other parts of the Central Provinces. As has already been seen, in 1842 Saugor had a small rising of its own, while in 1857 it was more disturbed than any District in the Province. The Dāngis and Bundelās were the descendants of gangs of free-booters, while the Lodhīs have in the past always been ready for a fight. Fifty years of unbroken tranquillity have, however, in a great measure removed these characteristics and these classes have settled down into respectable and peaceable cultivators. The principal castes are, among those wearing the sacred thread, Brāhmans, Rājputs and Baniās; among cultivating castes of good status, Dāngis, Ahīrs, Kurmīs, Lodhīs, and Kāchhis; and among those of lower status Khangārs, Chadārs and Telis. The primitive tribes are represented by the Gonds and Saonrs, and among the impure castes Chamārs muster strong.

Brahman: Jijhotia, Kanaujia, Sarwaria.

70. Brāhmans constitute 9 per cent. of the population, being the most numerous caste next to Chamārs, and own some 650 villages. The majority of the Brāhmans come from Northern India and belong to the Kanaujia branch of the Panch-Gaur or five northern divisions, subdivided into the Jijhotias, Kanaujias and Sarwarias. Among these the Jijhotias are most

numerous, and reckon Saugor as their home, as it was included in the territory of Jajhoti from which they take their name. Jijhotia Brāhmans are believed to have been dominant in this locality during the seventh century. Another etymology which they give themselves, but which is undoubtedly wrong, is from Jujhār Singh, a Bundelā chief, who performed a sacrifice and from whom 13 Kanaujia Brāhman boys accepted gifts. They were therefore degraded in rank and became the Jijhotias. The Sarwarias are so named from the river Sarjū in the United Provinces, about which they live. The Kanaujias eat meat, while the Jijhotias and Sarwarias do not. Nevertheless, the Kanaujias are considered the highest, and take daughters in marriage from Jijhotias without giving them. The Sarwarias do not usually intermarry with the other two subdivisions, though instances are known of their marrying with Kanaujias. The orthodox Sarwarias do not take presents, and do not give their daughters to families in villages from which they have themselves taken girls. In Damoh the Sarwarias are above the Kanaujias and sometimes take daughters from them. The Jijhotias plough with their own hands, while the Kanaujias rarely do this and the Sarwarias never. The Sarwarias will not smoke, though they chew tobacco. These subdivisions are usually the priests of the other castes in Saugor.

Sanādhya, Harenia, Laheria, Bhagore.

71. The Sanādhyas or Sanaurhias are another subdivision of northern Brāhmans, probably a branch of the Gaur. Many of them are thieves stealing, according to tradition, only in the daytime and not at night. One of their methods is said to be to beat a boy in the sight of a rich stranger. The boy runs crying and clings to the stranger asking him for help, and in the meantime picks his pocket. This character does not apply of course to the majority of Sanādhyas. Crooke[1] distinguishes the Sanādhyas and Sanaurhias, stating that the latter are a criminal con-

[1] Tribes and Castes of the N.-W. P. and Oudh, art. Sanaurhia.

fraternity, and are recruited from members of all except the impure castes, while the Sanādhyas are regular Brāhmans and not criminal. Adi-Gaurs or Harenias are a small local subdivision, so called it is said because they came from Hariāna beyond Delhi. They have taken to cultivation. They hold about twelve villages close together which usually contain forts, while their own houses are old and large and better built than the ordinary. The Laherias are another small subdivision who live principally in a village Semrā which is called Semrā Laheria on this account. They allow widow marriage, and have the custom called *Antā-Sānta* or exchanging girls in marriage between two families. They have no learning and cannot usually read or write. The Bhagore Brāhmans belong to Mālwā. They are usually native physicians, who are very popular in Saugor and muster strong, the people preferring them to English doctors except for operations. They are paid only when the patient recovers, and their medicines are said to be more palatable than European ones.

Maratha Brahmans.

72. The Marāthā Brāhmans date from the eighteenth century when Saugor was occupied by them. The most numerous subdivision are the Karhādas who come from Karhār to the south of Sātāra, and who include among them the former ruling family originating with Govind Rao Pandit. Saugor is the stronghold of Marāthā Brāhmans north of the Nerbudda. The Marāthā Brāhmans are generally landowners or engaged in Government or private service. They prefer Government service to any other occupation, and begin training their children for it from the earliest age. Many of the Marāthā Brāhmans have now left the District.

Telugu Brahmans.

73. The District contains a few Telugu Brāhmans who immigrated many generations ago, and are locally called Gokulasths. They now talk Hindī, but traces of Telugu still remain in their speech. The poet Padmākar who was born in Saugor

described himself as a Telugu poet resident in Bundelkhand. He is said to have been given a lakh of rupees by Rājā Raghunāth Rao for a couplet in which he stated that Raghunāth Rao gave away so many elephants in charity that Pārvatī hid her own son, the elephant-headed Ganesh, for fear lest Raghunāth Rao might also bestow him as a gift.

Khedawals.

74. There are also a number of Khedāwāl Brāhmans who are immigrants from Gujarāt. Their local headquarters are at Hattā in Damoh, and they say that the reason for their settling in Saugor and Damoh was as follows: On one occasion a Khedāwāl was passing from Gujarāt to Benāres, when he saw some diamonds lying in a field. He stopped and collected as many as he could, and informed the Rājā of Pannā, who gave him a *jāgīr* or estate and from that time other Khedāwāls came. The head of the Khedāwāls in Saugor is, at the time of writing, one Govardhan Bhat Dube whose ancestors were money-lenders to the Chiefs of the surrounding States. His father is said to have given the Rānī of Jhānsi a lakh of rupees as a present on Rakshābandhan day, and to have been addressed by her as her brother. The family is now reduced to extreme poverty. The Khedāwāls were usually the accountants of Mārwāris, and the agents of mālguzārs, corresponding to the Kāyasths elsewhere, and like them they have acquired a bad reputation for honesty—

Khedāwāl kā bachchā
Kabhī na bole sachchā

or 'A Khedāwāl's son cannot tell the truth.' The above description cannot of course be taken as applying to the majority of the caste at present, many of whom are gentlemen of high reputation and standing in the native community. Many of the Khedāwāls are now in Government service, and some are landowners. The Khedāwāls are very strict in their observance of caste rules, and do not smoke but only chew tobacco. If a Khedāwāl is imprisoned, it takes most of his life before he gets back to his caste. They generally have the title of Mehtā. The name Khedāwāl is derived from Khedā, a village in Gujarāt.

Brāhman families.

75. The leading families of Hindustāni Brāhmans are Rāmgulām and Bhaiyā Lāl Dube of Saugor, the Dhāna family, the Paterias of Khamaria, Bhaiyā Lāl Naik of Rehlī, Gaurī Shankar Deolia of Rehlī, and Rāmchandra Chaube of Khairāna. Among Marāthā Brāhmans the Jaisinghnagar Etāwa and Pithoria families, the Sūbhedārs of Sanodhā, and the Killai, Deorī and Khimlāsa families, and Gopāl Rao of Rehlī are the most important.

Rājput.

76. Rājputs form about 3 per cent. of the population and own some 230 villages. A large number of septs are represented in Saugor, and several of these are of comparatively pure blood, being allowed to intermarry with the Rājputs of Northern India and Rājputāna. The Chauhāns, Parihārs, Solankīs and Ponwārs are locally considered to be the four highest septs, and marry with each other and some of the other septs. The Ponwārs are divided into two classes, the Dhār Ponwārs who come from Ujjain, and ordinary Ponwārs who are of inferior status and marry with Bundelās. The Rājputs in Saugor retain the regular custom by which members of a sept may not marry among themselves but must marry those of another sept, and have not as a rule developed into castes, as the Ponwārs, Raghuvansis and others elsewhere. But the caste is very mixed, and has a number of subdivisions who are not proper Rājputs, besides inferior or illegitimate branches of the regular septs. It is said locally that any one who has no other caste calls himself a Rājput. The Bundelās, inferior Ponwārs and another class called Dhundeles marry with each other, and there are also said to be 13 other subcastes who do not intermarry with the 36 recognised tribes. Hence it is said, 'The

Rājput though he belong neither to the three subcastes, nor the 13 subcastes, yet calls himself a Rājput, and blows his own trumpet in his own house.'

Bundelā.

77. The most important class of Rājputs locally are the Bundelās, who have given their name to Bundelkhand. They rank below proper Rājputs, and are considered to be partly illegitimate. The Bundelās were apparently a tribe or confraternity of free-booters. Their character, as disclosed in a number of proverbial sayings and stories current regarding them, somewhat resembles that of the Scotch Highlanders as depicted by Stevenson. They are proud and penurious to the last degree, and quick to resent the smallest slight. They make good *shikāris* or sportsmen, but are so impatient of discipline that they have never found a vocation by enlisting in the Indian Army. Their characteristics are thus described in a doggerel verse. 'The 'Bundelās salute each other from miles apart, their pagris 'are cocked on the side of their head till they touch their 'shoulders. A Bundelā would dive into a well for the 'sake of a cowrie, but would fight with the Sardārs of Gov'ernment. He could not kill a rat, but boasts that he has 'conquered thousands. So it is better to keep quiet, because 'the Bundelā will only talk you down with his lies.' No Baniā could go past a Bundelā's house riding on a pony or holding up an umbrella; and all low caste persons who passed his house must salute it with the words 'Dīwān jū ko Rām Rām.' Women must take their shoes off to pass by. It is related that a few years ago a Bundelā was brought up before the Assistant Commissioner charged with assaulting a tahsīl process-server and threatening him with his sword. The Bundelā, who was very poor and wearing rags, was asked by the Assistant Commissioner whether he had threatened the man with his sword. He replied 'Certainly not. The sword is for gentlemen like you and me, of equal position. To him, if I had wished to beat him, I should have

taken my shoe.' Another story is that there was once a very overbearing tahsīldār of Khurai, who had a shoe 2½ feet long with which he used to collect the land-revenue. One day a Bundelā mālguzār appeared before him on some business. The tahsildār kept his seat. The Bundelā walked quietly up to the table, and said 'Will the Sarkār step aside with me a moment, as I have something private to say.' The tahsīldār got up and walked aside with him, on which the Bundelā said 'That is sufficient, I only wished to tell you that you should rise to receive me.' When the Bundelās are collected at a feast, they sit with their hands folded across their stomachs and their eyes turned up, and remain impassive while food is being put on their plates, and never say 'Enough' because they think that they would show themselves to be feeble men, if they refused to eat as much as was put before them. Much of the food is thus ultimately wasted and given to the sweepers, and this leads to great extravagance at marriages and other ceremonial occasions. The Lodhīs have a similar practice. The Bundelās were much feared and were not popular landlords, but they are now losing their old characteristics and settling down into respectable cultivators. During the famines they lost a number of their villages, and several of them died in the poor-house. The only important Bundelā families are those of Rājā Balwant Singh of Piparia in Kanjia, and Nanhe Rājā of Dari also in Khurai tahsīl.

Bāgri.

78. The Bāgris are another local subcaste, who are also found in Jubbulpore and Seonī. Crooke[1] states that they are the illegitimate offspring of Jādon Rājputs.

Baniā.

79. Baniās number over 4 per cent. of the population and own about 300 villages, being next to Brāhmans the largest land-holders. The principal subdivisions are the Parwārs, Golāpūrabs and Gahois, while others are Nemā, Oswāl, Agarwāl and Asāthi.

[1] Tribes and Castes of the N.-W. P., Vol. III., p. 9.

The Parwārs, Golāpūrabs and Oswāls are usually Jains and the others Hindus, the Oswāls being Swetāmbarī and the Parwārs and Golāpūrabs Digambarī Jains. The Parwār Baniās are the most influential class, and trace their origin from Tīkamgarh or Tehrī State in Bundelkhand. Several Parwārs are large landlords and are among the best and most liberal-minded in the District, notably Nathūrām Singhai of Etāwa, and Shrīmant Seth Mohan Lāl of Khurai. The Gahois are immigrants from Bundelkhand and are proverbially selfish. 'A Gahoi will deceive his own father.' While the Nemā Baniās have a reputation for being clever traders. 'Where a sheep grazes or a Nemā trades, what is there left for anybody else.' They are supposed to be dirty and to be peculiarly liable to ringworm. 'Let other Baniās be as they may be, but how could there be a Nemā without ringworm.' The Asāthis are said to be the descendants of an Ahīr who became a Baniā. It is told of the Asāthis that they first bury their dead, in accordance presumably with a former practice, and then exhume and burn the bodies.

Ardha jale, ardha gare
Jinkā nām Asāthi pare.

'He who is an Asāthi is half buried and half burnt.' But this practice if it really existed has now been abandoned. The Agarwāls are so called from the village Agrohā in the United Provinces from which they have immigrated. Trading and money-lending are the hereditary occupations of the Baniā, but many have now acquired villages and taken to agriculture. Starting with a nominal capital the Baniā soon makes money. 'If a Baniā gets a rupee he will have an income of eight rupees a month.' The way he does this is to buy a rupee's worth of stock in a town, and take it out early in the morning to a village, where he sits on the steps of the temple until he has sold it. Up till then he neither eats nor washes his face. He comes back in the evening after having eaten two or three pice worth of grain, and buys a fresh stock which he takes out to another village in the morning. Thus he turns over his capital several times a month, in a manner which would be abhorrent to the soul of an American financier. The Baniā never writes off debts even though his debtor may be a pauper, but goes on entering them up year by year in his account books and taking the debtor's acknowledgment. For he says *Purus Pāras* or 'Man is like the Philosopher's stone,' and his fortune may change any day. The Baniā is proverbially the Jew of India, and his traditional meanness and rapacity have given rise to a number of most uncomplimentary proverbs. 'A man who has a Baniā for a friend has no need of an enemy.' 'Borrow from a Bania and you are as good as ruined.' 'The rogue cheats strangers and the Baniā cheats his friends.' 'Kick a Baniā even if he is dead.' The Baniā, however, has many virtues, and if the bad specimens of his class are dishonest, the fault is mainly that of his clients whose ignorance and carelessness tempt him to take advantage of them. Baniā landlords are with some exceptions no worse than others, and several of them are considerably better.

Dāngi.

80. The Dāngis rank next to the Rājputs in status having formerly been dominant in Saugor which was sometimes known as Dāngīwāra after them. The caste is practically found only in this District. The legend of their origin is that on one occasion the chief of Garhpahrā detained the palanquins of 22 married women of different castes and kept them as his wives. The issue of the illicit intercourse were named Dāngis, and there are thus twenty-two subdivisions of these people. There are also three other subdivisions who claim descent from pure Rājputs, and who will take daughters in marriage from the remaining twenty-two but will not give their daughters to them. The name is said to be derived from *dāng* 'fraud' on account of the above deception or from *dāgi* 'stained.' A more probable derivation seems to be from *dāng*, a Persian word for hill; and the Dāngis may have been a set of robbers or free-booters in the Vindhyan hills, like

the Gūjars and Mewātis in Northern India, naturally recruiting their band from all classes of the population as is indicated by the story itself. '*Khet men bāmi, gaon men Dāngi,*' or 'A Dāngi in the village is like the hole of a snake in one's field' is a proverb which shows the estimation in which they were formerly held. They have now, however, developed into respectable landed proprietors, and have a more reputable legend of their origin of the usual Brahmanical type. The Dāngis are spirited but not unduly quarrelsome and are industrious and honest. They do not drink liquor, but eat the flesh of clean animals and permit widow-marriage, though some of them deny this. The Nahonias, Bhadorias and Nadiyās are the highest subdivisions and take daughters from the others, obtaining a large dowry with the girl which may amount to several hundreds of rupees, in return for the honour conferred. Pure Rājputs will, it is said, take daughters from Nahonias. The names of the subdivisions are local and derived from those of villages, and the groups are exogamous. There are no subcastes. The Dāngis live principally in the Khurai tahsīl in the five mahāls of Khimlāsa, Khurai, Eran, Dugāha and Mālthone which were formerly held by Dāngis. They are usually proprietors and tenants, and form between 4 and 5 per cent of the population. They hold some 250 villages. The leading families are those of Bilehrā descended from the chiefs of Garhpahrā, Rao Nārāyan Singh of Rehli, and the proprietors of Hinnode and Kanau in the Khurai tahsīl.

Lodhī.

81. The Lodhīs form about 8 per cent of the population, and hold 175 villages. They rank below the Dāngis in social position but somewhat above the Kurmis and other cultivating castes. The caste is found in large numbers in the United Provinces and Central India where it is known as Lodhā. The name Lodhī is derived by one writer,[1] from *lod* a clod,

[1] Nesfield's Brief View of the Caste System of the N.-W. P. and Oudh.

so that Lodhī would be the exact equivalent of 'clod-hopper.' Another derivation is from the bark of the *lodh* tree (*Symplocos racemosa*), the collection of which is one of their occupations in Northern India. Here they stand lowest in the list of agricultural castes, being, according to Mr. Nesfield, little better than a forest tribe, but in the Central Provinces the caste holds land, and aspires to Rājput origin. Several of them especially in Damoh and Jubbulpore formerly occupied the position of semi-independent chiefs and kept up contingents of matchlock-men and horsemen. According to a legend of their origin, however, the first Lodhī was created by Mahādeo from a scarecrow in a Kurmī woman's field and was given the vocation of a farm-servant, and married to a Kurmī girl. The Lodhīs are thus probably connected with the Kurmīs with whom they will eat food cooked without water. The Rajbhars, a low caste of labourers, also take food from Lodhīs, and seem to have some association with them. The principal subdivisions of the caste in Saugor are the Mahdele, Kerbania, Narbaria, Jaria, and Mahālodhīs. The Jaria and Mahālodhīs are endogamous divisions or subcastes, and are the lowest members of the caste. The other divisions are exogamous clans marrying outside the clan. The Mahdeles are the highest. The name of the Kerbanias is derived from Kerbanā in Damoh. The Mahdeles have the titles of Rājā and Dīwān, and the other clans those of Rao and Kunwar. These titles are derived from the Rājās of Pannā, and are sometimes still conferred by them. The Jarias and Mahālodhīs are the lowest and freely permit widow-marriage. The Mahālodhīs grow hemp, and will eat food cooked with water in the field, whereas the higher divisions will only eat it in the cooking-room. If a Mahālodhī takes somebody else's wife they only have to give a feast, and are readmitted into caste. The higher clans seclude their women, who when they go out wear long cloths covering their heads and reaching down to the feet. They are not allowed to wear ornaments of a cheaper metal than silver. The higher clans profess not to allow widow-marriage, but instances of it are known. They eat meat but do not drink liquor. The Lodhīs are fine looking men, and have still some appearance of having been soldiers. They are passionate and quarrelsome, but more so in Jubbulpore than in Saugor. This is put forcibly in the saying that 'A Lodhī's temper is as crooked as the stream of a bullock's urine.' They are generally agriculturists, but the bulk of them are not very prosperous as they are inclined to extravagance especially in their marriages. On such occasions they have the same custom as the Bundelās of never refusing any food that is set before them, a practice which leads to great waste. In Bandā it is said that the Lodhīs are so hospitable that they will never turn a caste-fellow away from the house. But when he has stayed with them some time and they are tired of him, they give him food cooked with water,[1] and he understands the hint and takes his departure. Many Lodhī girls are not married until they are 20 or more, owing perhaps to the expense entailed. Sometimes they are then married to a boy ten years younger than themselves. The Lodhīs are found all over the District. The Imjhirā family of Narsinghpur which was distinguished by its loyalty in the Mutiny has a large estate in Saugor. The attitude of this family was exceptional, as Lodhī landholders were as a rule among the most disaffected. Other leading families are those of Sihorā and Mohlī, while the mālguzārs of Pātan and Jhāgrī in the Bandā tahsīl were formerly also important landholders but now only have small estates.

Kurmī.

82. The Kurmīs number 4½ per cent of the population and hold about 100 villages. Their local subcastes are the Usrete, Gahoi and Santorā. The Usrete are also called Havelia because they are found principally in the wheat-growing tracts of the Northern Districts. The Gahois are most numerous in Saugor. The

1 Which he cannot eat.

Santorās grow hemp and are looked down on by the others. The Kurmī is the cultivator *par excellence*, his name according to one derivation being from the Sanskrit *krishi* and having this meaning. They are thrifty and hardworking, peaceably disposed and averse to litigation, while according to the saying they are easily intimidated: 'If you ask a Kurmī for anything he will not give you so much as a hair, but if you take him by the scuff of the neck he will give you all he has.' The Kurmīs are below the Dāngis and Lodhīs, about equal to the Ahīrs and somewhat above the Kāchhis and Mālis. Their women work in the fields and are a great help in cultivation. 'Good is the caste of the Kurmin; with a hoe in her hand, she goes to the fields and works with her husband.' Kurmī women are very strong. It is thus of great advantage to a Kurmī to have two or three wives, and polygamy is comparatively common. Girls are married very young, sometimes at one or two and frequently at four or five years of age. It is said that when a Kurmī gets rich he will do three things, the first being to marry his daughter very young at great expense, the second to build himself the largest house he can afford, and the third to buy the best bullocks. They are said to view adultery with another man of the caste very leniently, the husband often taking his wife back after feasting the caste fellows, while the seducer must pay the same penalty. A Kurmī will sometimes take his wife back also if she has gone wrong with a Brāhman, but not if the man is of any other caste.

Ahīr.

83. Ahīrs constitute about 5 per cent. of the population, being the third caste in point of numbers, and own 60 villages. They are believed to have been formerly dominant in Saugor, and the fort of Rehlī is said to have been built by the Faulādia Ahīrs, of whom some families still reside in the vicinity, and bear the title of Rao conferred on them by the Marāthās. Khamaria near Rehlī is supposed to have been the capital of the Faulādia Ahīrs, and it is said

that their descendants still return at intervals to take away buried treasure. The local subdivisions of the Ahīrs are Goal, Dhopā, Bharotia, Kamaria and others. The Goals drink liquor, but the Dhopās and some other subcastes do not. The Dhopās are the highest subcaste and do not permit widow-marriage. The Ghosis are an inferior branch of the caste who keep buffaloes, and probably became differentiated by taking to this special occupation. The Dauwā Ahīrs are the offspring of a Bundelā father and Ahīr mother. Such unions are still frequent, and their offspring become Dauwā Ahīrs and form a separate subcaste, from whom Brāhmans will take water. An Ahīr woman who is kept by a Bundelā is called Pardwārin or one coming from another house. The Ahīrs proper tend and graze cattle while the Goals keep cattle for the sale of milk. Ahīr women are tattooed at the Diwāli in honour of Krishna. At this time some Ahīrs put on a special dress strung with cowries, and go round the village singing and dancing. The caste worships Kārakh Deo who is the god of cattle, and wherever they go they make a platform, and put a stone on it to represent Kārakh Deo. When cattle fall sick, the owner goes to an Ahīr and presents *sīdha* or a day's food to him as an offering for the recovery of the cattle. During their marriages the bridegroom is wrapped in a black blanket while he is rubbed with oil and turmeric. The Ahīrs are supposed to be very stupid, and self-sufficient, and the following story is told of them. The head of the caste in one village was one Lāl Bujhakkar[1] with a great local reputation for wisdom. During the night an elephant happened to pass through this village, and next morning the Ahīrs found his footprints, but as they had never seen an elephant they were much perplexed as to what they were. So they said 'Let us go and ask our uncle Lāl Bujhakkar and he will tell us.' So Lāl Bujhakkar was brought, and after gazing at

[1] A name meaning a wise man who is generally referred to.

the footprints for a long time he spoke 'Nobody could have explained this but me, but happily I, Lāl Bujhakkar, know everything. A black-buck has tied four *chakkīs* (grinding stones) to his feet and jumped through the village with them.'

84. The Kāchhis form about 7 per cent of the population. They are believed to be an occupational offshoot of Kurmīs, and their special profession is to grow vegetables and garden crops on small patches of irrigated land, at which they are very skilful. They rank somewhat below the Kurmīs, and rarely become mālguzārs. They reside principally near Saugor, but also all over the District. In Saugor itself there are a few families of Muraos who are a branch of Kāchhis, deriving their name from *mūra*, a radish. The Kāchhis are quiet and well-disposed.

Kāchhi.

85. Mālis only number a few hundred persons in Saugor, their place as vegetable-growers being taken by the Kāchhis. The Mālis generally live in towns and keep vegetable gardens just outside. They sell flowers, and the Māli girls are very good flower-sellers, being famous for their coquetry. The Mālis also prepare the *maur* or marriage crown both for the boy and girl at the time of the marriage ceremony. These crowns are made of leaves of the date-palm. In return the Māli gets a present of a rupee, a piece of cloth and a day's food. The men are employed in Jain temples and work under the priest. They sweep the temple, clean the utensils, and do other menial work. This service, however, does not affect their religion and they continue to be Hindus. They are also employed for worshipping Devī and Mahādeo in Hindu temples.

Māli.

86. Khangārs number some 5,000 persons or 1 per cent of the population and Chadārs 14,000 or 3 per cent. These castes are usually

Khangār and Chadār.

employed as village watchmen. The Khangārs are probably an illegitimate offshoot of some higher caste. They say that their ancestors were formerly rulers in Bundelkhand, but were all slaughtered except one woman who gave birth to a child under a *kusum* tree (*Schleichera trijuga*), and was taken in by a *fakīr* to whom she represented herself as a Dāngi. The *fakīr* sent her to a Dāngi neighbour who gave her shelter and allowed her to join in a marriage ceremony then in progress in his house. Hence the custom still prevails among the Dāngis of giving the *maihar* or marriage-cake to a Khangār at their marriages as to one of the family. While the *fakīrs*, in memory of their ancestor who on this one occasion acted as giver instead of receiver, do not beg for alms at the marriage of a Khangār's daughter. The Khangārs revere the kusum tree and will not wear cloths dyed with safflower. This is no doubt a totemistic survival. The Khangārs were professional thieves in Marāthā times, and several proverbs remain to attest this. 'The Khangār is strong only when he possesses a *khūnta*' (a pointed iron rod to break through the wall of a house). 'The Sonār and the Khangār only flourish together' because the Sonār acts as receiver of the property stolen by the Khangār. They are said to have had different ways of breaking into a house, those who got through the roof being called 'Chhappartor,' while others who broke through the side-walls were called 'Khonpāphor.' The caste have now however generally relinquished their criminal practices and are field labourers and village watchmen. The Chadārs are considered to be somewhat lower than the Khangārs, the former being called 'kotwār' and the latter 'kotwāl.' Formerly the office of the 'kotwāl' was more honourable, and he did not perform the menial duties of the 'kotwār.' The Chadārs are largely engaged in weaving coarse country cloth, and are sometimes called 'Chirār' an abbreviation of the Sanskrit *chīrkār* or weaver.

Gond.[1] 87. The Gonds number between 20,000 and 30,000 persons or 4 to 5 per cent of the population, and hold 90 odd villages. They reside generally in the forest tracts bordering the District. Three divisions are found in Saugor, the Rāj-Gonds, Khatulhās and Bhois. The Rāj-Gonds were the ruling subdivision, but they are now found in great numbers, and it is clear that anyone who managed to acquire property has been allowed to become a Rāj-Gond. They are largely Hinduised, and some of them outdo even the Hindus in their ceremonial observances. The Khatulhās belonged to the Khatolā Gond State in Bijāwar. They sometimes intermarry with Rāj-Gonds, though the latter generally regard them as lower than themselves. The Bhoi or Pārsi Gonds are found in the Rehlī tahsīl, and are the most primitive members of the tribe. Their honorific title is 'Daroī'. They keep fowls, and the higher castes sometimes consider their touch to be defiling. The Gonds, however, have a pride of their own, and no outsider, not even a Brāhman or Rājput, can become a Gond. Neither a Gond nor a Saonr will eat the flesh of an animal which has been touched by a Chamār after death, even though its skin may not have been taken off. The Gond septs are exogamous and named after animals or plants in their own language, the meaning of which they have now forgotten, and hence there is no totemism among them. The whole tribe however worship the sāj, mahuā, mango and achār trees and will not cut or burn them. All the Gonds worship Burā Deo who is said to live in a kohā tree in the forest. To him cocoanuts, liquor, vermilion, and goats are offered, it being necessary that the worshipper should sever the head of the goat with one blow. As elsewhere, the Gonds in Saugor have the peculiar custom of celebrating the marriage at the bridegroom's house instead of the bride's. The Hinduised

[1] The bulk of the paragraph on Gonds is taken from a note kindly furnished by Major Sutherland.

Rāj-Gonds have now abandoned this practice, but the Bhoi Gonds adhere to it. When a Rāj-Gond is to be married, if the bridegroom is prevented by any unforeseen cause from attending the marriage ceremony, he sends his sword to represent him, and the sword being carried round the marriage post with the bride, the marriage is considered to be properly celebrated. The practice still sometimes obtains, when a Rāj-Gond or Khatulhā Gond is married, of sending two or three other girls with the wife, who live with the husband, and become his wives, but with an inferior status, their sons inheriting in the absence of issue by the proper wife. The principal Gond family is that of Pitehrā in the south of the District. A portion of this estate, including the village of Pitehrā,[1] has recently been transferred to Narsinghpur. The Rao of Bharrai is the only other Gond landowner of importance.

Saonr.

88. The Saonrs or Sawarās number some 13,000 persons or about 3 per cent of the population. As compared with those in the east of the Province they are somewhat backward and uncivilised in Saugor, and rank below Gonds though they do not eat fowls, pigs or dead cattle. 'Rāwat' which is sometimes returned as a caste name, appears merely to be a title adopted by the better class of Saonrs. The Saonrs formerly practised shifting cultivation, but this is now prohibited. They are wretched cultivators and still sow juār with a pointed stick, which, they say, was the implement given to them for this purpose by Mahādeo. Most of them collect and sell forest produce, and they are very clever at climbing trees and rocks to get honey. 'It is the Saonr who can drive the black bees from their hive.' They also make charcoal and dig up a root called *baichāndi* which they sell to the confectioners for sweetmeats. They perform the *bhānwar* ceremony or walking round the sacred

[1] Nearly the whole of this estate has passed out of the hands of its Gond proprietors.

pole at their marriages, at which a Brāhman is present. Poor Saonrs when they cannot afford to feast their guests give them a small piece of cake, which they put in their turbans as a sign of acceptance in lieu of hospitality. To those guests to whom it is indispensable to present something they give five cowries. Formerly they allotted as a dowry to their daughters a certain portion of forest, with the exclusive right of collecting its produce. The Saonrs worship Bhawāni under various names and also Dūlha Deo. Their gods are represented by earthen platforms under large trees or on rocks. Most of these are dedicated to the spirits of persons who have died a violent death or were distinguished sorcerers. Like the Baigā the Saonr is a great sorcerer. 'Verily, the Saonr is a cup of poison.' To appease the gods of disease they were accustomed to set fire to the forest. If a man has died a violent death they raise a small platform under a teak or sāj tree, the ghost of the deceased man then taking up its residence in the tree, which must not be cut down. They generally burn their dead.

Chamār.

89. Chamārs mainly constitute the menial and labouring class and number 55,000 persons or nearly 12 per cent of the population. They are as a rule miserably poor and not a single Chamār owns a village, though one is in the possession of a Mochī. A very few of them are tenants and the vast majority despised and bullied helots. They serve as village drudges, and are generally selected for the performance of *bigār* or forced labour. The woman of the Dohar and Jatwā subcastes act as midwives. They are the only class who will remove the carcasses of dead cattle, which they eat without regard to the disease from which the animal may have died. They also castrate cattle, and cure hides. They prepare the threshing floors and in return are given the droppings of the cattle while threshing is going on; and they wash out from these the undigested grain. The Chamārs are very strong and make the best farm-servants and

coolies for earth work. It is a proverb that 'the Chamār has half a rib more than other men.' The Chamār does not touch the corpse of a horse, dog, or uncloven-footed animal, nor does he kill a cow though he eats its flesh. A Chamār who once killed a calf accidentally had to go to the Ganges to purify himself. Cattle-poisoning is consequently very rare in Saugor. The Chamār is not considered so impure in Saugor as in the south and east of the Province, and he is allowed to go into all rooms of the house except the cooking and eating rooms. Besides the ordinary village gods, they have a special family god whose image in the shape of a lump of clay is kept in every household.

Criminal classes.

90. Among the criminal classes the Khangārs and Sanaurhias have already been mentioned, but it is probable that only a small minority of them are now professional criminals. The Bernīs or village dancing-girls have also a bad reputation as being inclined to crime and much addicted to drink. Saonrs are said to be addicted to thieving. Muhammadan Fakirs often become thieves if they take to opium-smoking. There are a number of eunuchs in Saugor who are always Muhammadans by religion. They dress like women, shave the hair of their face and call themselves by women's names. They are fairly well-to-do and beg at marriages and births. Some of them are said to practise unnatural vice when young, but they are not thieves and do not appear in the Courts. As in other Districts wandering gangs of Baluchis and Afghāns are met with. The Baluchis are great thieves and will steal anything they find in a house. They purchase articles in the bazar and retail them at exorbitant rates and also sell false jewellery. These gangs do not now visit Baluchistān, and recruit any outsider to join them. Their ostensible business is to sell ponies. They formerly kidnapped children, and even now children are not allowed outside the house when they come to a village. Their women wear a handkerchief drawn tightly over their heads. They speak a dialect of Persian. It is reported that

at their marriages the boy and girl dance together for two or three hours every day for a week while musical instruments are played. The Afghāns act like swindling commission agents, taking round common articles and selling them to servants and ignorant people for more than their real value. They make the debt payable by instalments, and collect money by threats of personal violence. But they do not commit ordinary thefts.

SOCIAL LIFE AND CUSTOMS.

Marriage ceremonies.

91. The marriages of boys are now sometimes not performed until they are twenty years old, but fifteen is considered to be the proper age for boys and nine for girls. If the parents are badly off, the marriage is usually delayed, but the bridegroom is arranged for three or four years before the ceremony takes place. The *sagai* or betrothal is the preliminary to a marriage, and the barber and *pandit* or Brāhman priest must be employed in it. The barber acts as a go-between or marriage agent and describes the character and person of the bride and bridegroom to the other's family, while the pandit casts their horoscopes. The barber, however, is not now relied on, as he may take a present from one of the parties to arrange the marriage, in spite of some physical defect or other drawback which he conceals. A member of the family therefore usually accompanies the barber. The full ceremonial of a marriage is gone through in nearly all castes in Saugor, whereas in other Districts the lower castes do not adhere to the procedure prescribed for orthodox Hindus. All over the District when the women of a bridal party go out to perform ceremonies they abuse with the most obscene language any respectable man whom they meet or whose house they pass. Similarly when the marriage guests are feasting, the women sing obscene songs from inside the house, and sometimes drench the guests with water, or throw handfuls of gram-flour and betel-nut and sugar cakes at them. Among the lower castes

they smear the faces of the guests with turmeric or make impressions with their fingers on their backs after dipping them in turmeric and water. After the procession has gone to the bride's house the women of the bridegroom's party who stay behind sometimes dress up a young girl as a boy and go round to the houses of their neighbours, dancing to the accompaniment of a drum and singing obscene songs. The bride always goes to her husband's house for a short time after the ceremony, in order to give his family an opportunity of seeing her, as the women of the bridegroom's family do not accompany the marriage party. If she is under age, the *gaunā* or going away ceremony is performed in the 1st, 3rd or 5th year after marriage, the bridegroom with a small party going to the bride's house to fetch her after the performance of a sacrifice.

Widow marriage and kept women.

92. Widow marriage is not permitted by Brāhmans, Rājputs, Kāyasths, Baniās, Sonārs and Lodhis, but all other castes allow it. It has been ruled that the child of a Lodhi by a kept woman can inherit. The marriage takes place in the dark fortnight, and only men and other widows take part in it. The widow is brought to her future husband's house, where he puts glass bangles on her wrists, and presents her with new clothes and she becomes his wife. The custom of keeping women has, however, until lately been common in all castes. The Dauwā Ahīrs are a special subcaste formed of the offspring of Bundelā fathers from Ahīr women. There are usually several of these persons attached to the houses of leading Bundelā families with whom they exercise a great influence. Similarly the Benaikayās are an offshoot of Parwār Baniās, being the children of widows who are kept by men of the caste. They often have their own temples as they are not allowed to enter the regular temples, or in any case to touch the god. There are a number of illegitimate children of Brāhmans who are called Doglās, and who usually act as the servants of Marāthā Brāhmans. As the latter will not take water from any but

another Brāhman, they experience considerable difficulty in obtaining servants, and are glad to avail themselves of such persons without enquiring too closely into their statement that they are Brāhmans. Men in good position who keep maidservants, belonging generally to the Dhīmar caste, have illicit intercourse with them occasionally. Hence the proverb 'The king's son draws water, and the water-bearer's son sits on the throne,' similar intrigues on the part of high-born women with their servants being not unknown. Another class of persons are called Kunwars, these being the offspring of the Marāthā Brāhman Pandits who were formerly rulers of Saugor, by their kept women. They form a separate caste and will not eat *katchā* food from Marāthā Brāhmans though they are their offspring.

Ceremonies at birth.

93. The following account of birth ceremonies is taken from Major Sutherland's note:—'The 'barber's wife is summoned as soon as 'the pains of labour are felt, and when she has determined 'that it has set in, hands over the case to her colleague the 'Basorin who remains in the lying-in room until the 10th day 'after delivery. To hasten delivery the abdomen is rubbed, and 'if it is delayed it is believed that some evil influence is at work. 'To avert this the patient calls on the name of the family god 'or her *gurū*[1] or on the spirit of any *satī*[2] who is locally famous. 'Or she may be given water to drink in which the feet of her 'husband, her mother-in-law or a young unmarried girl have 'been washed. Or a piece of paper with a drawing of the 'double triangle may be bound on her body as a charm. No 'special ceremonies follow the birth of a daughter, but when 'a son is born the event is heralded by the beating of a brass 'tray to scare away evil spirits, while around the heads of the 'mother and child are waved seven times against the sun's 'course, mustard seed, *ajwain* (*Carum copticum*), rock salt, 'sulphur, wheat-bran and hair cut from somebody's armpit, all

[1] Spiritual adviser. | [2] A widow who has been burnt on her husband's pyre.

'of which are known to be powerful averters of evil. These 'substances are then consumed in the brazier which stands in 'the lying-in room near or under the patient's cot. The child 'is then bathed with warm water, and when dry, fumigated 'with the smoke of the ajwain-seeds which have been thrown 'on to the brazier. After this it receives a dose of *ghūti*, a 'mixture of senna and carminatives. Thereafter for the first '24 hours it is given small doses of cow's milk, the first milk 'of the mother being considered to be highly injurious to her 'child. The placenta are buried in a corner of the lying-in 'room and thus the heart strings of the child are attached to 'its birth-place. During the ten days during which she 'remains in the lying-in room the mother is not allowed to 'drink cold water but is given a mixture of ginger, ajwain and 'other articles boiled in water to drink, and sweetmeats of 'cocoanut, ginger, ajwain and chironji to eat. After seven days 'she is bathed in hot water in which nīm leaves and ajwain 'seeds have been boiled and is then given new clothes and 'light food to eat. The rejoicings for the birth are held on 'the 10th day, the near relatives being invited and given a feast. 'In the evening the women of the village come and sing songs 'suitable to the occasion to the accompaniment of drums. 'The relatives of the family bring presents of small silver 'bangles, caps, coats, handkerchiefs and toys of brass or wood 'for the child. These are accepted by the parents and cash 'payments are made, generally amounting to double the value 'of the things received. Other relatives have guns with blank 'cartridge fired on to the walls of the house to show their 'joy.'

Customs at death.

94. The following description of death ceremonies is also taken from Major Sutherland's note:—'When a man is near his 'end, gifts to Brāhmans are made by him or by his son 'on his behalf. These, if he is a rich man, consist of 'five cows with their calves, marked on the forehead and 'hoofs with turmeric and with garlands of flowers round

'their necks. When it is evident that the dying man 'has but a few minutes to live, he is laid on a woollen 'blanket which is spread on the ground, so that his passing 'may be easy. In his mouth are placed a piece of gold, some 'leaves of the *tulsī* or basīl plant, and the *panchāmrita*, or 'milk, curds, ghī, sugar and honey. The dying man must lie 'with his head to the north and his feet to the south. So 'valuable as a means of securing a pure death is the presence 'of a piece of gold in the mouth, that some castes have small 'pieces of gold inserted into a couple of their upper teeth, in 'order that wherever and whenever they may die, the gold 'may be present to purify them. The dying man keeps on 'repeating "Rām, Rām, Sitārām."'

Funeral rites.

95. In all castes except among the Gonds as soon as a death has occurred, the corpse is bathed, clothed, and smeared with a mixture of powdered sandalwood, camphor and spices. A bier is then constructed of the wood of the teak or *sāj* (*Terminalia tomentosa*), two side pieces being made, on which are bound with hemp or string five or seven cross-pieces according to the height of the deceased. On the bier is laid straw, over which is spread a piece of newly purchased white cotton cloth of fine texture; the corpse is laid on this and covered with a piece of the same cloth. The covered corpse is tied securely on the bier, the hands being crossed on the breast with the thumbs and great toes tied together. The funeral procession then starts for the burning-ghāt, the son of the deceased walking in front, clad in a piece of the cloth from which the corpse's coverings have been taken. In his hand he carries an earthen pot suspended from a wooden triangle of bamboo, to which three cords of *palās* fibre are attached to hold it by. The pot contains smouldering cowdung cakes, obtained from outside the house, and destined to furnish the fire with which the pyre will be kindled. After him come the four corpse-bearers, and after them the relatives and friends of the deceased. At some convenient spot, usually under a pīpal

tree, the procession halts, the bier is laid on the ground, and two pice coins and five small pebbles are left.

Cremation.

96. The procession then proceeds to the cremation ground, and when this is reached, the corpse is taken from the bier and placed on the pyre. The cloth which covered it, and that on which it lay are given to a sweeper who is always present to receive this perquisite. To the corpse's mouth, eyes, ears, nostrils and throat is applied a mixture of barley flour, ghi, sesamum seeds and powdered sandalwood. Logs are then piled on the corpse and the pyre fired by the son. The fire is first applied to the head end of the pyre, and then resin is strewn over all, and it is fired in several places. When a woman is cremated the foot of the pyre is fired first. When the body is half-consumed the son takes up a piece of wood and with it strikes the skull seven times to break it and give exit to the soul. The son then takes up on his right shoulder an earthen pot full of water, in the bottom of which is a small hole. He walks round the pyre three times in the direction of the sun's course and stands facing to the south, and dashes the pot to the ground crying out in his grief 'Oh my father.' This is the only expression of sorrow which is permitted during the ceremony. While this is going on *mantras* or sacred verses are recited by the officiating Brāhman. When the corpse is nearly consumed all the assembly throw the *panch lakariyā* (pieces of wood or sprigs of tulsī) on to the pyre making obeisance to the deceased and saying '*Swarg ko jao*' or 'Ascend to heaven.' After the ceremony is concluded, the procession repairs to the nearest river or tank, and after bathing come to the house of the deceased where they find *nim* leaves (*Melia indica*) set ready, and chew them. They condole with the bereaved ones, extolling the virtues of the deceased, and then return to their homes. When they are gone the women of the family bathe, the bangles of the widow are broken, the vermilion on the parting of her hair

and the glass ornament (*tiklī*) on her forehead are removed, and she is clad in white clothing of coarse texture to show that henceforth she is only a widow.

Mourning.

97. On the third day after the cremation, or if that be a Sunday or a Wednesday or a day noted in the almanac as inauspicious, then on the fourth day the son, who has been living apart from the others, proceeds to the cremation ground, where, after bathing, he sprinkles the ashes of the pyre with milk. The lower castes sprinkle water or wheat. The ashes and bones of the deceased are then collected and placed in a silken bag, the lower castes depositing them in an earthen pot. The bag and its contents are either taken straight to the Ganges or Nerbudda or buried in a convenient spot, and taken there within ten days, or even after that, if the journey has to be postponed. If this occurs no marriage ceremony can be performed in the family until the ashes are disposed of. The son or brother of the deceased takes them to the river and returns with Ganges water in a tightly closed brass or copper vessel. The vessel is worshipped and a small feast is given, after which the water is used for some religious ceremony. In most castes, on the first day, the son cooks for himself a mess of pulse and rice, of which he eats some and gives the remainder to a dog, a cow or a young unmarried girl.

Provision for the soul.

98. On the 3rd day the *pindās* or sacrificial cakes are offered with the recitation of appropriate verses on the banks of a tank or river, and this goes on till the tenth day. On the evening of the third day, the son goes accompanied by a Brahman and a barber and carrying a key to avert evil, to a *pīpal* tree (*Ficus religiosa*), on whose branches he hangs two earthen pots by strings of palās-fibre. One pot is full of water which trickles out through a hole in the bottom, while the other contains an earthen lamp. On each succeeding night the son replenishes the contents of these pots, which are intended to

refresh the spirit of the deceased and to light it on its way to the lower world.

Return of the soul.

99. Some castes observe the following custom on the evening of the third day. The ashes of the cooking place are carefully sifted and the fine powder thus obtained is spread on a brass tray, which is left overnight on the spot where the deceased breathed his last, or near the cooking-place. In the morning the layer of ashes is inspected and if what appears to be a hand or foot-print is seen, it is held that the spirit of the deceased has visited the house. Some castes look for hand-prints, some for foot-prints, and some for both, and Nais look for the print of a cow's hoof, which when seen is held to prove that the deceased in consideration of his singular merits, has been reborn a cow. On the 10th day the males of the family bathe at the river or tank and undergo ceremonial shaving, the entire head from the left ear across the crown to the right ear being shaved. This ceremony is obligatory on a man whose father, mother, uncle or elder brother has died, but the death of a wife, sister, son, daughter or younger brother does not entail its performance. In the evening a feast is held for the family and their menial servants. A portion of the viands is set apart in leaf plates on the spot where the deceased breathed his last, and after a while this portion is given to a cow. Among the lower castes the feast is held on the third day, and the deceased's portion is removed to a distance from the house and left on the road leading to the cremation ground.

Gifts for the dead.

100. The period of mourning is 3 days in low castes, 5 days among Saonrs, 8 among Gonds, and 10 in the case of the higher castes. On the 11th day the ceremony of purification takes place when the whole house is whitewashed, all clothes washed, and the earthen pots are thrown away and replaced by new ones. On this day if the family can afford it a *dān* or gift is made to a Brāhman consisting of a new cot and bedding

with a cloth, an umbrella to shield the spirit from the sun's rays, a copper vessel full of water to quench its thirst, a brass lamp to guide it on its journey, and a blanket, shoes and such articles as the deceased used. Such gifts are accepted only by Katyā or Mahā-Brāhmans who are looked down on by other Brāhmans. On the 13th day a feast is given, all the relations and friends who took part in the cremation ceremony being invited, and each being given a brass lotā, or if this cannot be managed a few copper coins. Among Brāhmans only 13 persons are invited.

Burial.

101. The bodies of children who have died before cutting their teeth are buried, and sometimes of those under five years old. The bodies of persons who have died of small-pox or leprosy are always buried. If a person has died by hanging or drowning, or from the bite of a snake, his body is burnt without any rites, but in order that his soul may be saved the *hom* sacrifice is performed subsequently to the cremation.

Houses.

102. The house of a *mālguzār* or good tenant stands in a courtyard or *angan* 45 to 60 feet square and surrounded by a brick or mud wall. The plan of a typical house is shown below:—

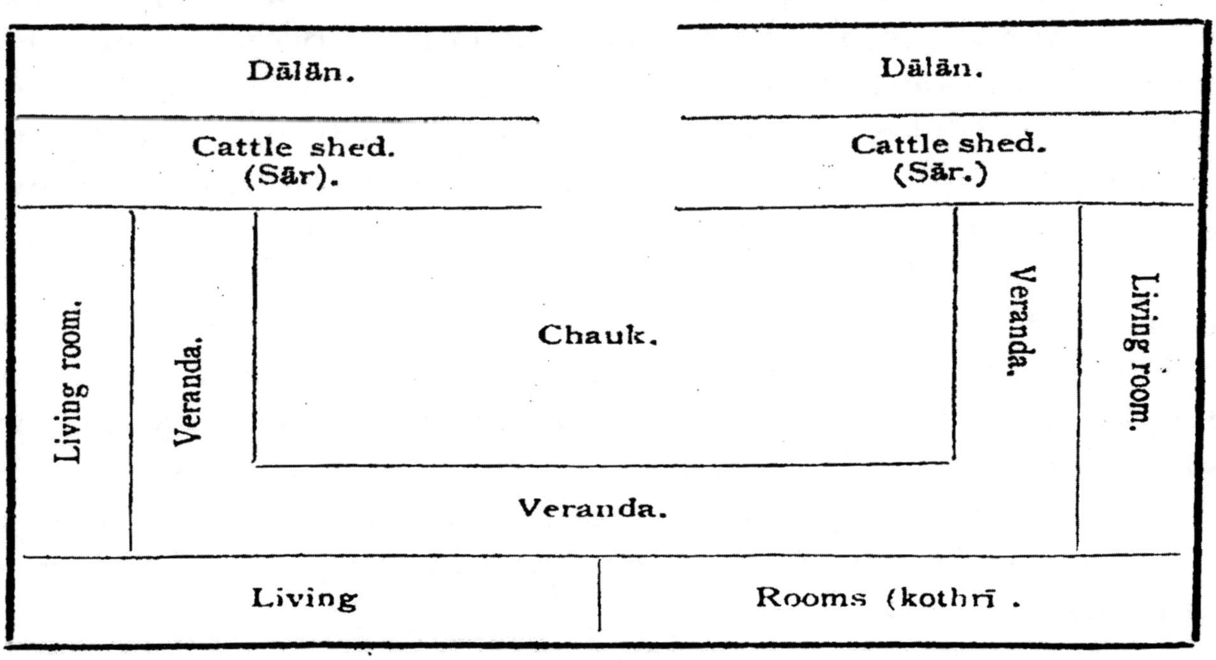

The *dālān* or hall is for the reception of visitors. One of the living rooms is set spart for storing grain. Those who keep their women secluded have a door at the back of the courtyard for their use. Cooking is done in one of the rooms, and there are no chimneys, the smoke escaping through the tiles. They bathe either in the *chauk* or central courtyard, or go out and bathe in a tank or river or at a well. Hot water is not usually used for bathing except by invalids. The family usually sleep inside the house in the winter, and outside in the hot weather. A poor mālguzār or tenant only has two rooms with a veranda in front, one of which is used by the family, while cattle are kept in the other. The poorest tenants have only one room in which both men and cattle reside. A mālguzār's house as shown above costs Rs. 200 to Rs. 250 when the walls are of mud, and Rs. 400 to Rs. 500 when they are of bricks. The house of an average tenant costs Rs. 30 or Rs. 40. Nearly all houses are tiled, thatch being avoided owing to the risk of fire. Poor tenants do repairs to their houses themselves, sometimes even making the tiles. Such a house lasts for 15 or 20 years, being repaired annually. Houses in towns are usually more costly than in villages and also better built. A house should not face south as this is unlucky. Some families have a prejudice against a second storey, some will not have stone houses, and others will not have their courtyards paved. The well-to-do consult a Brāhman as to the selection of a site for a new house. The foundation stone is laid with some ceremony, it being lucky that it should be laid by a man who has been faithful to his wife. Small pieces of new cloth of various colours are tied on to the eaves while the walls are being built, and marks of charcoal are made on the door-frame to avert the evil eye, which might cause the walls to crack or the stone to split. New houses are occupied on auspicious days, a ceremony of purification being first performed accompanied by the feeding of Brāhmans.

103. The following graphic description of a tenant's house is furnished by Major Sutherland:—'It is apparent that the standard 'of comfort in Saugor is much lower than in Europe, when 'one has seen a villager's house. Single-storied, with mud 'walls, and a roof covered with ill-made and ill-baked tiles, it 'stands in its little compound if he be a man of means, or end 'to end with another house of the same kind if he be poor. 'The interior is dark, for light is admitted only by the low 'door, and the smoke-stained ceiling contributes to the gloom. 'The floor is of beaten earth, well plastered with cowdung, 'the plastering being repeated weekly. In one corner of the 'room we may see a large box in which are kept the gar-'ments of the family; with it may be a tin tube containing 'the title-deeds of the owner, and the certificates which have 'been given to him and his forefathers by Government 'officials. Carefully arranged in their places are the brass 'cooking-pots, water-pots and plates, well polished with 'mud and water applied with plenty of elbow-grease by the 'careful housewife. Poor tenants frequently only have one 'or two brass plates and cups and an iron girdle, while all 'the rest of their vessels are of earthenware. Near these 'lies the fireplace, a horse-shoe like mound of mud, with a 'high rim on which to rest the pot. In a niche in the wall 'lies a bundle of papers, carefully tied up in red-coloured 'coarse cloth. These the master of the house has brought 'back from the tahsīl town with him; they are receipts for 'rents paid to the mālguzār, and with them lies the horoscope 'of the son of the house. At the back of the house is a 'small compound, and in this the string cots of the family 'are lying exposed to the sun; for insects are frequently 'found in them, and sleep is disturbed, if the cots be not 'thoroughly sun-heated at least once a week. In the com-'pound, too, is a small raised altar-like edifice in which grows 'a sprig of the sacred *tulsī* (*Ocimum sanctum*). In the back 'veranda lie several earthenware pots full of water from the

Houses and furniture.

'village well, and in a niche in the wall is coiled the rope 'which is fastened to the neck of the pot when it is lowered 'into the well. Resting against the compound walls, and 'also it may be against the walls of the house, are cakes of 'cowdung on which the finger-prints of the women who 'made them are clearly visible. The jungle is near at hand 'so there are but a few sticks lying piled up in a corner. 'These are useful when hot fire is needed, but for nursing 'the spark throughout the day cowdung cakes are used. 'Chairs and tables there are none, nor would the good people 'know how to use them if they had them. In one niche, 'however, there is evidence of civilisation; a bottle bought 'at the weekly market for 2 annas, contains some of the 'wonderful earth-oil which comes from "Vilāyat," and which 'is burnt in little tin lamps on high days and holidays. For 'ordinary use there is an earthenware saucer half filled with 'til or linseed oil, into which dips a strand of cotton-thread 'whose other end rests on the margin of the saucer, and 'when lit gives a feeble light and volumes of smoke, less 'noisome however than that given off when the kerosine 'lamplet is lighted.[1] Tenants usually do not have cots but 'sleep on the ground, spreading kodon-straw on it for 'warmth. They have no bedding except a *gudrī* or mattress 'made of old rags and clothes sewn together. In winter 'they put it over them, and sleep on it in summer. Mālgu-'zārs have a *razai* or quilt and a *doria* or thick cloth like 'those used for covering carts, with a cot to sleep on. A 'mālguzār's cooking and eating vessels may be worth Rs. 30 'or Rs. 40, though well-to-do persons who entertain largely on 'festive occasions, keep a much more extensive supply.'

Food.

104. Persons who do not cultivate with their own hands have only two daily meals, one at midday and the other at 8 or 9 in the evening. Agriculturists require a third meal in the

[1] Kerosine oil is now commonly used for lighting purposes being cheaper than vegetable oil.

early morning before going out to the fields. Before the recent bad years mālguzārs and tenants frequently ate wheat twice a day, and rice on festivals, but now the cultivating classes cannot usually afford wheat and have substituted juār and kodon for it. These are made in thick *chapātis*, their flour not being sufficiently adhesive for thin ones. Pulses are eaten with the *chapātis*, or if these cannot be obtained they are dipped into butter-milk. If *chapātis* cannot be afforded at both meals, *ghorua* or the flour of kodon and juār boiled into a paste with water, is substituted for them, a smaller quantity of this being sufficient to allay hunger. Farm-servants eat this when they can afford it, and if not they eat mahuā-flowers. These are sometimes boiled in water, and the juice is then strained off and mixed with half-ground flour, and they are also pounded and made into *chapātis* with flour and water. Mālguzārs have both pulses and vegetables with their food, which otherwise resembles that of tenants. The leaves of the young gram-plants make a very favourite vegetable and are eaten raw either moist or dried. In times of scarcity the poorer classes eat tamarind leaves, the pith of the banyan tree, the bark of the *semar* tree (*Bombax malabaricum*), the fruit of the *babūl* (*Acacia arabica*) and other articles. An agriculturist will eat 2 lbs. of grain a day, if he can get it, and if grain is at 30 seers a rupee his food with the addition of salt, pepper and oil will cost Rs. 1-8 a month. This includes good food on festivals. Tobacco costs two annas a month. Women do not smoke in Saugor.

Clothes.

105. Mālguzārs usually wear a *bandī* or *angarkhā* and a *dhotī*. The *angarkhā* is a long coat reaching to the knees and with flaps folding over the breast and tied with strings. The *bandī* is a short *angarkhā* reaching to the hips. In the cold weather these are frequently stuffed with cotton and dyed dark green (*amowā*) or dark blue (*surmai*) so as not to show the dirt. For visits of ceremony a pair of *paijāmas*

are worn. Nothing is usually worn under the *angarkhā* in the country, but townspeople have a *kurtā* or shirt. Government servants wear coats, with a *dupattā* or handkerchief trailing over the shoulders. Followers of the *nayi roshinī* or 'new culture' now carry handkerchiefs in their pockets. Coats are of any colour, of serge or wool as well as cotton. High officials now wear a coat and trousers. A long coat like a frock coat but buttoning up is called *sherwāni;* this is worn with loose trousers, and is called 'Aligarh fashion,' as it is the dress of Muhammadan students from the College. Tenants wear a *bandī* or *mirzai,* the two terms being synonymous, or a *nimastīn* or half-sleeved waistcoat with buttons in front. Formerly the *nimastīn* had only *ghundīs* or small pieces of cloth made up into balls, which were the precursors of the button. Wearing the *dhotī* pulled half way up to the thighs is called 'cultivator's fashion.' Mālguzārs and tenants usually wear a *pagrī or dupattā* and very few wear caps. A cap coming down to the neck behind and covering the ears is an old fashion, but is now seldom worn. This is called *topā* and is sometimes stuffed with cotton. Most people wear *dupattās* or head-cloths of short pieces of cloth tied loosely. Cultivators wear it low and close round the head, and educated people wear it high up. The ordinary Saugor *pagrī* is tied close round the head with slight projections at the sides. The tenant wears his *dupattā* with a large projection on one side, and in it they carry their *chilam* or pipe-bowl, and also small quantities of vegetables, salt or condiments purchased at the bazar. In case of necessity they can also transform their *dupattā* into a *dhotī,* or tie up a bundle of grass with it, or tie their *lotā* to it to draw water from a well. An ordinary mālguzār will have the following clothes annually—one cold weather *bandī* at Rs. 1-4-0, two hot weather *bandīs* at Re. 1 each, one *dupattā* at Re. 1, an *angarkhā* every two years at Rs. 2-8-0 and two pairs of shoes at Rs. 1-4-0, making a total expenditure of Rs. 8 a year. Tenants will spend half as much as this. Farm-servants wear a *dhotī* and *dupattā* on the head and a *bandī* if they can get one. They will not go bare-headed. Many farm-servants wear their master's old clothes.

Shoes.[1]

106. The Saugor or Bundelkhandī shoe has large flaps coming high up the leg in front and behind and large turned-in toes. The two flaps are tied round the leg above the ankle so that they will not come off in the mud. Their object is to keep out thorns, while the toe-piece prevents the feet from being bruised by rocks and stones. All agriculturists have a blanket to keep out the rain in the monsoon months, and for warmth in the cold weather.

Women's clothes.

107. Women wear a *lahengā* or skirt made of coarse cloth called *kasbī*, usually red, and an *orhnī* or shoulder-cloth of the same material. Hand-woven cloth is still usually worn in the interior. The skirt is sometimes drawn up through the leg behind so as to give it a divided appearance; this is called *kachhotā*. On the upper part of the body they wear an *angia* which is like a *cholī* or breast-cloth, but is tied up behind. High-caste women draw the *orhnī* right over the head so that the face cannot be seen. When a woman goes before a respectable person she covers her head. Women of respectable families wear a *pichhorā* over the *orhnī* when visiting their relations. This is a sheet of fine white cloth reaching from the head to the ankles. It is sometimes dyed yellow or red. When a girl is married the bridegroom's family give her expensive clothes to wear at festivals and her own people give her ordinary clothes, but usually not more than will last for a year. Whenever she goes back to her father's house after her marriage, he gives her one or two cloths if he can afford it. A woman will have two pairs of *lahengās* and *orhnīs* a year, costing about Rs. 6. *Angias* cost scarcely anything as they are made

---

[1] A full description of the Bundelkhandī shoe is given in the Monograph on the Leather Industry in the Central Provinces by Mr. Chenevix Trench, C.S.

up from old pieces of cloth. A mālguzār's wife will have three pairs and also a pair of *dhotīs* costing Rs. 2-8-0. Women of the middle and lower classes wear ornaments of bell-metal, a mixture of copper and zinc, which are very popular. Some women wear brass and zinc ornaments, and well-to-do persons have them of silver or gold.

LEADING FAMILIES.

Marāthā Brāhmans. The Sūbhedār and Tālukdār families.

108. Among the leading families the Marāthā Brāhmans, the offspring of the old governing class whom we succeeded, are strongly represented. The descendant of Govind Rao Pandit, the well-known governor of Saugor, resides in Jubbulpore with a political pension and is generally designated as Rājā of Saugor. The Sūbhedār family of Sanodhā are descended from Vināyak Rao, who was the agent of Rukmā Bai and Rādha Bai, the widows of Abba Sāhib. Vināyak Rao was a Karhāda Brāhman and related to the Saugor Rājās, and the Sūbhedār family are thus a junior branch of the Rāj family. Vināyak Rao had two sons, Ganpat Rao and Moreshwar Rao and the present representative Rao Venkat Rao Sāhib is a son of Moreshwar Rao. He is the proprietor of seven villages and an Honorary Magistrate, enjoys a political pension, and is much respected by the native community. Government letters are sent to him in a velvet cover, and nobody smokes in front of him at a private party, or gives money to a dancing-girl in his presence. Another branch of the family are the descendants of Ganpat Rao whose son Rāmchandra Rao also receives a pension. The Tālukdār family of Jaisinghnagar is the next in importance. The ancestor of this family was one Anant Rao whose daughter Rukmā Bai married Raghunāth Rao Abba, Sāhib of Saugor. On the cession it was proposed to grant the Jaisinghnagar pargana to Rukmā Bai but she preferred a cash pension. The Jaisinghnagar estate was accordingly conferred on Ganpat Rao, a grandson of Anant Rao. The present representatives of the family Rāmchandra Rao,

Govind Rao and Ganpat Rao are the grandsons of Ganpat Rao. The estate contains 57 villages, 28 of which are held on ordinary mālguzāri tenure, while in the others the family are superior proprietors, the inferior proprietary right having been granted to the old village headmen when the estate was settled.

Etāwa and Pithoria families.

109. Another important family is that of Etāwa, whose ancestor Rāmchandra Ballāl received this pargana at the cession as a reward for assistance rendered to the British, and exercised civil and criminal jurisdiction in it. The late proprietor Raghunāth Rao or Bhao Sāhib was addicted to drink and involved the estate in debt. A half share in the bulk of the villages has been sold outright to the Parwār money-lenders Nathūrām Singhai and Rai Sāhib Seth Mohan Lāl, and the other half share mortgaged with possession for eighteen years. Three villages have been reserved for the support of the widow and her family and they have also some property in Kurwai State. The Shrimant family of Pithoria are also of good standing. They are Deshasth Brāhmans and the Pithoria estate was conferred on their ancestor in exchange for the Panch Mahāls of Deorī which he held at the time of the cession, and which were made over to Sindhia. The family are now divided into three branches, the eldest of which is represented by Mādho Rao. The estate is involved beyond hope of redemption and the family only retain a few villages. The title of Shrimant is said to have been conferred on one of their ancestors by the Peshwā as a reward for taking Kolāba.

Other Marāthā Brāhmans.

110. The Fadnavis family of Deori is also of some standing. The estate was granted to their ancestor by the Peshwā and part of it was formerly revenue-free. The present representative Govind Rao[1] is an Honorary Magistrate and a leading member of the Deorī Municipality. He holds 13 villages and is

[1] This gentleman has recently died.

somewhat in debt. The family are Kokanasth Brāhmans. Rao Gopāl Rao and Rao Govind Rao, proprietors of Rehlī, belong to an old Karhāda Brāhman family who were related to the Governor of Saugor, Govind Pandit. Their ancestors were Māmlatdārs of Rehlī and held a considerable estate. They also enjoyed a political pension which was forfeited on suspicion of complicity in the Mutiny. The father of the present proprietors Krishna Rao was an Honorary Magistrate at Saugor, and Gopāl Rao enjoyed a similar distinction at Rehlī. The brothers now own three villages and are slightly indebted. Kāshīnāth and Vishwanāth Dixit, residents of Saugor, are the representatives of a Marāthā Brāhman family of good standing who were priests of the Sūbhedār family. They have seats in Darbār and own a few villages.

Hindustāni Brāhmans

111. Among Hindustāni Brāhmans one of the most important families is that of Dhāna. Kanhyā Lāl Tiwāri, the founder of its fortunes, rendered conspicuous services in the Mutiny for which he received a title and estate composed of confiscated villages belonging to the Rājā of Sahajpur. His grand-daughter, Rajo Bai, married a resident of Jubbulpore, and on her death the estate was involved in litigation and finally awarded to Hīra Lāl and Banshīdhar, the nephews of Kanhyā Lāl. Hīra Lāl shortly afterwards died and his son Balīchand, the present representative, succeeded him. He and his brother own about 35 villages. Bhaiyā Lāl Naik of Rehlī, a Sanādhya Brāhman, is the representative of a well-known family. The title of Naik is said to have been awarded by the Marāthās to commemorate the assistance given by him in the conquest of Bhind. Girdhāri Lāl Naik, father of Bhaiyā Lāl, did good service in the Mutiny by raising 200 men and holding the fort and town of Rehlī. For this he was given proprietary rights in the villages of Kumrai and Sahajpur Khurd, and received a special certificate in recognition of his services in 1877. Bhaiyā Lāl,

the son of Girdhāri Lāl, is the proprietor of 12 villages, the principal of which are Khamaria and Barkhedā. The family consists of four brothers. Another Sanādhya Brāhman family is that of Mahūna. Gourī Shanker Deolia, the present representative, holds shares in 12 villages and has considerable money-lending transactions. He is a member of the District Council and the Rehlī Local Board. The Pateria family of Khamaria are Jijhotia Brāhmans and are at present represented by two brothers Gayā Prasād Pateria and Jagannāth Pateria. The former has a few villages and is also a moneylender, while the latter has 17 or 18 villages in Saugor and Damoh, but is indebted and some of his villages are mortgaged to Gayā Prasād. Hāthi Sao Nand Kishore of Dhurmār, in Bandā tahsīl, owns some villages and has moneylending transactions in that tahsīl, though he resides principally in Bijāwar State, and has more business there and in Pannā than in Saugor. His family is called Hāthi Sao because Bakht Balī Rājā of Shāhgarh gave his father the honour of riding through the town on an elephant in recognition of a loan made to him in 1853. The present representative lives jointly with a cousin and two sons. The Jijhotia Brāhmans of Pindarua in Bandā tahsīl were formerly Dīwāns of the Rājās of Garhākotā and Shāhgarh and received from them a grant of several villages revenue-free. The present representative is Thākur Mardan Singh who holds shares in five villages. Har Prasād, Sanādhya Brāhman, the lambardār of Saugor, has seven villages. He is an Honorary Magistrate, a Member of the District Council and Municipal Committee, and is a good landlord. Biseshwar Dayāl Misra, Kanaujia Brāhman of Mokalpur, is a leading banker in Saugor town and holds about ten villages. He is reputed to be a respectable man and not exorbitant. The only notable family of Mārwāri or Pallīwāl Brāhmans is that of Seth Khet Singh of Khurai, which settled there about a century ago. Khet Singh is a member of the Khurai Municipal Committee, owns over 20 villages and has extensive loan transactions. He distinguished himself by his liberal conduct in the debtors' conciliation proceedings.

Rājput and Bundelā families.

112. The Rājput and Bundelā families, though historically among the most important in the District, are as a rule not prosperous. Rājā Balwant Singh Bundelā of Piprāsar belongs to an old family, and holds five very small villages, granted by the Gwalior Darbār, and continued as a revenue-free grant by the British Government in recognition of his assistance in the colonisation of the Kanjia pargana. He is very poor and derives a bare subsistence from the proceeds of his forests. Rai Bahādur Thākur Mahārāj Singh of Tīla, who has lately died, was one of the leading citizens of Saugor and took great interest in all public business. He acted as an intelligence officer for the British during the Mutiny. He possessed about five villages, now held by his sons. Another old Bundelā family is that of Dari in Khurai, now represented by Jangjit or Nanhe Rājā of Dari. He owns about ten villages and his estate is involved beyond hope of redemption. The family bear the old title of Sawai Dīwān or Head Dīwān, Dīwān being the designation of the younger brother of a Rājā among Rājputs and Lodhīs. The Bundelā family of Garholī is one of high standing in the caste, but they hold only one or two villages and their estate is mismanaged. The present representative, Dīwān Jālam Singh, was in Pannā during the Mutiny and gave assistance to the British. His nephew and heir, Nirpat Singh, is indolent and a confirmed gānja smoker. Rao Nirbhaya Singh Bundelā of Baraithā is related to the Shāhgarh family. He is a respectable man and lends money and grain.

Dāngi families

113. Among the Dāngis the family of the Rājā of Bilehrā is historically perhaps the most important in the District, as they are the representatives of the old Dāngi rulers of Saugor who were ousted by the Marāthās. Bilehrā and four other villages were granted as a jāgīr to the deposed family and have been

continued revenue-free to them by the British Government. The present representative is Ratan Singh, an adopted son. He possesses two villages in mālguzāri right in addition to the Bilehrā estate. A dispute concerning the division of the estate has been raised by the widows of the late proprietors and litigation has been begun. The late Rai Sāhib Nirpat Singh Dāngi of Baheria was one of the best landlords in the District and was given a title in recognition of the considerate manner in which he treated his tenants during the scarcity of 1894. The present representative, Rao Nārāyan Singh, is partly paralysed and incapable of managing his own affairs. The estate which consists of 12 whole villages and parts of four others is under the Court of Wards. Thākur Bakhat Singh of Jhāgri in Bandā tahsīl is a Nahonia Dāngi. The Nahonias are one of the highest clans and claim to give their daughters to Rājputs. He owns shares in six villages.

Lodhī families.

114. Among Lodhī families may be mentioned those of Mohli, Pātan and Imjhirā. Thākur Khalak Singh of Mohlī owns about ten villages, which were held by his father Hamīr Singh on quit-rent tenure on condition of preserving order in the surrounding country. The grant lapsed at Hamīr Singh's death and the villages are now held in ordinary proprietary right. Rao Mahārāj Singh and Dīwān Pratāp Singh of Pātan belong to an old family; one of their ancestors took the fort of Dhāmoni for the Nāgpur Rājā Raghujī Rao and obtained a grant of 48 villages in Saugor and Jubbulpore. On the cession, the family were awarded a pension of Rs. 2,400 by the East India Company, and this continued until the Mutiny, when it was forfeited on account of the rebellion of one of their members. They now only hold the village of Pātan. Rao Mahārāj Singh is the head of the Baneria Lodhīs, who derive their name from Banerā, a village in Tīkamgarh State. He affixes the *tīka* or mark on the forehead to members of his clan when they succeed to their property. He is related to the Indrāna family of Jubbulpore. The Lodhī family of Imjhirā in

Narsinghpur have 13 villages in Saugor, the principal of which is Marh Piparia. The present representative is Rānī Saraswatī, widow of Rājā Bahādur Bhānu Partāp Singh; the family obtained the title and a remission of revenue for their services in the Mutiny, when Rao Sūrat Singh stubbornly resisted the Saugor mutineers at Imjhirā. The estate was for a considerable period under the Court of Wards and is now managed by the father of the widow.

Baniā families.

115. Several Baniās are large landlords, especially in the Khurai tahsīl. Rājā Gokul Dās of Jubbulpore holds about 100 villages in Saugor. Shrīmant Seth Mohan Lāl of Khurai is the leading banker of the tahsīl, and has an estate of some 50 villages. He is a member of the Khurai Municipality and the District Council has contributed substantial sums to various public objects, and was distinguished by his liberality in the debtors' conciliation proceedings. The title Shrīmant Seth was awarded to him by the Jain community for having performed the car festival four times. Nathū Rām Nand Lāl Singhai of Etāwa is a liberal and high-principled landlord, chiefly noted for the large embankments constructed by him on the Etāwa estate, of which he is part proprietor and mortgagee. He is a very old man and somewhat heavily involved. Rai Sāhib Seth Mohan Lāl of Rondhā in the Khurai tahsīl is co-proprietor and mortgagee of the Etāwa estate with Nathū Rām. He is also heavily involved, and is a good and considerate landlord. He received his title for his liberality to his tenants in 1894. Bihāri Lāl of Saugor and his nephew Chunnī Lāl are Agarwāl Baniās. The founder of the family was a Commissariat agent. They hold a number of villages belonging to the estate of Bhaiyā Lāl Dube and are large Public Works contractors and manage the tonga services to Pachmarhī and Betūl. Litigation has arisen between the uncle and nephew.

Gond families.

116. The principal Gond family is that of Pitehrā, whose present representative is Rānī Chandra Motī, widow of Rājā Rājendra Singh.

The ancestors of this family were driven out of Deorī by the Marāthās and awarded the *tappā* or estate of Baleh consisting of 53 villages. The estate was subsequently increased to 104 villages. During the minority of Rājendra Singh the estate was managed by the Court of Wards and a considerable balance was handed over to him on his coming of age. This he dissipated and again plunged the estate heavily into debt. It was mortgaged to Azīmullā Khān of Saugor and Bansī Lāl Abīrchand, and with the exception of 13 villages the whole estate has recently passed into their hands. The widow has adopted a son Indrajit Singh and the adoption has been recognised. Pitehrā itself and some other villages near it have recently been transferred to Narsinghpur. Rao Gajrāj Singh of Bharrai, Rāj-Gond, is the representative of another old family. He is heavily involved and the estate has been foreclosed.

Muhammadan families.

117. Muhammadan mālguzārs are not numerous. Tālewar Khān of Hirankhedā is the only important member of this class who is of old standing. His estate is involved. Muhammad Azīmullā Khān of Saugor has purchased a number of villages in the last few years and is mortgagee of the Pitehrā estate. His family belongs to Bhopāl. Khān Sāhib Muhammad Abdul Rahmān Khān, Vakil of Rehlī, and Khān Sāhib Hāji Khudā Baksh, retired Assistant Superintendent of Police and Honorary Magistrate of Saugor are other leading members of the Muhammadan community.

Kāyasths.

118. Munshī Bhawāni Prasād, Kāyasth of Deorī, is an Honorary Magistrate and holds five or six villages. His family belongs to Chhindwāra District.

CHAPTER IV.

AGRICULTURE.

SOILS.

System of Classification.

119. At the 30 years' settlement, fields were classified according to soil only, the local names of the various soils being adopted. These were *mār, kābar, mund, rathia, raiyān, patarua* and *bhatua*. No distinctions based on crops or positions were recognised. In Mr. De Brett's settlement a far more elaborate classification was adopted, and soils were distinguished, according to their composition, the crops they actually carried, and their position, names and differences known and appreciated by the people being adhered to throughout. Nine soils were distinguished and named respectively *mār, kābar, mund awal, mund dovam, rathia, raiyān, patarua, bhatua* and *kachhār*. The distinguishing characteristics of these soils were as follows.

Mār.

120. Mār is a clayey soil of first-rate fertility occurring in level country, with a greyish-black colour and great depth. It is very retentive of moisture, does not crack much, and takes a long time to become fit for ploughing after rain. If much rain falls in the cold weather, wheat on mār soil suffers from rust. This soil is very uncommon and covers only one per cent of the cultivated area, being found principally in the Khurai tahsīl, in the Jharai, Khurai, Etāwa, Eran and Khimlāsa groups and in the Rehli group in the tahsīl of that name. In the Bandā and Saugor tahsils it is very rarely met with.

Kābar.

121. Kābar is first-rate black cotton soil composed of small particles, and is sticky (*chiktā*) when wet, and hard when dry. It is greasy and is used for cleaning the hair. Its clods are very hard, and break with a smooth fracture. It sometimes contains small pebbles of a black colour. Kābar covers only

two per cent of the cultivated area, and is found chiefly in the Rehlī tahsīl, being especially common in the Garhākotā, Rehlī, Chhirāri and Deorī groups. In the Bherā group of the Bandā tahsīl, there is also a considerable area of this soil.

Mund.

122. Mund is black or brown soil of good quality but inferior to mār or kābar. It differs from kābar in being of looser texture, as it consists of larger particles, and generally contains some admixture of limestone grit (*chunkankri*). It dries after rain more rapidly than mār. Mund is divided into two classes of which the first is black or nearly black soil containing little lime grit, while the second is of lighter colour, contains more limestone pebbles and sand, and therefore cracks less. Mund is the commonest soil and covers 56 per cent of the cultivated area, 27 per cent being of the first class and 29 of the second.

Rathia.

123. Rathia is an inferior kind of kābar of a brown colour, containing pebbles and grit, and forming, when dry, very hard clods. It is a difficult soil to cultivate, and if there is delay in ploughing, becomes too hard to be worked. It is said to wear out plough-cattle very fast. Rathia covers 5 per cent of the cultivated area, and is generally classed as fit to grow wheat.

Raiyān.

124. Raiyān is black soil generally containing some black stones, which is distinguished from mār, kābar or mund by its shallowness. It occurs in the neighbourhood of hills, and rock underlies the soil at a small depth. It forms very wide and deep cracks when it dries. Raiyān covers 10 per cent of the cultivated area, and carries both autumn and spring crops, but wheat sown on it requires cold weather rain.

Patarua.

125. Patarua or 'thin' soil is an inferior kind of mund, the best portions of which have been washed away by drainage. It

is brown in colour and of loose friable texture. It is generally found on uneven or raviny ground, and covers 21 per cent of the cultivated area. Good patarua can grow wheat in favourable seasons, but it is mainly devoted to inferior crops. Another kind of land classed as patarua, is light-coloured sandy soil, well suited for rice, which occurs near the Vindhyan hills.

Bhatua.

126. Bhatua is poor land generally of reddish colour and covered with cobble-stones. It covers 5 per cent of the cultivated area, and grows only the inferior autumn millets and oil-seeds.

Kachhār.

127. Kachhār is good soil situated on or below the banks of a river or stream, which is flooded during the rains and fertilised by the deposit of silt. It grows wheat and vegetables. Only good land is recorded as kachhār, poor soil on the banks of a stream being shown as patarua. The area of kachhār land is very small, being only 1,500 acres.

Gohāri or wheat land.

128. Land was also classed according to the crops grown on it. Fields which grew or had grown wheat were classed as 'gohāri,' rice fields as 'dhanāhi,' fruit and vegetable gardens and sugarcane fields as 'bāri' and other fields as 'mutfarikāt.' Land lying near the village site and manured by its drainage or in other ways was entered as 'geunrā,' to whatever class it might belong. In the whole District 690,000 acres or 64 per cent of the cultivated area were classed as wheat land, 22,000 acres or 2 per cent as rice land, 21,000 acres or 2 per cent as garden land, and 342,000 acres or 32 per cent as minor crop land. In practice land was only classed as capable of growing wheat when the records showed that this crop had actually been raised on it. Practically all the mār, kābar and first-class mund soil is classed as wheat-growing, much of the second-class mund, and a certain quantity of rathia and raiyān.

Position-classes of wheat land.

129. For wheat fields or gohāri land the following position-classes were adopted : *Sasirā*—if the field was a very good one lying low, and retaining moisture a long time ; only one per cent of the wheat land is in this position ; *tagar*—for a high-lying field damaged by drainage and *bharkīla*—for a field cut up by water channels or ravines ; these positions contain 13 per cent of the wheat-growing area ; *ujarhā*—for a field lying at a distance from the village and damaged by wild beasts ; 5 per cent of the wheat land is in this class ; *bandhia*—for a field embanked with a small bank, and *bandhān*—for a field embanked with a large bank ; only one per cent of the wheat-growing area was embanked at settlement ; *abpāshi*—irrigated ; only ½ per cent of the area is irrigated, and 2 per cent is classed as *geunrā* or receiving the drainage of the village ; *māmūli*—for a field not falling into any of the above classes ; this position contains 78 per cent of the wheat-growing area.

Of rice-land.

130. Rice land was classed as *tikrā* if highlying, *samān* if level, *jhilān* if lowlying and *abpāshi* when irrigated from a tank. About 3 per cent of the rice lands are irrigated and 33 per cent are within the geunrā area.

Minor crop and garden land.

131. The greater portion of the minor crop land is 'patarua' or 'bhatua', these two soils covering nearly 70 per cent of the whole area, and the remainder being second class mund, raiyān and rathia. There were no position classes for this land. Garden land was classed as *abpāshi* if irrigated, and *barāni* if unirrigated, and gardens were further classified according as they were for the production of (*a*) maize, vegetables or fruit, or (*b*) sugar-cane. The whole of a plot appropriated to the growth of sugarcane in rotation with other crops was classed as 'bāri gannā' and not merely that part of it which was under sugar-cane in any particular year.

132. The factors of value of these soils differ slightly in different tahsīls, but the following figures represent them fairly accurately.

Soil-factors.

Taking wheat land first, mār in the ordinary position had a factor of 36, kābar 34, mund I 32, mund II 26, rathia 24, raiyān 20, and patarua 16. In Rehlī, excluding Garhākota, kābar was lowered to 32, and in Khurai mund I to 30, while in Saugor mund II was raised to 28. In Nāharmow pargana of Rehlī tahsīl, rathia and raiyān were valued somewhat more highly. Kachhār was valued at 32 in Khurai and 34 in Rehlī. For the position of sasirā the factor was raised from 12½ to 25 per cent and for that of geunrā 30 per cent in the case of mund I, 40 for mund II, 50 for rathia and raiyān, and 75 for patarua For the tagar position the factors were lowered by 25 per cent while for bharkīla they were lowered 40 per cent. The ujarhā classification was reserved for fields in which heavy fencing is necessary to keep out wild animals, and in which persons have to live night and day to protect the crops. The factors were lowered 40 per cent for this position. Double-cropped rice land in the samān and jhilān positions is more valuable than wheat land and was given a special scale of factors. These were in the case of mund I, 40 for the samān and 48 for the jhilān position, for mund II 36 and 44 respectively, for rathia 32 and 40, for raiyān 24 and 32, and for patarua-jhilān 16. Patarua, tikrā and samān are the only soil-classes found usually with a single crop of rice and they were valued at 8 and 12. For land in the geunrā position these factors were raised from 30 to 75 per cent as in the case of wheat. The crops grown on miscellaneous or *mutfarikāt* land are the various autumn grains and also linseed, gram and *masūr* (lentil). The outturn depends very largely on the character of the season, the poorer soils failing in a dry year. The factors given were 21 for mund I, 16 for mund II, 14 for rathia, 12 for raiyān, 8 for patarua, and 4 for bhatua. For *mutfarikāt* land in the geunrā position the same increase per cent. was adopted as in the case of wheat and rice. For garden land the factors are slightly higher than for wheat, while if it is irrigated they were raised by 50 per cent in the case of the better, and 75 per cent in that of the inferior soils. Irrigated garden land in the geunrā position was raised another 25 to 50 per cent.

STATISTICS OF CULTIVATION.

Statistics of Cultivation.

133. Of the total area of the District over 750 square miles or 19 per cent are included in Government forest,[1] 220 square miles or 5½ per cent are classed as not available for cultivation, and over 1,200 square miles[2] or 31 per cent as culturable waste other than fallow. The remaining area amounting to more than 1,700 square miles or 11 lakhs of acres was occupied for cultivation in 1903-04. The occupied area has decreased by about a lakh of acres since Mr. De Brett's settlement (1892—94) when it amounted to about 60 per cent of the mālguzāri area. Owing to the hilly nature of the country, and the large tracts of stony and unproductive land, a considerable proportion of the area classed as culturable waste will never be able to produce crops of any value. Most of the good land is taken up and future extension of cultivation will be mainly to poorer soils. The maximum area recorded as occupied was 1,230,000 acres in 1894-95.

Closeness of Cultivation in different tracts.

134. Cultivation is on the whole closer in the Saugor and Rehlī tahsīls than in Khurai and Bandā. In the two former it exceeded 60 per cent of the available area at settlement, while in the two latter it was under 60 per cent. The most closely cultivated portions of the District were at that time the central part of the Khurai tahsīl, and the Garhākotā, Nāharmow and Deorī groups of the Rehlī tahsīl. Much land has since gone out of cultivation in Khurai, but with favourable seasons it should be recovered in a few years. The Saugor tahsīl was throughout

[1] The above statistics are for the year 1903-04.

[2] Excludes old fallow which is included in occupied area.

fairly closely cultivated, the worst group being that of Jaisinghnagar where only 57 per cent of the total area was occupied for cultivation. The least densely cultivated portion was the Dhāmoni group of the Bandā tahsīl, where nearly two-thirds of the total area was unoccupied. The crops here are much exposed to the depredations of wild animals, and it is popularly supposed that the whole country lies under the curse of a fakīr and will never prosper. The adjoining group of Barodia showed only 44 per cent of its area occupied and the Kanjia group in the north of the Khurai tahsīl 49 per cent. The Bharrai group of the Rehlī tahsīl is also a poor tract and had only 40 per cent of its total area occupied. This group contains a number of jungly villages belonging to the Rājā of Pitehrā, some of which have recently been transferred to Narsinghpur. In the Pithoria group of the Khurai tahsīl, which belongs to an old Marāthā family of good standing, 47 per cent of the total area was occupied for cultivation. Mr. De Brett considered that a considerable area of land was unnecessarily left fallow in the Khurai tahsīl owing to the prevalence of *kāns* grass (*Saccharum spontaneum*). The inhabitants affirm that it is impossible to prevent the invasion of this weed, and that it is certain to appear as soon as the land becomes in the least exhausted. The stiff land of Khurai is more suited to the grass than that of Saugor or Rehlī. But by the embankment of fields it should be possible to reclaim all such areas. Mr. De Brett also notes that in many parts of the District the demand is rather for tenants than land, and under such circumstances there is little inducement to careful husbandry or improvement of the soil. Taking these facts into consideration it appears that there is on the whole a fair scope for extension of cultivation in addition to the recovery of the ground lost since 1894-95.

Fallows.

135. Over 3 lakhs of acres or nearly a third of the whole occupied area were fallow in 1903-04, as against about 2 lakhs in

1893-94, which is probably the normal area. Nearly the whole increase is under old fallow, and must therefore be attributed to the absence of demand for land or capacity to cultivate it. Black-soil fields are rarely left fallow if their cultivation is practicable, and the old fallow probably consists mainly of land overrun by kāns grass. In the light soils on hilly ground in which the minor millets and inferior oilseeds are grown, periodical resting fallows are necessary, in the absence of manure, to allow the land to recuperate. A common practice is to leave such fields fallow every fourth year after cropping them for two years with kodon and one year with ramtilli or jagnī.

Progress of cropping.

136. The gross cropped area was 8 lakhs of acres in 1903-04, of which 20,000 were double-cropped. In 1893-94 the net cropped area was nearly 10½ lakhs of acres and that double-cropped 25,000. The District has therefore nearly 2½ lakhs of acres to recover before it reaches its normal state of prosperity, or any extension of tillage to land hitherto uncultivated is undertaken. At the 30 years' settlement (1867) the cropped area was 6¾ lakhs of acres and the increase up to 1893-94 was therefore 3¾ lakhs or 55 per cent including land double-cropped. Heavy increases took place during the currency of the 30 years' settlement in the area under the spring crops wheat, gram, and especially linseed, which was scarcely grown at all in 1866-67.

Double-cropping.

137. The maximum area recorded as bearing two crops was 38,000 acres in 1902-03. The practice of double-cropping is only followed in a limited area consisting of the rice-growing fields round the village site, and artificially embanked wheat fields or naturally depressed plots which catch the drainage of surrounding fields. The area double-cropped depends largely on the character of the autumn rains, and reaches its maximum when these are copious, as in 1902, when 13 inches were received between September and

November. The practice apparently hardly existed at all at the 30 years' settlement when only 40 acres were shown as bearing after-crops. The minimum area recorded since 1891 was 6,400 acres in the famine year of 1899-1900. The method of double-cropping adopted is either to sow catch crops of rice in the embanked wheat fields, or the spring grains gram, linseed, and masūr in rice fields after the rice has been cut.

Autumn and spring crops.

138. In 1893-94, 3½ lakhs of acres were sown with autumn and nearly 7 lakhs with spring crops. The subsequent run of bad wheat harvests led to a great increase in the popularity of juār which largely supplanted wheat, while a large area was also now devoted to jagnī, which is an inexpensive crop to grow. In 1897-98, 5 lakhs of acres were under autumn and only 2¾ lakhs under spring crops. Since then the spring crops have recovered their popularity to a certain extent and occupied 438,000 acres in 1903-04.

Statistics of crops.

139. In this year wheat covered 3 lakhs of acres or 37 per cent of the cropped area, juār over a lakh or 14 per cent, gram 90,000 or 12 per cent, til and kodon nearly 50,000 or 6 per cent each, linseed 36,000 or 4 per cent, rice 17,000 or 2 per cent, and cotton 13,000 or nearly 2 per cent. An important crop which is not shown separately in the returns is ramtilli or jagnī and this covered 72,000 acres in 1902-03. The corresponding figures for 1893-94 were wheat 5½ lakhs of acres or 52 per cent of the cropped area, juār 70,000 or 7 per cent, gram 70,000 or 7 per cent, til 70,000 or 7 per cent, linseed 40,000 or 4 per cent, kodon and kutki 60,000 or 6 per cent, rice 20,000 or 2 per cent and cotton 20,000 or 2 per cent. The decrease of 2½ lakhs of acres in the cropped area since 1893-94, is thus wholly accounted for by wheat, the variations in the other crops counterbalancing each other.

CROPS.

Wheat.

140. Wheat (*Triticum sativum*) has always been the principal staple of the District, covering, in former years, half of the whole cropped area and at present over a third. Four varieties are grown in the District known as *pissi*, *kathia*, *hānsia*, and *jalāliya*. *Pissi* is the most common variety and is the soft yellow grain usually grown for export. It is of two kinds *shikarhai* or bearded and *mundī* or plain. *Shikarhai* is the commoner variety and less liable to be eaten by animals. *Mundī* is sown in embanked fields because it is less liable to be affected by rust. *Kathia* and *hānsia* are both hard and bearded grains, the former being red and the latter yellow. *Jalāliya* is the large soft yellow grain preferred by native consumers.

Methods of cultivation.

141. Owing to the soft friable nature of the prevalent mund soil deep ploughing is unnecessary, and the *bakhar* or paring plough is usually employed in the preparation of the land for wheat. Between May and October the field is ordinarily ploughed once with the *nāgar* or regular plough and three to five times with the *bakhar*. If the field is overgrown with weeds or kāns grass two or three ploughings with the *nāgar* may be necessary. The seed is sown in October and the harvest lasts from the 15th March to the 15th April. Sowing is done by means of a small plough behind which a bamboo tube trails at the end of a string, being supported by the sower who drops the seed through a bowl at the top. After this nothing more is required until the harvest, except to watch the crop and keep off animals and birds. Wheat is frequently sown mixed with an admixture of gram or linseed. A crop of mixed wheat and gram is called *birrā*. The quantity of gram mixed is 5, 10 or 15 per cent of the whole quantity of the seed. The proportion in which the crop is divided for the agricultural statistics is 85 of wheat and 15 of gram. The quantity of linseed mixed is usually 5

per cent of the total. In cases where wheat is sown mixed with gram, the outturn of wheat is of course lowered, but as the addition of gram increases the productiveness of the wheat sown with it, there is a smaller proportion of decrease in the combined outturn. Wheat-fields are rarely embanked and such embankments as exist are usually only dams to prevent surface scouring. As a rule the fields are neither manured nor irrigated. A small quantity of irrigated wheat is grown in the Bandā tahsīl. In Saugor, good wheat land is cultivated 30 or 40 years without a fallow, but in Khurai, fields which have been cultivated continuously for a number of years, are liable to be attacked by kāns grass. Rust or *gerua* is the most common disease to which wheat is subject and is produced by rainy or cloudy weather when the plants are in ear. The grain turns a yellowish red. The progress of rust is very rapid, a whole field being destroyed in a single night. Heavy winds when wheat-plants are coming into ear are liable to shrivel the grain. Wheat is less liable to damage by *tusār* or frost than other grains, but hoar-frost sometimes dries up the ears or makes them very small; this disease is called *jhirī*. Fields in the vicinity of river banks are particularly liable to be damaged by frost. *Kuhar* or blight is caused by wet weather when the plant is in flower, the flowers rotting and dropping off. This disease is very rare. In very dry weather the roots of the plants are attacked by white ants; this is called *okrā*. Hail-storms occurring when wheat is in ear, sometimes destroy the whole crop. The seed sown to an acre of wheat is 100 lbs. and the standard outturn is 600 lbs. or six fold.

Gram.

142. Gram (*Cicer arietinum*) is at present the third crop in importance. Its cultivation has largely increased in recent years both alone and as a mixture with wheat. Three varieties of gram are locally distinguished, called respectively *haldia*, *imalia* and *parbatia*. *Haldia* has a yellowish and *imalia* a reddish grain, and that of *haldia* is the larger. *Parbatia* has a white soft grain and is grown only as a delicacy. The system of cultivation is similar

to that of wheat, but the ground is not so carefully prepared for gram, and it is also sown on poor soils which will not bear wheat. Gram is sometimes sown mixed with linseed in the proportion of a third. There is a considerable local demand for gram owing to the presence of a garrison in Saugor. While the plants are green the young shoots can be plucked and eaten as a vegetable without harming their growth. Gram is sown in September and October and harvested some 15 days before wheat. When it is in pod it is liable to the attacks of a green caterpillar called *illī*, if the weather is foggy and cloudy. Frost has also a severe effect upon gram, but the plants will grow again when attacked before they come into flower, and if there is rain afterwards a bumper crop may be obtained. Eighty lbs. of gram are sown to the acre, and the standard outturn is 500 lbs.

Linseed.

143. Linseed (*Linum usitatissimum*) has recently declined in popularity owing to the poor harvests. Two varieties are distinguished, the seed of one being white and of the other copper-coloured. The white seed has a white flower and the copper-coloured a blue flower. Linseed is sown on poor wheat land and other inferior soils, frequently in rotation with wheat. It is an exhausting crop and cannot be sown more than twice running in the same land. It is sometimes sown as a border to wheat-fields as cattle avoid it. The method of cultivation is the same as for wheat. It is sown at the same time as wheat, and ripens a little before it. It is more liable to rust than any other crop and also to frost, and to the attacks of white ants in very dry weather. The standard outturn per acre is 280 lbs.

Other spring crops.

144. The other spring crops are *masūr*, or lentil (*Ervum lens*), *tiurā* or *lākh* (*Lathyrus sativus*), and *batrā* or peas (*Pisum arvense*). These are grown occasionally on wheat land. Masūr is sown in low-lying fields and also as a second crop after rice. It requires a soil retentive of moisture. It has a small white

flower. The area under it is some 8,000 to 10,000 acres. Batrā is the large pea and mattar the small pea, but they are frequently not distinguished. Only about 2,000 acres are usually sown with peas. Peas have blue and white flowers. Tiurā is usually given to cattle and its consumption as a food in famine years has on several occasions produced a number of cases of incurable paralysis. The area under it varies from 1,000 to 4,000 acres, and has recently decreased. The flower is reddish blue. In the case of both tiurā, masūr and peas the quantity of seed sown and the outturns, approximate to those of gram. They are sown at the same time as wheat and harvested 20 to 30 days earlier.

Juar.

145. Juar (*Sorghum vulgare*) is the principal autumn crop and the second in importance in the District. Many varieties are locally distinguished. One of these is called *bandarbaith*, because it is so small that a monkey can sit down and pick off the pods. *Bāsmati* or 'sweet-smelling' is another variety, this being also the name of one of the best kinds of table rice. It yields a small crop. *Leburh* is another variety with very tall plants growing fast and ripening early. This is only cultivated in gardens and requires manure. *Jugnū* is a variety with a red grain, the word meaning glow-worm or fire-fly. *Bhūs* is a variety with a very long head, the grains of which are not exposed. Birds cannot eat it, but on the other hand pig like it best because it has the longest head. It has a small outturn. *Ernā* is a variety so named from *ernā* 'to twist' because the head twists as it hangs. Juār was formerly grown mainly in the Bandā tahsīl, but it is now distributed all over the District and is the principal crop in Kanjia and Mālthone. It is often grown on good land in rotation with wheat, and does particularly well in some cases in light-soil villages where wheat would not be equally successful. It is sometimes sown before the rains in hilly land and in black-soil fields after the rains have broken. The field is ploughed once with the *bakhar* before sowing unless it is much overgrown with weeds, when

the *nāgar* is used. The seed is sown broadcast and the *bakhar* is then dragged over the field either lightly right way up or upside down. When the plants are some inches high the field is ploughed lengthways and breadthways with the *nāgar*, the bullocks being muzzled and treading between the lines of the crop. A certain number of the plants are weeded out by this process, while the remainder are strengthened and the field is at the same time cleared of weeds. If the plough is not used the crop must be twice weeded by hand. Juār needs to be watched day and night after the plants have come into ear, and during the day for some time before this. It is frequently given out on contract to labourers who sow, watch, weed, reap and thresh the crop and receive half the produce. The harvest lasts during December. When the rainfall is heavy the seed sometimes rots in the ground or the leaves are attacked by green flies when the plant is coming into pod. This disease is called *bhinkā*. The stalks may also be attacked by a black caterpillar. *Kandua* or smut is not common in Saugor. When attacked by smut the flowers turn black. *Agia* is a little plant like grass with long leaves, and in a very dry year springs up in a field and causes the juār to wither. Only 8 to 12 lbs. of juār are sown to the acre and the standard outturn is 500 lbs.

Rice.

146. Rice (*Oryza sativa*) is usually grown in small plots round village sites which profit by the drainage which they receive. The crop though a small one is valuable, owing to the high prices obtained locally for rice. Eighty lbs. of seed are sown to the acre and the standard outturn is 900 lbs. of unhusked, which are estimated to yield 550 lbs. of husked rice.

Kodon.

147. *Kodon* (*Paspalum scrobiculatum*) and *kutkī* (*Panicum psilopodium*) are sown in the poor patarua and raiyān soils, being most largely cultivated in the north of Bandā and south-east of Rehlī tahsīls. *Lathāra* is a small variety of kodon. Kodon is usually sown alone, but is sometimes mixed with a small

quantity of juār. The crop is weeded once or twice and must also be watched. Ten to 15 lbs. of seed are sown to the acre and the standard outturn is 400 lbs. yielding 212 lbs. of husked grain. Kutkī is usually sown in the beginning of August and ripens towards the end of September. About 5 lbs. of seed are sown to the acre and the outturn is said to be forty fold.

Til and Ramtilli.

148. *Til* (*Sesamum indicum*) and *jagnī* or *ramtilli* (*Guizotia oleifera*) are important crops covering together over 15 per cent of the total area. They thrive on poor soil without involving much labour in cultivation and are also little liable to damage by wild animals. They are sown in newly broken up and imperfectly cleared land. Four varieties of til are locally distinguished, two having white seeds, one black, and one red. The red or *maghelī* til is sown in August and ripens in January, and the white and black varieties are sown in July and cut in November. The plants are liable to be rotted by heavy rainfall before they have come into pod, but after this they are not much affected by it. Ramtilli is sown towards the end of August and reaped in the cold weather. It has a very pretty yellow flower and the plants grow two or three feet high with thick stalks. From 2 to 4 lbs. of til are sown to the acre and about 6 lbs. of ramtilli. The standard outturn of til is 150 lbs., while ramtilli is said to yield 200 lbs. an acre. These oilseeds do well in dry seasons and generally gave moderate to fair outturns in the famine years.

Cotton.

149. Cotton (*Gossypium herbaceum*) is not an important crop in Saugor, and the recent increase in the foreign demand has caused no appreciable rise in its cultivation. It is grown principally in Rehli tahsil and to a less extent in Bandā, while Saugor and Khurai have scarcely any. Cotton-seed oil is used locally as a hair oil. The standard outturn is 180 lbs. of uncleaned, yielding 54 lbs. of cleaned cotton.

Sugarcane.

150. The cultivation of sugarcane (*Saccharum officinarum*, has diminished almost to vanishing point. At the 30 years' settlement it covered 5,500 acres, but the area under it decreased to 1,700 acres in 1893-94 and 300 in 1903-04. In many villages large abandoned stone mills may be seen, where no cane is now grown, while the wells dug for sugarcane are used for the irrigation of wheat. The reason for the decline in cultivation is that the *gur* or unrefined sugar locally produced is undersold by that imported from Northern India. Two varieties are grown—a foreign one called *angrezī* for eating, and a local one called *pachrangī* for the manufacture of gur.

Minor crops.

151. Among minor crops may be mentioned sanhemp which covered 7,500 acres in 1902-03. This is a profitable crop and is grown for export. 6,500 acres were devoted to maize in the same year. This grain is grown in garden-plots at the backs of houses. Several minor millets are cultivated here and there, the most important being *rāla* (*Panicum miliaceum*) with an area of 2,000 acres and *sawān* (*Panicum frumentaceum*) with a little more. The principal vegetables and condiments grown are coriander, chillies, brinjals (*Solanum melongena*), and *ajwain* (*Carum copticum*), each of which covers from 200 to 300 acres. Seventy-one acres are devoted to potatoes, and very high rents are paid by Kāchhis for the irrigated plots on which they produce this vegetable. About 3,000 acres included in holdings are covered by mango-groves, and of the 1,000 acres returned as groves, the bulk are probably mangoes. Guavas are grown on nearly 200 acres.

Total value of all the crops grown.

152. The following statement shows the valuation of the gross agricultural produce of the District in 1903-04 taking the standard outturn on the area cropped in that year, valued according to the prices ruling in 1903.

Gross Produce and its Value.

Details of crops.	Area (1903-04).	Standard outturn per acre.	Gross produce.	Value rate per rupee.	Gross value.	Value of crop per acre.		
	Thousands of acres.	lbs.	Thousands of lbs.	lbs.	Thousands of Rs.	Rs.	a.	p.
Wheat ...	289	600	173,589	31	5,646	19	5	8
Gram ...	93	500	46,698	47	994	10	10	3
Juar ...	110	500	54,779	54	1,014	9	4	2
Rice (cleaned) ...	17	600	9,900	20	495	30	0	0
Linseed ...	36	280	10,094	21	481	13	5	4
Til ...	46	150	6,847	24	285	6	4	0
Sugarcane (gur) ...	315	1,500	473	20	24	75	0	0
Cotton (cleaned)...	13	60	798	5	160	12	0	0
Kodon (cleaned)...	45	220	9,843	25	394	8	12	10
Minor food grains	35	250	8,871	60	148	4	2	8
Miscellaneous food crops ...	329	250	82	60	1	4	2	8
Gardens ...	5	...	...	...	99	20	0	0
Miscellaneous non-food crops ...	113	...	...	...	564	5	0	0
Total ...	803 including double-cropped area.	...	321,974	...	1,03,04	...		

A comparison of this statement with the similar one given on page 22 of Mr. De Brett's Settlement Report is of considerable interest. The total value of a normal harvest on the cropped area of 1903-04 was just over a crore of rupees. At the time of settlement it amounted, according to Mr. DeBrett's calculation, to a crore and a half. The harvest of the District had therefore been reduced in value by a third.

The wheat crop was worth only 56 lakhs instead of 83. Juār was so cheap in 1903 that the large increase in its area did not produce any addition to the value of the harvest sufficient to counterbalance the loss on wheat. The value of the harvest was only 10 lakhs as against 7 lakhs at settlement. The linseed crop yielded only 5 lakhs as against 8, and gram 10 lakhs as against 11½. It may be noted, however, that the year 1903 witnessed a substantial fall in prices, and the value of the harvest in 1902-03 was considerably higher, amounting when computed in the same manner to Rs. 119 lakhs.

Agricultural implements.

153. The agricultural implements used are the following:—The *hal* or plough is employed for deep ploughing, and the *bakhar* or paring plough for ordinary preparation of a field. The *nāri* is a smaller plough with a sowing-tube tied behind it. *Parainā* is the goad, pointed at one end and with a flat piece of iron at the other for cleaning the earth off the *hal* or *bakhar*. The plough-share is called *phār* and the share of the *nāri* is *phār* or *kusia*. The strip of iron attached to the *bakhar* is known as *pāns*. The pole to which the yoke is fixed is *harīs* and the handle of the plough is *muthia* and that of the *bakhar*, *nijonā*. *Jua* is the yoke which is in two pieces, one of which goes over the neck of the bullocks and the other under. *Pācha* is a rake with five spikes used for drawing the grain into the winnowing baskets after it has been threshed. *Obī* is the spud used for fencing the threshing-floor. *Hansia* is a sickle, *kulhādi* an axe, *kodāli* a pick-axe, and *phaorā* a hoe. *Kus* is the large iron spud elsewhere called *sabbal*.

Manure.

154. Manure is not so much used as it might be. The droppings of cattle are only kept for manure during the four months of the rainy season, and for the other eight months are made into cakes for fuel. Rice, cotton and vegetables are manured, but not usually the spring crops.

IRRIGATION.

155. The irrigated area varies from about 5,000 to 8,000 acres, practically the whole of which is watered from wells. There are some 2,000 durable and 1,500 temporary wells, and the area irrigated from each averages between one and two acres. Saugor is one of the few Districts in which there are more durable than temporary wells. Well irrigation is practised principally in the northern half of the Bandā tahsil, and next to Bandā in Saugor, while the number of wells in Khurai and Rehli is small. In Bandā the Persian wheel is used to raise the water, and elsewhere the ordinary *mot* or leather bag. The durable wells are lined with masonry. The average depth of a well is 30 to 35 feet, its width 10 to 12 feet, and the cost of construction about Rs. 300. The subsoil water is said to be met with at a depth of 20 feet from the surface in Saugor tahsīl, from 20 to 40 feet in Bandā, and from 30 to 35 feet in Rehlī. In Khurai it appears to be deeper. Rock is generally met with at a short distance below ground, and this makes the sinking of wells expensive. The cost of temporary wells is of course much smaller. The crops irrigated are generally sugarcane, garden crops and vegetables. In Bandā, a little wheat and barley are grown as irrigated crops in small fields near the village site, the soil in the north being too shallow to carry them without assistance. Wells appear to be less numerous now than formerly, and the decay of sugarcane cultivation is assigned as a reason for their decrease. It is stated that in 1899-1900 many of the wells failed.

Wells.

156. There are between one and two hundred tanks in the District, but the bulk of these are not used for irrigation, and the area watered from tanks is insignificant. The crop irrigated is generally rice. No use is as yet made of the rivers, whose bed is so far below the level of the country as to make the cost of raising water prohibitive. The system of embanking wheat-

Tanks.

fields is, however, in reality a method of irrigation, and it is to the encouragement of this that the efforts of Government are mainly directed.

Embanked fields.

157. The practice of embanking land for spring crops is of comparatively recent introduction and has found most favour in Khurai, where the clayey soil is probably adapted to the construction of firm embankments, and the surface is level enough to get an even distribution of water. Embanked fields require very little labour in cultivation, all that is necessary being to pass the *bakhar* or paring plough over them once before sowing. They make the cultivator independent of the September and October rains as the ground cannot dry up. And the outturn in an ordinary year is substantially increased. In a dry year when many fields cannot be sown, the cultivator with embanked fields will reap large profits. On the other hand, the crops in embanked fields are more liable to damage from rust, attacks of which are not infrequent in Saugor, and possibly also from frost, which appears to affect particularly crops standing in damp ground. These disadvantages, however, are held to be more than counterbalanced by the advantages accruing from embankments. During the recent bad seasons, much wheat land, especially in the Khurai tahsil, has been overrun by the destructive *kāns* grass (*Saccharum spontaneum*), and the embanking of fields is a method of reclaiming this land, as the grass is killed by keeping the field under water for one season.

Two methods of embanking.

158. There are two methods of embanking fields. The first, which is most widely practised in the Jubbulpore Havelī, is to enclose the field on all sides by an embankment about 3 feet high. The embankments are intended to hold up all the rain water that falls on the fields and to retain a maximum depth of about 1½ feet. The water is drained off about

a fortnight before sowing. This system is only successful when the surface is very level. The second system, which is generally followed in Saugor, is to construct embankments of 6 or 7 feet high on the lower sides of large fields having a slight slope. The slope should ordinarily not be more than 1 in 200, otherwise the expense is largely increased. The embankments are constructed on contours with flank and partition banks to divide the area above them into fields of a suitable size. Spill channels should be provided round the upper ends of the main and divisional spurs. The embankments hold from 3 to 4 feet of water immediately above them when the fields are full. This water is held up during the rains to saturate the land submerged above the embankments. In the month of October it is let out, and used to give the fields below the embankments a watering before sowing. The lower fields are usually surrounded by small banks of from 1½ to 3 feet high, and are cropped with early rice during the rains, thus giving double crops. The cost of constructing such embankments is taken to be about Rs. 20 per acre protected, but in the case of large embankments within which water is held up to 10 feet or more it may amount to Rs. 50 an acre. The Jubbulpore embankments are somewhat cheaper.

Outturn and assessments.

159. Wheat is the crop principally sown in these embanked fields. In Saugor at last settlement (1892—94) no extra rate was imposed on embanked fields with a view to encouraging the extension of the practice. In Jubbulpore the soil factor was raised by 50 per cent for the large embankments of the Havelí, but this apparently was as compared with wheat land in a sloping position, and therefore of comparatively inferior quality. The returns of crop experiments showed that on the same soils the outturn in embanked fields was increased by about 20 per cent. At Mr. De Brett's settlement only 1,100 acres of wheat land were recorded as having large embankments and 7,500 acres as having small ones. The embanked fields were fairly

distributed over Saugor, Rehlī and Khurai tahsīls. Since the settlement, some more embankments have been undertaken in the Khurai tahsīl, Nathū Rām Singhai of Etāwa having in particular taken up this form of improvement. Some embankments were constructed experimentally in 1902-03 by Government on land overgrown with kāns grass.

CATTLE.

Breeds and prices.

160. Most of the cattle used in the District are bred locally, though the richer cultivators buy imported animals of the Gwalior and Bhopāl breeds, and also from the neighbourhood of the Ken river in Pannā State. The large white cattle from Bhopāl are called 'Sankhā' bullocks. The prevailing colour of the Saugor breed is light grey. They are small animals and of no particular quality, but are suited to the strong and rocky ground, on which imported cattle do not do well. Gwalior and Bhopāl cattle are most used in the stiff clayey soil of Khurai. Bulls are not as a rule kept for breeding, which is carried on indiscriminately from the young bullocks before castration. The practice of letting loose a bull on the death of a high-caste Hindu was formerly in vogue. These bulls were held sacred and allowed to wander where they pleased, and they thus served to some extent for breeding purposes. But such animals would no longer be permitted to damage the crops and would be sent to the pound and bought up by the butchers for slaughter, so the custom of letting them loose has died out. Occasionally when a cultivator has a strong steer he keeps him for a year or two extra before gelding him and gets calves from him. The price of an ordinary pair of local bullocks is Rs. 40 to 50 when they are fit for work. Gwalior or Sankhā cattle cost from Rs. 100 to Rs. 200 a pair. The working life of a pair of Saugor bullocks is seven or eight years from the time they are trained to cultivation, and that of the imported bullocks a year or two longer. They are castrated at three

or four years old. The cultivating castes will castrate cattle in Saugor in contradistinction to most Districts, where this operation is performed by some low caste as Gonds, Chamārs or Māngs. Chamārs, however, often do it here also. The testicles are clasped in a pair of iron pincers and pounded to pulp with a stone. The animal remains ill for a week or a fortnight and is not put to work for two months. Brāhmans and Rājputs will not castrate cattle with their own hands, and Baniās will not do it at all, but sell their young bulls and buy oxen. Nose-strings are not used either for plough or cart work, but a cord is passed round the forehead below the horns. The people think that the use of nose-strings tends to weaken the animal, but this of course is a pure delusion. They have thus very little control over cart bullocks and cannot stop or turn them easily.

Food.

161. Cattle usually get nothing but grass, with wheat-chaff in the hot weather. Though juār is largely grown, the stalks as a rule are not cut, but are left standing in the fields or only the upper half is cut and given to cattle. The forests afford sufficient grazing. Cattle are usually sent to the forests in the rains, especially from the black-soil tracts, as their feet sink into the soft ground and they are tormented by flies. When rain falls the plough-bullocks are sent for. Cows are kept for milk, and cow's milk is drunk, probably because it is not rich enough for making ghī. A cow only gives 1 or 2 lbs. of milk a day. Its price is from Rs. 6 to Rs. 15.

Statistics of plough-cattle.

162. In 1902-03 the District contained 96,000 plough-cattle or a pair for every 16 acres cultivated. The number of cows was 132,000; this figure is large in comparison with those of other Districts, and is at the rate of more than one cow to each householder and 68 to a village.

Buffaloes.

163. Buffaloes are kept by all classes, but not used for cultivation. The she-buffaloes are valued for their milk from which ghī is made. The young males or *parās* are disposed of very cheaply to the caste of Basdewās, who drive them in large herds to Chhattisgarh and dispose of them at remunerative prices. Male calves are said to be very delicate and difficult to rear, but this is probably because no attention is paid to them. Barren she-buffaloes are used as pack-animals. A cow buffalo costs from Rs. 25 to Rs. 50 and will give 4 or 5 seers of milk if it is well fed on oilcake. A buffalo in calf gives milk for a year and is then dry for another year, the interval for a cow being 8 or 9 months. The number of cow buffaloes in 1902-03 was 62,000, and was the highest in the Province.

Ponies.

164. Ponies are bred in the District but to a much less extent than formerly, when every mālguzār who could afford it kept a mare for riding. Since roads have been made they prefer to travel in bullock-carts. Ponies are also used by Baniās as pack-animals, for the carriage of grain and ghī. Such ponies only cost Rs. 5 to Rs. 10 each. Stallions are never castrated. A considerable number of imported animals of fairly good class were also formerly kept, but there are now very few. Breeding stallions were until lately supplied by Government, but the results obtained were very inadequate, and it has been decided to discontinue the practice of maintaining them. The number of horses and ponies in 1902-03 was 7,975 or about 4 to each inhabited village.

Sheep and Goats.

165. Sheep are kept only by the Gadaria or shepherd caste, and goats by this and other low castes of Hindus and by Muhammadans. No use is made of their manure. Goats are kept mainly for food, and their milk is drunk and also sold to the Halwais or confectioners. Blankets are made from the wool of sheep

and used by all agriculturists. In 1902-03 there were 15,000 sheep and 20,000 goats.

Donkeys.

166. Donkeys are only kept by Gadherā Kumhārs, Khatíks or vegetable-sellers, Dhobīs, and Sunkars and Beldārs or masons, and used for the carriage of their stock-in-trade as grain, lime, bricks and tiles, earth and vegetables. The donkey makes a very good beast of burden, and its price is from Rs. 5 to Rs. 20. The milk is not drunk, but is sometimes given as medicine to children. The donkey is impure, and no Hindus except those mentioned keep him. He is the animal on which Sitala, the goddess of small-pox, rides. 'Khachchars' or mules are the offspring of a donkey sire and a horse dam, that is to say, they are in reality jennets. They are only bred from a donkey stallion kept up by Government. High-caste Hindus frequently object to having their mares covered by a donkey, but the stock are much more valuable than ponies, the mule of a small mare fetching Rs. 60 or Rs. 70 and of a large one Rs. 200 or Rs. 300. They are sold to the cavalry and artillery. Hindus will not usually ride on mules in Saugor. In 1902-03 there were 425 mules and 1,270 donkeys in the District.

Cattle Disease.

167. The local names of the commoner diseases of cattle are *māla* and *chechak* for rinderpest, *baikarā* for foot-and-mouth disease, *ghatsarap*, *bhaonrā* or *parsujā* for anthrax, and *sunkā* for pleuro-pneumonia. Rinderpest is common, buffaloes suffering more from it than cattle, especially the young males. The animals generally die within a week, and if they live to twelve days will probably survive. The owners feed them on oilcake, ghī and rice-water and worship Devī. Foot-and-mouth disease is not usually fatal but is worst in the hot weather. The animal is tied up near water, so that its feet stand in the mud, and is given ghī mixed with pepper and linseed oil to eat while lime and tobacco or coal-tar and 'dikāmali' gum are rubbed in

the ulcerated parts of the feet, or a decoction of nīm-seeds pounded and boiled in linseed oil. The disease more commonly attacks the feet. The different forms of anthrax are considered locally as different diseases. It is called *bhaonrā* when the head gets giddy and the animal runs in circles, and *parsujā* or *ghatsarap* when the throat is swollen. The latter form is said to be comparatively rare. The local remedy is to brand the throat with a hot iron, but the animal nearly always dies. Buffaloes are said to suffer from a disease called locally *illai.* Their nostrils get pierced, and maggots appear in them. A piece of grass covered with butter and vermilion is thrust up the nostrils. Cultivating cattle die more frequently than others, and the most unhealthy time is the early part of the rains, when they eat the young grass. A veterinary dispensary is maintained by the District Council at Saugor.

Carts.

168. Carts are of two kinds, *rahrua* and *chhakrā.* The rahrua cart is a primitive one, and its wheels are solid disks of wood in three pieces joined by wooden spikes, and without tyres. Their narrow sharp edges are very injurious to the roads. Chhakrās have only come into use on a large scale in the last 15 years or since the construction of good roads. They are the ordinary country carts. Light trotting-carts are as yet unknown, nor are the bullocks trained to trot. The price of a rahrua cart is Rs. 4 and of a chhakrā cart Rs. 15.

Cattle Fairs.

169. A large annual cattle fair is held at Garhākotā, and a weekly cattle-market at Khurai besides one or two less important bazars. A notice of these is contained in the section on markets and fairs.

CHAPTER V.

LOANS, PRICES, WAGES, &c.

LOANS.

Land Improvement and Agricultural Loans.

170. As over the rest of the Province, Government action in the supply of capital for agriculture has only assumed important dimensions during the last decade. Between 1871 and 1891 the loans granted under the Land Improvement Loans Act amounted only to Rs. 19,000, and those under the Agriculturists' Loans Act to Rs. 26,000. Between 1891 and 1895 large advances were made under the latter Act, the total amounting to Rs. 4 lakhs of which Rs. 3½ lakhs were borrowed in 1894-95. From 1896 to 1901 a further sum of nearly Rs. 3 lakhs was given out, and Rs. 96,000 more, between 1901 and 1903, the total advances of agricultural loans since 1871 thus amounting to Rs. 8·13 lakhs. Under the Land Improvement Loans Act, only Rs. 22,000 were given out between 1891 and 1901. The scope for work under this Act is somewhat limited in wheat-growing Districts, and the embankment of fields, the main object for which they are taken, has made little progress in Saugor until a very recent period. During 1901-02, however, Rs. 30,000 were distributed in loans for the reclamation of fields overgrown with kāns grass. The total advances under both acts up to 1902-03 thus amounted to Rs. 8·75 lakhs. Of this sum Rs. 6·25 lakhs have been recovered, Rs. 2 lakhs are outstanding and some Rs. 50,000 have been remitted. Of the interest due on the loans Rs. 70,000 have been recovered and Rs. 10,000 remitted.

Sanads for improvements.

171. Fifty-one sanads or certificates in all have been granted for the improvement of land and other works of public utility since 1895. Of these 12 were given in 1898-99 and 14 in 1901-02. Out of the whole number 17 were awarded

for making *bandhāns* or large field embankments, combined in four cases with the construction of wells. Eight sanads were given for making *bandhias* or small embankments, nine for the construction of wells and one for a tank and well. In the remaining cases the work for which the sanads were granted is not recorded. Viewed generally, this is not a very substantial list of improvements, but as already mentioned the people have only lately begun to look with favour on the practice of embanking fields, while since the decay in the cultivation of sugarcane, much of the incentive to construct wells has vanished. The wells, originally dug for watering sugarcane, are now used, since the water is available, for the irrigation of wheat and other crops, but the people do not consider it worth while to make new wells for this purpose.

Rates of interest on private loans.

172. The rates of interest on cash loans advanced by bankers are 6 to 9 per cent on the pledge of jewels, 12 per cent on mortgage of land or loans to substantial proprietors, and 18 to 24 per cent on loans to small proprietors and tenants. Frequently in the case of poor tenants, one anna in the rupee is deducted by the lender at the time of giving the loan, and this transaction is not entered in the deed. As a rule bonds or deeds are written for loans, but they are dispensed with if the borrower deposits a pledge in the shape of jewels. If the borrower is a substantial and reliable man loans are also made without a document, and an attested entry in the lender's account-books is considered sufficient. Railway and other contractors and cattle-dealers like Basdewās, who only borrow money for short periods have to pay very high rates of interest. The Basdewās take loans for four or five months and are charged between 2 and 4 per cent per month.

Grain loans.

173. For loans of seed-grain for the spring crops, the rate of interest is usually *sawai* or 25 per cent for the period between seed-

time and harvest. For the first loan to a new borrower 50 per cent is sometimes charged. Since the price of grain has begun to vary greatly between seed-time and harvest, a practice has arisen, chiefly in the Khurai tahsil, of fixing cash rates for a loan of seed-grain, and stipulating that the loan shall be repaid in grain valued at the same cash rate. In this manner the grain interest sometimes amounts to nearly 100 per cent. This method of advancing seed-grain has been introduced in the villages belonging to Rājā Gokul Dās. For loans of seed-grain for the autumn crops, the rate of interest is usually 100 per cent. This is partly, as in the case of juār, owing to the insignificance of the transaction and the small quantity of seed required. The regular moneylenders do not deal largely in advances of these grains and they are frequently made by the tenants to each other, the same rate of interest being charged. Very few tenants keep their own seed in Saugor, and the bulk of them regularly borrow it every year. Loans for subsistence while the crops are on the ground are called *khawai*. These are made repayable at harvest with 25 per cent interest in grain. The *bandhwār* system of making loans, to be repaid in kind at a fixed rate, is largely resorted to by dealers in *ghī* or clarified butter. The loan is made in cash and is repayable in *ghī* at a fixed rate some 25 per cent cheaper than the price at the time of making the loan.

174. A large number of Baniās carry on money-lending transactions, some of whom have acquired substantial estates, while others do not own villages; a few of the leading mālguzārs of other castes are also moneylenders. The principal capitalists in the Saugor tahsīl are Biseshwar Dayāl Misra Kanaujia Brāhman of Saugor, Bihāri Lāl Chunnī Lāl Gomashtās Agarwāl Baniās of Saugor, Ratanlāl Dālchand Khandelwāl Baniā of Saugor, Balīchand and Benīprasād Tiwāri Jijhotia Brāhmans of Dhāna, Muhammad Azīmullā Khān of Saugor, Sagun Mal Lakshmichand Oswāl Baniās of Rāhatgarh, and Bihāri Misra

Money-lenders.

Sarwaria Brāhman of Dongāsarā. In the Rehlī tahsīl, Gayā Prasād and Baijnāth Patel Jijhotia Brāhmans of Khamaria have very large dealings, and next in importance to them is Lālchand Parwār Baniā of Keslī. Several of the Saugor bankers also carry on dealings in Rehli. In Khurai, Rājā Gokul Dās of Jubbulpore has extensive transactions, and Shrimant Seth Mohan Lāl Parwār Baniā of Khurai, Khet Singh Pallīwāl Brāhman of Khurai, Nathūrām Singhai Parwār Baniā of Etāwa, and Rai Sāhib Seth Mohan Lāl Parwār Baniā of Rondhā are the other leading bankers. The last two are now in somewhat poor circumstances, owing partly to their own liberality to their tenants, and to their debtors in the conciliation proceedings. Most of the above firms hold a large number of villages and the Baniās as a class are very powerful and influential in Khurai tahsīl. Kālūrām Gurhā of Khurai, and Pannā Lāl Chaudhrī Parwār Baniā of Mālthone, also have extensive transactions. In Bandā, Hāthi Sao Nand Kishore Jijhotia Brāhman of Dhurmār, Dālchand Singhai Parwār Baniā of Binaikā, and Kāre Singhai Golāpūrab Baniā of Hirāpur, are the principal local bankers, but the dealings of all these are on a very small scale compared with those of the other tahsils. Seth Kanak Mal of Saugor has a shop in Bandā.

Indebtedness of the Agricultural classes

175. The series of bad years, through which the District has passed, has affected moneylenders, mālguzārs and tenants alike. Before the bad years commencing in 1892-93, there was already a considerable amount of indebtedness due to want of providence and extravagant expenditure on marriages. This has enormously increased since the famines. During the decade ending 1901, the population decreased by 20 per cent, the area under cultivation by 20 per cent, and the cropped area by 26 per cent, while the acreage of wheat shrank to little more than half its former total. The realisations of income tax decreased by nearly half. In Khurai

tahsil it was estimated in 1903 that a considerable majority of landlords and tenants were involved, and in other parts of the District, though the mālguzārs were better off, the indebtedness among tenants was not much less. While some of the leading moneylenders maintained their position or acquired fresh property, several sustained large losses and themselves became involved. Many villages in the Khurai tahsil present an eloquently desolate appearance, more than half the houses standing empty. Very little of the jewellery pawned during the famines has been redeemed, and it is a comparatively rare sight to meet a person wearing gold and silver or even good clothes, while bell-metal has largely been substituted for the precious metals as the material for ornaments. Few landowners can now afford to keep good horses or ponies, and the inferior millets have been largely substituted as food-grains for wheat, which was formerly consumed even by the labouring classes. No exact statistics of the transfers of villages could be obtained, but such as have been furnished appear to show that a very large number of villages have changed hands in recent years. This is borne out by the fact that several large estates have lately been acquired through loan transactions, notably those of Gokul Dās, Azimullā Khān, and some of the villages belonging to Shrīmant Seth Mohan Lāl and Seth Khet Singh of Khurai. At the same time some of the largest estates as those of Etāwa, Pithoria and Pitehrā have either been lost by their owners or are heavily involved.

Conciliation proceedings.

176. Proceedings undertaken with the object of reducing the debts of proprietors and tenants, who would otherwise have become bankrupt, were inaugurated in the Khurai tahsil and the Dhāmoni pargana of the Bandā tahsīl, the most affected portions of the District, by Mr. Fuller when Commissioner of Jubbulpore in 1898. In that year, loans were advanced by Government to tenants and cultivating proprietors, conditionally on the release of

private debts by other creditors. The idea gained favour and was followed by the spontaneous release by various large creditors, of irrecoverable debts, so that in all Rs. 7·96 lakhs of debt were remitted. In 1900 and 1901 a regular scheme of conciliation of the debts of proprietors in the Khurai tahsil and the Dhāmoni pargana of Bandā was initiated and carried through by Rao Bahādur Rāmbhau Meghashām and Rao Sāhib Gangā Singh, Extra Assistant Commissioners. The circumstances of 583 villages, owned by 1,390 shareholders, were examined. The debts of 502 of these were settled by arbitration; 56 were well off and out of debt, 749 only owed such debts as they were able to pay without assistance, 50 did not wish for any assistance, and 33 had debts for which nothing could be done owing to their creditors declining to submit to arbitration These figures are of interest as showing that in what was undoubtedly the worst tract of the District, considerably less than half of the proprietors were very heavily involved. The debts of 502 shareholders in 294 villages which were included in the conciliation scheme, reached, however, the very large total of Rs. 9·40 lakhs. Of this Rs. 6·40 lakhs or 68 per cent were remitted, no less than 76 per cent of the remitted debt being secured by mortgage or decree. This amount of debt aggregated three times the estimated selling value of the property. The creditors who were most conspicuous for their liberality in remission and the assistance given by them to the Government officers, were Rai Sāhib Mohan Lāl, Seth Khet Singh and Shrīmant Seth Mohan Lāl. Proceedings were subsequently taken by tahsildārs in each of the four tahsils, the inquiry being confined to persons who were indebted for loans to Government. These resulted in the remission of Rs. 27,000 of Government loans and something over a lakh of rupees of private loans. A large number of proprietors and tenants were thus saved from ruin, and with moderately favourable seasons and care and industry on their own part, should be able to extricate themselves from debt.

PRICES.

Rise in prices during the 30 years' settlement. Wheat.

177. Mr. De Brett considered that the general rise in the prices of grain during the currency of the 30 years' settlement might be taken at 75 to 100 per cent. This result was arrived at by a scrutiny of the account books of leading proprietors, and it was generally concurred in by the people. The retail prices, recorded in the returns as ruling at Saugor, did not accurately represent the amount which the cultivators obtained for their produce, as it included the cost of carriage of the grain to market. The rate at which cultivators obtained credit for their grain with the mālguzārs at the yearly settlement of accounts, is usually fixed by a *panchāyat* or committee of neighbouring mālguzārs and tenants, and is a wholesale rate somewhat lower than the market-price. The prices arrived at by the Settlement Officer for the five years 1857—62 preceding the 30 years' settlement were wheat 79 lbs., pissi 88 lbs. and gram 95 lbs.; while for the five years preceding the last settlement (1887—92) the corresponding rates were wheat 37 lbs., pissi 36 lbs. and gram 45 lbs. This was equivalent to a rise in prices of 117 per cent for wheat, 141 per cent for pissi and 109 per cent for gram. The quinquennium immediately preceding the 30 years' settlement was one of especially low prices. In the years before 1857 there had been poor crops, while in those succeeding 1862, prices rose with a bound owing to the increased European demand ensuing on the American War. These prices were, however, normal at that period. They have never fallen again to anything approaching the same level, owing to various causes. The high prices of the sixties were sustained by the scarcity of 1867-68 and continued until 1869, when a gradual fall set in, which was, however, checked by the demand for grain arising in 1878 and 1879 from the famines of those years in the North-Western Provinces and Madras. For the years 1862-67 the average

price of wheat was 38 lbs. per rupee, during 1867—72 it was 46 lbs., during 1872—77, 55 lbs., during 1877—82, 51 lbs., during 1882—87, 58 lbs., and during 1887—92, 36 lbs. The cheapest period between 1862 and 1892 was thus the quinquennium 1882—87 when prices were only 38 per cent higher than in 1857—62. The above figures are for Saugor tahsīl, and while the rates in other tahsils presented in past years slight variations, the results for the whole period were nearly the same.

Other grains.

178. The variations in the prices of other grains approximated to that of wheat, but the rates for pissi wheat rose, as has already been seen, in a special degree in consequence of the demand for export. Gram has generally been from 5 to 10 lbs. per rupee cheaper than wheat, while juār has differed much more largely from wheat, ranging from 2 to 17 lbs. per rupee cheaper. It is noteworthy that at the 30 years' settlement juār was very little cheaper than wheat, the difference being only 2 lbs. during the years 1862—66. The explanation apparently consists in the fact that as juār was in no demand for export, its price was not subsequently forced up as that of wheat has been; and it seems a reasonable conclusion, that at this time juār was not considered so much inferior to wheat as a food-grain as is the case at present, and that the superior estimation in which wheat is held is partly a result of its increased price.

Variation in prices in the interior.

179. It may be noted also that the statistics given by Mr. De Brett show that the prices taken from mālguzārs' account books, and which represent the wholesale rate received by the producer, ranged from 6 to 12 lbs. per rupee less than the market-prices recorded at Saugor, this difference being equivalent to an increase of 23 per cent on the former rate. The difference apparently represents the cost of carriage to Saugor and the middleman's profit, and the conclusion is that the latter item must have been very

considerable. Mr. Cleveland notes that in the interior, prices ranged from one to two seers a rupee lower than at Saugor at the time of attestation; and this figure perhaps shows that with the increased competition in trade, the tenants are gradually realising the true market value of their produce.

Course of prices since 1892.

180. The figures of prices since 1892 are the official ones returned at Saugor. The official return of the price of wheat was 31 lbs. per rupee during the quinquennium 1887—92. It was already rising in the later years and had reached 25 lbs. in 1891. During the following years it gradually increased till the famine of 1897 when 16½ lbs. was recorded. This again fell to 25 lbs. in the following year and rose to 20 lbs. in 1900. Since then it has gradually declined, and in 1903 the rate was 30 lbs. or the lowest since 1889. The price assumed at Mr. De Brett's settlement was 37 lbs., but in comparing this with the official figures, from 2 to 4 lbs. must be added for the difference between the rural and headquarters rates, and the conclusion is that in 1903 prices were very little higher than at settlement. Since 1891 the price of gram has ranged between 2 and 14½ lbs. per rupee cheaper than wheat, the lowest difference of 2 lbs. being in 1897, when gram was 19 lbs., and the highest of 14 lbs. in 1903 when gram was 45 lbs.[1] In years of scarcity gram is thus scarcely cheaper than wheat, but when the harvests are good, the foreign demand for wheat sends it up 50 per cent. higher than gram. During the same period the price of juār has ranged between 25 lbs. in 1897 and 1900, and 59 lbs. in 1903. The lowest figure ever recorded for juār was 85 lbs. in 1881, and it was cheaper in 1903, than in 30 out of the last 40 years. As already noticed its relative cheapness in proportion to wheat has been much greater in recent years than formerly. Rice is expensive in Saugor, and as a food-grain

[1] The exact prices in 1903 were: wheat 30·4 lbs., gram 44·8 lbs.

is a luxury of the better classes. Its price is seldom cheaper than 21 or 22 lbs. to the rupee. The highest rate recorded since 1891 was 14 lbs. in 1897. The price of linseed was 20 lbs. in 1891 and in most years of the decade it has been above that. This oilseed has largely increased in value since about 1888, and its cultivation was very popular in the early nineties, but since then it has greatly declined, notwithstanding that the price has remained at its former level. Til, however, is now also a very valuable crop, and is apparently a safer agricultural investment than linseed. The price of cotton has ranged between 4·6 and 6·4 lbs. since 1891, the rates at Saugor having apparently been more uniform than in the Nāgpur Districts.

Prices of miscellaneous articles.

181. Salt was 18 lbs. to the rupee or a little more from 1891 to 1896, and since then has declined to 20 and 22 lbs. and finally to 24 lbs. in 1903, this last fall being due to the reduction of the duty. *Gur* or unrefined sugar varies from 16 lbs. to 40 lbs. a rupee, the rates being different at different seasons of the year. Saugor *gur* is from 2 to 4 lbs. more expensive than that imported, and very little is now produced. *Gur* is more consumed than sugar at present, but the popularity of the latter is increasing. Mirzāpur sugar is from 7 to 8 lbs. a rupee and Mauritius sugar from 8 to 10 lbs. Milk is sold at 32 lbs. a rupee in Saugor and pure milk at 26 lbs. Milk is not generally sold in villages. The Gaolis water the milk which they sell, except that supplied to the confectioners. Milk is cheapest in the rains when it falls to 40 lbs. a rupee and most expensive in the hot weather, especially when a number of marriages are in progress. The rate for *ghī* or melted butter is 3 lbs. a rupee in Saugor, and 3½ lbs. in the interior. It has substantially increased in price during the last decade. Grass is sold at the rate of 1,000 to 1,200 *pūlas* or bundles to the rupee in Saugor and 1,500 in the interior. A cartload of firewood containing from 5 to 8 maunds or 400 to 640 lbs.

costs Re. 1 to Rs. 1-8. Firewood is only sold in towns. Tenants bring firewood from the forests in their own carts, the expenditure on one cartload being the license fee of 2 annas in Government forest and 4 annas for labour, or 6 annas in all. A family of five persons will obtain 6 or 7 cartloads of firewood in the year. One cartload would last about a month if used by itself and is eked out by cowdung cakes and pickings from mālguzāri forest. Head-loads of firewood are sold only in towns. A head-load weighs from 40 to 60 lbs. and costs from 1½ to 3 annas in Saugor, and 2 to 3 pice in small towns.

WAGES.

182. In 1893 the average wages of an able-bodied agricultural labourer were shown as Rs. 4-8 a month, and those of the skilled artisans like masons, carpenters, and blacksmiths, as Rs. 9-8 to Rs. 10. In 1903 a labourer received Rs. 5 a month, and the artisans Rs. 12-8. These rates, however, are probably those prevalent in Saugor and perhaps one or two other towns, and the customary wages in the interior for agricultural labour are lower, whether calculated in cash or grain.

Published statistics.

183. Farm-servants are called locally *harwāha*. They are engaged either for six or twelve months, the contract being made at the end of *Jeth* (May-June). Small tenants engage a farm-servant for six months, while landowners take some for six and some for twelve months, the number required during the rains being larger than in the cold weather. Farm-servants are usually paid in cash and the wages are from Rs. 2-8 to Rs. 3 a month; in addition to this, a blanket and a pair of shoes worth Rs. 2 and sometimes a *mirzai* or waistcoat are given annually. While sowing is proceeding, the farm-servant receives daily a *khowa* or double handful of grain equivalent to about a pound; and similarly during the harvest, he receives daily one sheaf giving about two pounds of

Farm-servants.

grain. When sowing is finished, the farm-servants assemble in the courtyard or outside under a tree and receive a good meal at the master's expense and a present of 2 lbs. of grain. The farm-servant has no special right to glean. Anyone may glean, but if the field is thickly strewn, the owner gets it done himself. In Mālthone, the wages of a farm-servant are lower and he receives only Rs. 2 per month and the above perquisites. Formerly it is said that the farm-servant had a plot sown with 20 lbs. of grain for him, in addition to his wages. But this custom has now ceased, and his wages are consequently lower than they were. If paid in grain, the farm-servant receives 6 *seis* or 120 lbs. mixed grain monthly. During the famines, wages sank to 5 *seis* or 100 lbs. and this was paid in gram or juār or sometimes even partly in mahuā. In Bandā, however, the cash wages of farm-servants have risen from Rs. 1-8 or Rs. 2 to Rs. 2-8 or Rs. 3. Generally, it may be concluded that the wages of farm-servants have not kept pace with the rise in prices. The explanation of this fact is, however, probably the general poverty of agriculturists, and the decrease in the demand for labour owing to the quantity of land which has gone out of cultivation.

Herdsmen.

184. The herdsman is called *baredī*. Boys are usually employed as herdsmen as they are obtained for a lower wage. The monthly rate of pay is from 12 annas for a boy to Rs. 3 for a full-grown man. The *baredī* also receives a little of the previous night's food in the morning, either cold *chapātis*, or wheat, rice, or juār boiled in buttermilk. He receives his blanket and pair of shoes annually, and sometimes an old coat or head-cloth. When a male calf is born he gets 2 pice and his food, and for the birth of a female calf, a new cloth, or at least 4 pice. When salt is given to the cattle once a fortnight the *baredī* gets an eighth share. Those who have a number of cattle keep a private herdsman, and large landowners have three or four, one for each class of animal. For the small cultivators there are one

or more herdsmen who take the village cattle to graze. The hire is 2 pice a month for a calf, one anna for a cow, and two annas for a buffalo. The herdsman receives a small present at Diwāli. In the morning the herdsman gives a call, and the owners let out their cattle, who assemble at the village standing-ground, and when he brings them back at night, each man goes and takes his own cattle home. Those who have their cattle milked and tied up by the herdsman have to pay something more. The herdsman must also search for missing cattle, but he is not responsible for their loss, and occasionally he colludes with cattle-thieves. During the rains cattle are sent to graze in the jungles at night in order to increase the supply of milk.

Gobarwali.

185. Another agricultural servant is the *gobarwāli.* She is usually a woman and gets from 8 annas to Rs. 2 a month, and a set of clothes worth about Rs. 2 a year, with the same presents of grain as the farm-servant. She cleans out the cattle-stalls, collects the manure, and makes the *kandās* or cowdung cakes. She also sweeps the courtyard in the mornings, prepares the buttermilk, and helps to grind wheat. During the rains she spreads ashes or dry earth in the stalls.

Field labourers.

186. The agricultural labourer is called *mazdūr.* The usual custom in the case of the autumn crops is to give them out on the *bhagia* system, the labourer doing the weeding, watching, and harvesting, and receiving a third or half of the crop after deducting the seed. Usually the labourer takes two acres in this way, and a tenant with a holding of ten acres will give four acres to two *bhagias,* and reserve six acres in the centre of the holding for himself. The cash wages of a casual agricultural labourer are 4 to 5 pice a day, and for this he works only from a little before midday to evening. For harvesting special rates are paid. The daily wage for cutting juār is a sheaf of 30 or 40 stalks yielding 4 lbs. of grain. For rice or kodon, 5 lbs. of

unhusked grain are paid. For cutting the spring crops, two sheaves or 4 lbs. are given, while the man who binds the sheaves and the water-carrier receive 3 lbs. each, there being one binder to every three reapers and one water-carrier to every 20 or 30 reapers. For gram one *karpā* or heap of heads containing about 5 lbs. is given. Watchers of the autumn crops at night receive Re. 1 a month, and they are able to do some work during the day as well. For watching the spring crops by day *moghias* or fowlers are frequently employed. They take a contract of the whole village for watching the crops from seed-time until harvest, and receive a *sei* or 20 lbs. of grain per plough of 13 acres. The customary wage for earthwork in the construction of field embankments is a rupee for a hundred by one by one cubits or 337 cubic feet of earth excavated. But labour can now be obtained at the rate of a rupee for 400 cubic feet.

Seasons of employment.

187. The seasons of slack and full employment for agricultural labourers are somewhat as follows: Beginning from August there is a good demand for labour in this month and the first part of September for weeding the autumn crops. By the time weeding is finished, the sowing of the spring crops begins, the customary date being Dasahrā, which may be about the middle of September. By the time the spring crops are sown towards the end of October, the harvesting of the autumn grains, first juār and then rice, til, and other crops commences. The harvest lasts till the end of December and a slack period then ensues during January and February. During this time many labourers collect grass and fuel for sale, while others are employed in threshing the crops. The fruits of the wild plum tree and of the bushes *makoi* (*Zizyphus Œnoplia*) and *karondā* (*Carrissa Carandas*) also ripen at this time and form a welcome aid to the sustenance of the poor. With the beginning of March comes the spring harvest and

full employment is then available for everybody for two months. During May the threshing of the spring crops affords some employment, and a certain amount is obtained in embanking fields. This is also the time of the mahuā crop, the most important food product afforded by the forests. Mahuā trees are most plentiful in the Bandā tahsīl and labourers from other tracts go there to pick it and also to Bundelkhand. The people go out to gather the flowers in the early morning and coming back about 9 A.M., do any other work that they may have. Another very slack period is during June and July, the sowing of the autumn crops not causing any very large demand for labour. The little weed *chakorā* (*Cassia Tora*) grows at this time, and also the *sawān* grass (*Panicum Crus-Galli*) the seeds of which the people gather by sweeping a bent bamboo attached to a basket over the heads of the grass. The earnings of the spring harvest, during which each labourer gets two or three days' food for a day's work, also last through the hot weather. A certain amount of emigration takes place to the Nerbudda valley at the time of the wheat harvest, and to Lalitpur for cutting the juār. In a tract devoted mainly to autumn crops the end of the hot weather and the beginning of the rains is the hardest time for the casual labourer, but in wheat country the pinch is most felt in January and February during the Hindu months of Pūs and Māgh, and hence they say punningly Mā(g)hia parā or "Trouble has come."

Village servants.

188. Another important class to whom customary wages are paid are the village artisans and servants. Setting aside the patwāri or accountant and kotwār or watchman, who now receive cash stipends and are practically in the employment of Government, the principal village servants are the Lohār or blacksmith, the Barhai or carpenter, the Nai or barber, the Dhīmar or water-bearer, the Dhobī or washerman, and the Purohit and Pandā or village priests. The Kumhār or potter and Basor or basket-

maker do not usually receive customary dues but sell their wares, while the Chamār is the general village drudge.

The Lohār.

189. The Lohār mends the iron implements of agriculture, the ploughshare, axe, sickle, goad and other articles. For doing this he receives a yearly contribution of one *sei* or 20 lbs. of grain per plough, together with a handful of grain at sowing time and a sheaf at harvest of both the autumn and spring crops. The total comes to 26 lbs. Near Saugor he gets 9 large *chauthias* or 22½ lbs. and 10 lbs. extra. This does not cover the making of new implements for which he must be separately paid or at least supplied with the material. At the Diwāli festival the Lohār prepares small iron nails and drives one into the threshold of every tenant, for doing which he receives a small present. The nail is supposed to keep evil spirits out of the house.

The Carpenter.

190. The Barhai mends the plough and *bakhar* or paring-plough and the other wooden implements of agriculture. He also makes new ones, the wood being supplied to him. For making carts or the woodwork of houses he must be paid separately. At Diwāli the Barhai makes a wooden peg about 6 inches long and drives it into the floor inside the door of the house, and for this he gets a present of a pound of grain. Frequently the village has no Barhai and the Lohār does the carpentering work as well as his own.

The Barber.

191. The Nai is the most important of all the village servants. He receives 20 lbs. of grain per year for each adult male in the family, or in some villages 22½ lbs. per plough, besides the usual 4 or 5 lbs. at seed-time and harvest. And on days when he shaves the men he gets some food. Ordinary cultivators are shaved once a fortnight. Besides this the Nai arranges marriages, carries the invitations for the wedding, supplies leaf-plates and cups for the wedding, carries the torch for the marriage procession, spreads the carpet in the marriage shed, fills the *huqqās* of

all the guests, and performs various other offices. One of the ordinary duties of the Nai is to rub or apply massage to the legs of his clients in the evening, and when he goes to a house to do this he gets his food. The Nain or barber's wife is equally useful. She invites the women on festive occasions, washes the clothes of female guests at weddings, dresses women, ties their hair and puts lac-dye on their feet and *menhdī* or pounded henna on their fingers. When a child is born the duties of the Nain begin when the days of pollution are over and the midwife leaves. She then attends on the mother and child and rubs them with oil. Large villages have two or three barbers, but in the case of small ones there is only one barber to every three or four villages, and he goes round to them on different days.

The Water-bearer.

192. The Dhimar is usually the mālguzār's servant, but sometimes he receives contributions from the tenants. From the mālguzār he receives a plot of rent-free land or wages. In large villages each house has a *ghinochī* or tripod containing *gharās* or earthen vessels for water. These the Dhimar fills up once in the morning and once in the evening. For this he receives 2 or 3 annas a month. The Dhīmar also brings water for Government servants when they come to the village, and cleans their cooking vessels and prepares the hearth with fresh cowdung and water in order to cleanse it. If he cleans the mālguzār's vessels he gets his food for doing so. When the tenants have marriages he performs the same household duties, and receives a present of Rs. 1 or 2 and some clothes if the families are well off, and also his food every day while the marriage is in progress. The Dhimar's duty is also to carry back the palanquins in which the bridegroom and bride return from the wedding. He is the regular 'banhgi-bardār' or bearer in the old sense, and carries the mālguzār's vessels and other things in a *banhgī* [1] when he

[1] Two loops of rope to hold baskets or bundles suspended from a wooden cross-bar across the shoulders.

goes on a journey. Dhīmars are usually personal servants. In cooking he is allowed to knead the food. He may enter any part of the house, including the cooking-place and the women's rooms. He addresses his mistress as 'mother.' When he lights a pipe he takes the first pull and then offers it to his master, presenting it with his left hand placed under his right elbow in token of respect. Another business of the Dhīmar's is to take sweet potatoes and boiled plums to the fields at harvest-time and sell them. He supplies water to the reapers and receives three sheaves a day in payment. The Dhīmar is not a good agriculturist, and generally restricts himself to the cultivation of a garden plot. He has a monopoly of growing *singhāra* or water-nuts in tanks. He is also a fisherman, and makes his own nets, weaving them at leisure on a stick while he is walking along, or while he is sitting smoking and talking. Town Dhīmars are addicted to drink, and there can be no marriage or *panchāyat* without liquor. They also smoke gānja.

The Washerman.

193. The Dhobī is engaged when there is a birth or death. These events cause impurity and hence all the clothes of all members of the household must be washed when the impurity ceases. When a man dies the Dhobī receives eight annas, and for a woman four annas, and similar rates in the case of the birth of a male or female child. For ordinary washing he gets half as much as the Barhai or Lohār, that is 12 or 13 lbs. of grain annually. When he brings home clothes he is also given a meal, and well-to-do persons give him their old clothes as a present. In return for this he washes all the clothes of the family at intervals of one or two months, except their loin-cloths and women's bodices which the people wash themselves daily. He washes clothes by rubbing them with wood ashes at night and beating them out in water with a stick in the morning. Silk clothes are washed with the nut of the *rītha* tree (*Sapindus emarginatus*) which gives a lather like soap. When the

Dhobī brings back the clean clothes, they are sometimes sprinkled with water before being touched in order to free them from the impurity caused by the touch of the Dhobī. The Dhobī may come as far as the veranda but not into the house. Among some of the higher castes on the occasion of a marriage the elder members of the bridegroom's family go with the bride to the Dhobin's house. She presents the bride with betel-leaf and in return is given clothes with a rupee. The ceremony is called *sohāg* or 'good fortune' and the present from the Dhobin is supposed to be lucky. The Dhobī himself is an unlucky person to see on going out in the morning, and the *sohāg* ceremony is perhaps intended to neutralise the effect of this, and to show that even those who ordinarily cause evil fortune are propitiatory to the marriage.

The Bamboo-worker.

194. The Basor is not a village servant and sells the baskets which he makes in the ordinary manner. He acts however as the village musician, and plays at marriages. The band usually consists of four men, and they get two annas a day each and their food. The Basorin or Basor's wife is the village midwife, and she receives one rupee for the birth of a boy and 8 annas for a girl, besides her food while she is in attendance. The Basor takes the winding sheet of dead persons, and also picks up the copper coins or cowries which are thrown over the corpse by the mourners on its way to the burning-ghāt.

The Potter.

195. The Kumhār also is not a regular village servant and sells his pots in the ordinary manner. But he sometimes takes the soiled grass from the stalls of the cattle and gives pots free to the cultivator in exchange. On Aktī day at the beginning of the agricultural year, the Kumhār presents five pots with covers on them to each tenant and receives 2½ lbs. of grain in exchange. One of these the tenant fills with water and presents to a Brāhman, and

the rest he reserves for his own purposes. The Kumhārs are divided into two sub-castes, Gadherās and Bardias, who keep donkeys and buffaloes respectively as pack-animals. The former are considered unclean, but not the latter. On the occasion of a wedding the bridegroom's party take the bride to the Kumhārin's house as part of the *sohāg* ceremony. The Kumhār seats the bride on his wheel and turns it round with her seven times. The Kumhārin presents her with seven pots which are taken back to the house and used in the *bhānwar* ceremony. They are filled with water and are supposed to represent the seven seas. In return for this she receives a present of clothes.

The Village Priest.

196. The Purohit is the village priest and may be any kind of Hindustāni Brāhman. A Purohit is appointed for every village, even though in the case of small villages he may not reside in it. The Purohit points out the auspicious days for sowing, winnowing, laying the foundations of a house, bringing cowdung cakes into the house, occupying a new house, erecting a new hearth in the house, weaning a new-born child, cutting its hair, and giving it a name. His usual fee for such services is 2 pice, but poor people simply give him a little grain or an areca-nut. When a calamity occurs the Purohit is hired to recite the 'Durgā Pāth' or a collection of hymns in honour of Devī, either at his own house or at that of the tenant. During the first fortnight of Kunwār,[1] when 'Pitripaksh' or the worship of ancestors takes place, the Purohit is fed by all the villagers, and takes his choice daily out of four or five houses to which he is invited, while the others give him some grain. At this period he sits by the village tank and repeats verses while the people make libations of water. He receives two handfuls of grain at sowing time and two sheaves at harvest, and about the same amount when the

[1] September-October.

grain is removed from the threshing floor. The Pandā is the priest of the village gods and especially Devī, and he officiates at the village festivals in the manner described in the section on religion. For this he receives his expenses and some payment, and the usual presents at seed-time and harvest, but no regular contributions.

The Chamār.

197. The Chamār is not a village servant, but has a place in the village economy as he takes the skins of dead cattle. In return for this he has to mend the shoes of the family, and the plough gear and to supply annually a *jot* or neck-rope; for new shoes he must be paid. He also has to do the *bhet-bigār* or attendance on Government officers and to carry messages from his own village to the next, but not further unless he is specially paid. He usually supplies one pair of shoes annually to the mālguzār and one or two pairs to the kotwār. In some villages the tenant is entitled to receive half the skin after it has been cured.

Total payments by tenants.

198. The following is a rough estimate of the amounts expended by a tenant on payments for labour, and to the village servants. The tenant is supposed to have a holding of 24 acres, consisting of 13 acres of rabī land, 7 acres of kharif land and 4 acres of fallow. Such a tenant should have four bullocks; he might be expected to keep a farm-servant for six months from June to December. And for two months during the two sowing seasons he will employ a boy to graze his plough-cattle during the intervals of cultivation, making them over to the village grazier for the rest of the year. The tenant's own labour is excluded from computation.

Particulars of payments.	Payment in grain.	Payment in cash.
	Lbs.	Rs. a. p.
Purohit or village priest	5	
Nai (barber) including his perquisites	52	
Barhai (carpenter) do. do.	59	
Lohār (black-smith) do. do.	59	
Dhobī washerman) do. do.	34	
One farm-servant at Rs. 3 per month for six months	...	18 0 0
His perquisites—shoes and blanket	...	2 0 0
His grain perquisites	74	
Grazier's fees for 4 bullocks at 1 anna per bullock per month for ten months	...	2 8 0
Grazier's fees for two months of the two sowing seasons (a boy at Rs. 2 a month)	...	4 0 0
1st weeding of 7 acres of kharīf land at 6 coolies for one day for every acre=42 coolies at 1 anna each.	...	2 10 0
2nd weeding do. do. do.	...	2 10 0
Rakhwāli (watching) of kharīf crops during the day for one month at two seis or 24 seers per plough for the entire season	48	
Rakhwāli (watching) for kharīf crops during the night at Rs 2 per month	...	2 0 0
Rakhwāli of rabī crops for one month at night at Rs. 2 per month	...	2 0 0
Reaping of rabī crops at 5 per cent of the mixed produce	299	
Reaping of kharīf crops at 5 per cent of the produce	210	
Feed of 4 bullocks (oilcake at one seer per bullock for two months at 25 seers a rupee ...	480	

Abstract.

	Rs.	a	p.
Total cash payments	35	12	0
Total grain payments 840 lbs.=420 seers at 18 seers per rupee	23	5	4
Oilcake 480 lbs.=240 seers at 25 seers a rupee.	9	10	0
Total ...	68	11	4

The tenant's payments for labour will thus amount to Rs. 68 odd. The value of the crop on 7 acres of land sown with autumn grains, one acre rice, three acres of juār and three acres of kodon is Rs. 56. The value of 13 acres of spring grains, eight acres wheat, three acres gram, and two acres linseed is Rs. 225. The total value of the crop is thus Rs. 281, and the cost of labour is nearly 25 per cent of the value of the produce. The rent may be taken at Rs. 26-4 on an average of Rs. 1-1-6 per occupied acre or rather less than a tenth of the produce. The value of seed-grain including interest at 25 per cent on rice and the spring grains is Rs. 44-4 or between a sixth and a seventh of the produce. The total expenditure on labour, seed-grain and rent is thus Rs. 139 or rather less than half the produce.

MANUFACTURES.

Cotton.

199. The cotton industry is not important in Saugor, only three Districts in the Province having a smaller number of cotton-spinners and weavers. The decrease has been very marked during the last decade. A little thread is still spun by hand, generally by women in their spare time, and used in the manufacture of coarse carpets, bags and cloths. Raw cotton which has been stuffed in quilts (*razai* and *toshak*) is afterwards spun into thread for *newār*-cloth and cart-covers. But for weaving ordinary wearing cloth, mill-spun thread is now solely used. Cloth is woven to some extent in large villages all over the District, but the chief centres are in Rehli tahsil, Rehli itself, Deori and Gourjhāmar each having some hundred houses of weavers, while in Garhākotā there are about twice this number. White *dhotīs* with red borders for children, and red cloths with black borders for women are principally woven. Garhākotā was described in 1850 as a 'chief cotton-mart,' the principal articles woven being *addās* or cloths in red, white and blue stripes, which were made into *lahengās* or skirts for women.

Very few of these are however made now. The weaving castes are principally Korīs and Chadārs, who weave only coarse cloth. There are only a few hundred Koshtīs in the District, and a few houses of Momins or Muhammadan weavers in Saugor. These sometimes make head-cloths with gold and silver thread.

Dyeing.

200. Cotton cloths are dyed in Rehlī, Garhākotā, and Gourjhāmar, but the industry is also decaying. The colours produced in Garhākotā and Gourjhāmar from the water of the Sonār are considered to be especially good. Saugor is said to have been famous for its dyeing industry, and to have had a large export trade in former times, but this has now altogether vanished. Many of the weavers now buy coloured thread. The cloths generally dyed are women's *sāris*, men's head-cloths, and cloths dyed green (*amowā*) and blue (*surmai*) for warm coats, and yellow for lining. Mārwāri and Muhammadan women are fond of bright and gay colours, and their clothes are generally treated with fugitive agents so that they may be dyed several times. The three dyeing castes are all represented; the Rangrezes who are Muhammadans by faith, and whose customs are a curious mixture of those of Hindus and Musalmāns, both dye and print, and also the Chhīpas, while the Rangāris only dye. The Rangrezes had a brisk trade when Banjārās in large numbers used to travel over the District, as the Banjārā women were good customers. Saugor has a considerable number of Rangrezes, but the term is partly an occupational one, and a Rangrez as soon as he ceased to carry on dyeing would probably return himself only as a Muhammadan. *Kusum* or safflower which was formerly extensively used as a dyeing agent is now scarcely ever employed owing to its cost, and indigo and *al* (*Morinda citrifolia*) though not entirely discarded are being supplanted by aniline dyes. In 1890-91 there were 400 acres under indigo and other dyes, but practically none are grown now.

Wool.

201. Coarse country blankets are woven from the wool of sheep by the Gadarias or shepherd caste, who combine this occupation with sheep-tending. The local supply is insufficient and blankets are imported from Bundelkhand. Those made in the District are somewhat inferior to the imported article. They are black, white, or chequered in black and white. In Khurai tahsīl blankets of a superior quality are made and sold for Rs. 2 or Rs. 3, the ordinary ones costing 17 or 18 annas. The Khurai blankets are called *rāl*. Some Pinjārās in Saugor city make *numdahs* of unspun wool, which are covered with cloth to form native saddles. The scutched wool is spread on cloth and sprinkled with a solution of soap, the cloth being then kneaded with the hands and feet to make the thickness uniform. The *numdahs* are sold in pairs, one black and the other white, and a pair weighing 2 lbs. costs 11 annas, the wool being worth 8 annas.

Gold and Silver work.

202. Saugor had formerly a large industry of gold and silver workers, but they are now hard put to it to make a living. It is estimated that the number of houses of Sonārs has fallen from 200 to 100 and of these not more than 70 are engaged in their own profession. There are a few Sonārs also in Khurai and Etāwa and one or two in most large villages. The Sonārs have partly taken to working in brass, but they make only small articles such as chains, bells, and little boxes. They have also become cultivators, and drive the plough themselves, a practice which has the effect of spoiling their hands and also prevents them from giving their sons a proper training. To be a good Sonār the hands must be trained from early youth to acquire the necessary delicacy of touch. The Sonār's son sits all day with his father, watching him work and handling the ornaments. Formerly the Sonār never touched a plough. The ornaments made in Saugor are heavier than elsewhere, and also different in shape. Gold ornaments are made by hammering and are usually hollow,

the interior being filled up with lac. Silver ornaments are made by hammering and casting; they are now frequently cast hollow, so as to make them cheaper. Gilt and nickel-silver ornaments are imported ready made and worn by the poorer classes. In Saugor there are a few *Jadias* who set precious stones.

Bell-metal.

203. Ornaments are now also largely made of bell-metal by the subcaste of Audhia Sonārs. Bell-metal is an alloy of copper and tin or pewter, which is made locally. When used for ornaments, the proportion of tin or pewter is increased so as to make them of a light colour, resembling silver as far as may be. Women of the higher castes may wear bell-metal ornaments only on their ankles and feet, and Marāthā and Khedāwāl Brāhmans may not wear them at all. The lower castes wear them all over the body. Eating and drinking vessels are also made of bell-metal, but they cannot be used for cooking as they will not stand fire. They are also brittle and break when dropped. In Saugor bell-metal vessels are considered to be liable to pollution like earthen vessels and cannot be lent to outsiders. Bell-metal vessels are always made by casting. The payment for making ornaments is only 1 pice per 5 tolas weight, if the purchaser provides the metal. When sold by weight the rate is Rs. 1-4 per seer (2 lbs.) for large ornaments and Rs. 4 or Rs. 5 for small ones. The Audhia Sonārs are looked down on by the rest of the caste and do not wear the sacred thread. There are bell-metal industries in Saugor, Tigorā, Jaisingh-nagar, Rāhatgarh, Isharwāra, Deorī, Khurai, Khimlāsa, Mālthone, and other places.

Brass and Copper work.

204. The number of workers in brass and copper is comparatively small. Water pots and dishes are made by the hammering process, while drinking and cooking pots, instruments, idols and toys are mainly cast. Copper horns for use as musical instruments are made in Mālthone

and sent outside the District, and also an instrument like a bugle called *turhī* which is used by Bairāgis. Brass is imported in sheets, and old vessels are bought by the Kasārs at half price and recast. Brass is also manufactured locally, by mixing copper and zinc in varying proportions. A mixture of three parts of copper with two of zinc gives the best and most valuable brass. Brass vessels are only used for carrying and storing water by the richer classes, most people having earthen *gharās*. A brass water-vessel in Saugor is shaped like a *lotā* and does not bulge out as in the Southern Districts. Numbers of brass and copper vessels are also imported. Brass-working industries exist at Saugor, Khurai and Etāwa, and a small amount of work is done at Garhākotā and Rehlī.

Iron work.

205. Most villages have a Lohār or blacksmith who makes and mends agricultural implements. Imported iron is now principally used and many articles are imported ready-made by Bohrās, but cooking utensils made of the iron smelted at Hīrāpur and Baraithā are preferred to the imported articles. Ornamental iron nut-cutters are made at Deorī from Tendūkhedā iron, and were formerly exported to other Districts, but only two or three families now make them. Some Lohārs in the towns can make good locks.

Carpentering and wood work.

206. Carpenters are found in most villages, who make the wooden implements of agriculture and are remunerated as village servants. Saugor had in 1891 more carpenters than any District except Jubbulpore and Nāgpur, but the census of 1901 showed a heavy decrease, and this class must have suffered very severely in the famines. There are a few good carpenters in towns who turn out high-class work and English furniture. Ornamental wood-carving is also done to order, and some of the Jain temples contain very good specimens of this work. At Bagrohī in Bandā, *pālkis*, carts, and other articles are made of teak-wood and sent to Saugor and

Bijāwar. Kunderās or turners make tops, toys, cups, chess-men, huqqās and other articles, and also do lacquer-work. Bamboo-workers also muster strong in Saugor as compared with other Districts, but their numbers have similarly declined during the last decade; bamboo-work is the business of the caste of Basors who also act as musicians, while their women are midwives. All kinds of baskets are made, and winnowing fans, matting, and screens or *chiks*. Brooms of bamboo are used by sweepers for clearing the roads, but for the house the brooms of palm-leaf made by Kuchbandhias are employed; the Kuchbandhias also make mats and brushes for white-washing walls from the same material, and circular holders for vessels from *munj* grass (*Saccharum ciliare*). The large bamboo baskets elsewhere used for storing grain are not found in Saugor, where it is kept in earthenware receptacles.

Pottery.

207. The number of potters is also very large in Saugor, being exceeded only in one or two Districts. Nearly every village has a Kumhār to supply its requirements for earthenware vessels, which are used extensively for cooking and storing water. Black and red clays are used, and mixed with an almost equal quantity of horse-dung. The vessels are coloured red, white, yellow or black before being baked. The quality of the earthenware is generally superior to that of the Southern Districts, and the pottery of Shāhgarh, owing to some quality in the clay, has a special reputation for strength and durability. The Kumhārs also make bricks and tiles, but the tenants frequently make these for themselves, especially the unbaked square bricks called *chaukā*. At the Diwāli festival the Kumhārs make a variety of clay figures and ornaments and give them a glittering whitish colour with lime and mica, while the Mochīs make painted dolls and images of gods and animals.

Bangles.

208. Glass bangles are made in Pithoria, Garholā, Garhākotā, and Rāhatgarh, the Hindu bangle-makers being known as Kacherās and the Muhammadans as Sīsgars. Balls of rough glass are

obtained from Cawnpore. The bangles made locally are now being superseded by those of transparent glass which are imported from Austria. *Kachonias* or glass beads are made at Garholā and exported to Northern India, where they are worn in bracelets. In Saugor they are only worn by children and there is little demand for them. Rude glass bottles are made for holding scented oils and medicines. Lac bangles are made by the caste of Lakherās, but are worn as a rule only during the month of *Shrāwan* (July-August). Beads and necklaces of lac, and ornaments for the ears and head are worn by children and women of the lower castes.

Leather-workers.

209. The leather industry in Saugor is also numerically the most important in the Province numbering about 12,000 persons. It is, however, not an organised but a village industry, families of Chamārs living in every group of three or four villages. They make the articles of leather used in agriculture, and also shoes. The Saugor or Bundelkhandī shoe is very distinctive, coming high up the leg both before and behind, and having a large turned-in toe. The better class of shoes have ornamental designs worked with silk and cotton thread and lace, and sometimes with red wool (*banāt*). Shoes are principally made in Rāhatgarh and Saugor. The leather industry has also declined very seriously in recent years, partly on account of the large demand for raw hides for export, as numbers of animals are now sold alive to the butchers, and their skins are thus lost to the Chamār.

Markets and Fairs. Weekly markets.

210. The important weekly bazars or markets of the Saugor tahsīl are those of Saugor, Rāhatgarh, Karrāpur, Shāhpur, Narīaolī Dhāna, Jaisinghnagar, Bilehrā, Pāmākherī and Surkhi. In Saugor itself different markets are held for special articles, as corn and thread. The most important one is on Wednesdays, when cattle are sold beside other articles. Cattle are also sold at the Rāhatgarh market, as well as locally manufactured iron articles, and leather shoes. Karrāpur is a large grain

market and grain for export is sold there. The leading bazars of Khurai tahsil are those of Khurai, Etāwa, Mālthone, Khimlāsa and Pithoria. The Khurai weekly cattle market is the largest in the District, 6,000 to 7,000 head of cattle being brought from Gwalior, Bhopāl and other States, and sold to local purchasers for export to Chhattīsgarh and the United Provinces; many cattle are also sold for slaughter. The following figures show the number of cattle sold at Khurai and the total amount realised during the years 1901-03:—

STATEMENT.

Year.	No. of cattle sold.	Value of cattle sold.
		Rs.
1901 ...	58,648	4,25,891
1902 ...	33,678	3,68,806
1903 ...	30,772	4,61,423

Registration of cattle is optional, and fees are levied at the rate of a pice in a rupee of the selling price. The realisations amount to about Rs. 2,000 a year. Hides are sold at Niwāri in Khurai tahsil. In Rehlī tahsil, Deorī, Garhākotā, Chāndpur, Rehlī, Gourjhāmar, Keslī and Maharājpur are important markets. Cattle are sold at Kesli and Deorī. Bandā and Shāhgarh are the leading markets of Bandā tahsil. Cattle are sold at Shāhgarh, and also gold and silver ornaments and brass and copper vessels. Grain for export is not usually sold in the weekly markets. The Baniās travel about to villages to purchase it, and many tenants take their grain to Saugor in their own carts.

Fairs—Garhākotā.

211. A considerable number of small fairs are held annually in the District, the bulk of these consisting however only of insignificant local gatherings for religious purposes. There are

16 fairs in all, the most important of which are those of Garhākotā, Rāngir, Bhāpel, and Garhpahrā.[1] The Garhākotā fair is one of the largest in the Province, and lasts from Basant Panchmī to Holī or for 40 days in January and February. It is principally a cattle fair, but rice, spices and groceries are also sold. Thousands of cattle are brought for sale and purchased by dealers who attend from all parts of the country, buy up the animals for the sake of their skins, slaughter them on the spot and export the skins and bones. The flesh is dried and sent to Bombay and Burma. The attendance has varied between 13,000 and 35,000 persons in different years, and people come from Chhattīsgarh, the United Provinces and Bombay. The number of cattle brought for sale to the fair has been as high as thirty or forty thousand, but has declined in recent years. Statistics of the business done at the fair in the years 1901-03 are shown below.

STATEMENT.

Year.	No. of cattle sold.	Value of cattle sold.	Weight of other articles sold.	Value of other articles sold.
		Rs.	Mds.	Rs.
1901 ...	19,894	1,88,031	9,261	29,266
1902 ...	14,609	1,66,895	6,869	33,198
1903 ...	11,582	1,27,184	7,175	32,129

Temporary shops or booths are opened for the sale of cloth, metal-ware, provisions, sweetmeats, vegetables, toys and dolls.

Other fairs.

212. Two fairs are held annually at Rāngir in Rehlī tahsīl on the last two days of the Naorātra of Kunwār and Chait, or in September and March. The latter is the more important and the attendance averages some 20,000 persons, while

[1] See also Gazetteer articles on the above places and on Bīna, Deorī, Jhāgri, Jaitpur, Rehlī, Saugor, Singrāwan, Tinsua and Uldan.

about 300 temporary shops are opened. A fairly important fair is held at Bhāpel on the Saugor-Rāhatgarh road on the last day of Kārtik (November). This is called the Phuler fair and the average attendance is about 10,000 persons, but has greatly decreased since 1883 when as many as 60,000 persons were present. Temporary shops are opened for the sale of vessels and provisions. The Garhpahrā fair is held on the four Tuesdays in the month of Asārh (June-July) in honour of Mahābīr or Hanumān. The third Tuesday is the most important day, and the attendance then ranges between 3,000 and 9,000, the average being 4,000. The fair is not important from a commercial point of view, as only provisions and toys are sold. A fair is held at Uldan in Rehlī tahsīl on Til Sankrānt in January, lasting for three or four days. The attendance is from 5,000 to 10,000 and a certain quantity of merchandise is sold. A Jain fair is held at Bīna near Deorī in November or December at which some 2,000 or 3,000 Jains assemble.

Weights and measures—Grain Measures.

213. The grain measures in ordinary use are the following:—

One *polī* or *poholī* = 25 tolās.

One *pai* or *adhelī* = 2 *polīs* = 50 tolās.

One *chauthia* = 2 *pais* = 100 tolās or $1\frac{1}{4}$ seers.

One *kuraiyā* or *pailā* = 4 *chauthias* or 5 seers.

One *sei* = 2 *kuraiyās* or 10 seers.

One *māni* = 20 *seis* or 5 maunds.

In Rehlī the *chauthia* contains 105 tolās, and the *kuraiyā* $4\frac{1}{2}$ *chauthias*, and the *māni* is thus equivalent to 6 maunds. There is also a large *māni* in use, which is sometimes called "Saugor *nāp*." This is double the size of the small *māni* and therefore contains 10 maunds, and 12 maunds in Rehlī. This *māni* is still 20 *seis*, but the *sei* contains 4 *kuraiyās*, while an intermediate measure, the *kuro* or *pailā*, has 2 *kuraiyās*, thus containing 10 seers and being equivalent to the Nāgpur *kuro*. The *kuraiyā* and *chauthia* are the measures commonly in use. Stamped brass *kuraiyās*, *chauthias* and *pais* have been issued by Government. The equivalent weights given for the above measures of capacity are for wheat. Thus a measure of a *māni* of wheat is equivalent to 200 seers weight of the grain. But an equivalent bulk of other grains often weighs either more or less than wheat, and in such cases the *māni* contains in their case more or less than 200 seers. A *māni* of urad contains 215 to 225 seers, one of rice 210 to 220, of mūng 210 to 215, of gram and makkā about 200, of juār 190 to 200, of linseed 165, and of jagnī 150 seers. The wheat grown in Khurai is said to be heavier than in the rest of the District, so that a *māni* of this grain is equivalent to 210 seers.

Other measures.

214. The *kos* contains three miles in Saugor and is sometimes called the 'Gondi kos.' Distances smaller than a *kos* may be spoken of as so many *khets* (fields), a *khet* being two to three furlongs. The old measures of area were:

20 *kachwānsis* = 1 *biswānsi*.

20 *biswānsis* = 1 *biswā*.

20 *biswās* = 1 *bīgha*.

The *bīgha* is practically equivalent to an acre, and the *kachwānsi* rather more than half a square yard. But mālguzārs and intelligent tenants now talk of areas in acres and decimals of an acre; while the common practice of the people is to express area in terms of the seed capacity of the land. A *māni* of land is in this manner equivalent to 4 acres, and in Khurai to 3 acres; this being the area of land in which a *māni* measure of wheat is sown. Another method is to talk of a *hal* or plough of land, that is the area which can be cultivated with a plough of two bullocks. A plough is equivalent to three *mānis* or 12 acres of ordinary land, and to 8 or 10 acres of *rathia* soil, which is somewhat difficult to cultivate. In Khurai the plough is said to be only 6 acres owing to the stiffness of the soil.

Miscellaneous weights.

215. The precious metals and jewels are sold by the *tolā*. One *tolā* contains 12 *māshas* or 96 *rattīs*. The *tolā* of gold differs from the standard tolā weight by one *rattī*. That is, it is equivalent to $1\frac{1}{96}$ times an ordinary tolā or rupee weight. For silver the ordinary tolā is used. The cheaper metals, and ghī and other solid articles are sold by weight in seers and maunds. But for weighing hemp and cotton a *pakkā* seer of 100 tolās is employed, and for other articles the *katchā* or Government seer of 80 tolās. The price of oil is quoted by weight, but it is usually sold by measurement. A pot containing 1 chittack of oil is called a *chhatkī*, one of 2 chittacks a *kaiyā*, one of 4 chittacks a *pauwā*, and one containing a seer weight a *serā*.

TRADE.

Exports and Imports.

216. Previous to 1870, in which year the Great Indian Peninsula Railway from Bombay to Jubbulpore was opened, exports were chiefly in the direction of Rājputāna and Bundelkhand and towards Mirzāpur through Damoh. Saugor was then the centre of the salt trade between Rājputāna and the Northern Districts of the Central Provinces. Large quantities of salt were brought to Saugor by Banjārās on pack-bullocks, and they took away wheat and oilseeds in exchange. In the south of the District a considerable quantity of cotton was grown and sent to Mirzāpur and Bombay. There was scarcely any trade in grain from here, though small quantities were sometimes exported to Bundelkhand. The District imported its spices and groceries from the Western Presidency, but sugar (*gur*) was manufactured locally. Cotton cloths were also sent to adjoining Districts, and *sarotās* (nut-cutters) from Deorī, and there was some trade in *al* (*Morinda citrifolia*). Silk and woollen cloth was generally imported. The salt customs line was abolished in 1874, and from this time duty was levied at the place of manufacture; as a consequence, the importance of Saugor

as a centre for the salt trade completely vanished, and with it the trade in the export of grain to Rājputāna to pay for the salt. The imports of salt in 1867-68 exceeded 2½ lakhs of maunds and were valued at Rs. 10½ lakhs. By 1875 the grain trade with Rājputāna had practically ceased, and for some time trade was very dull owing to the absence of any outlet for the surplus grain. In 1877 and 1878 the Saugor grain-holders learnt to adapt themselves to the altered circumstances, and from that time up to 1888 the surplus grain of the District was exported to Bombay through Karelī. In years of bad harvests in Bhopāl and Gwalior, part of it would be diverted to these States. The Bhopāl-Jhānsi line of the Indian Midland Railway was opened in 1889, and the branch from Bīna to Saugor in the same year. The extension to Damoh was completed in 1895. Trade immediately took advantage of the new route and the exports for 1891 from Saugor, Nariaolī and Mundrā stations and from Karelī were 11 lakhs of maunds, while the highest recorded exports from Karelī in 1885 had been 9½ lakhs. The imports for 1891 by both lines were 3 lakhs of maunds, as against 2 lakhs, the highest total through Karelī. The bulk of the trade of the District now reaches the railway at Saugor and other stations on the Bīna-Katnī line, though the exports of the southern part of the Rehlī tahsīl still go to Karelī.

Statistics available.

217. Figures of bulk of the exports and imports from and to Karelī station for the years 1870—91 and for the Saugor, Nariaolī and Mundrā stations for 1889—91, are given on pages 28-29 of Mr. De Brett's Settlement Report. The railway returns are available only for the years 1901, 1902, 1903, and the figures for the first two of these years were still so much affected by the collapse of the export trade in grain caused by the famines that they are of little value for a general notice of trade. The exports and imports for 1903 of all important articles are available for the stations of Saugor, Khurai, Bina and Bamora and the statistics here

given are taken from these returns. A considerable proportion of the trade of Bīmora station is with the adjoining Native States, but on the other hand, parts of the Saugor District send their produce to Karelī and Patharia stations.

Exports—Wheat and other grains.

218. The principal exports are now wheat, oilseeds and ghī.[1] The exports of wheat were formerly of more importance than all others combined, but during and after the famine years they shrank into insignificance. Thus in 1901 and 1902 the value of wheat exported was less than a lakh of rupees. In 1902 the Khurai tahsīl did not grow enough wheat for its own requirements and imported it from Cawnpore. When the trade of Saugor went to Karelī station, the largest bulk of wheat exported was 7½ lakhs of maunds in 1885, this being the period when the English demand for Indian wheat became very strong, partly owing to the Russian war scare. In 1903 the weight of wheat exported was just over 4 lakhs of maunds, and it was valued at Rs. 10½ lakhs. The position of 1885 had therefore by no means been recovered in 1903, but the area under wheat has decreased to less than half its former figure. It is probable that in 1891 the exports of wheat reached 10 lakhs of maunds as the exports from Saugor, Nariaolī, and Mundrā were nearly 6 lakhs. The exports of other grains and pulses outside wheat were just under 4 lakhs of maunds in 1903, and were valued at Rs. 8 lakhs. This included one lakh of maunds of juār and 2¾ lakhs of gram and pulses, the bulk of which must be gram as the quantity of pulses grown is small. No such figures as these were ever approached in the time of the Karelī trade. Taken together the exports of grain were 8 lakhs of maunds or about the same as the quantity exported from Karelī in 1885. Nearly all the wheat exported goes to Saugor station, while other grains are also sent from Bīna, Khurai and Bīmora.

---

[1] The following figures do not include the returns of some small stations whose exports amount to about ten per cent of the total.

Gram and juār are thus now staple export grains and have practically made up for the shrinkage in the exports of wheat.

Oilseeds.

219. The exports of oilseeds in 1903 were just under 2 lakhs of maunds, valued at Rs. 7½ lakhs. These figures are larger than any recorded from Karelī. Til and linseed are the oilseeds exported, the figures for til being 113,000 and for linseed 62,000 maunds, valued, respectively, at Rs. 4·33 and Rs. 2·62 lakhs. No other oilseeds are exported in considerable quantities. The exports of rape and mustard were 8,000 maunds valued at Rs. 34,000. The total exports of grain and oilseeds in 1903 were thus just under 10 lakhs of maunds valued at Rs. 26 lakhs. The figures for 1901 and 1902 are so far below this that they afford no basis for comparison. The year 1903 was the first one after the famines in which trade was really good, and it is probable that the above quantities are well below these which the District could export after several years of good seasons.

Other articles.

220. Ghī is also a staple of very great importance. The exports of this were 61,000 maunds valued at Rs. 14 lakhs in 1903, as against 82,000 maunds valued at Rs. 18½ lakhs in 1902. In the latter year the exports of ghī were considerably more valuable than those of grain and oilseeds combined. Ghī is principally made from the milk of she-buffaloes who are bred for this purpose, the young males being neglected or sold cheaply to the wandering caste of Basdewās who drive them to Chhattīsgarh and sell them for cultivation. The article next in importance among exports is raw cotton, the figures of which were 16,000 maunds valued at Rs. 2¼ lakhs in 1903 as against 6,000 maunds value Rs. 1 lakh in 1901. The former figure was the result of a bumper crop and is equivalent to the produce of the whole acreage under cotton in the District. But the bulk of the cotton exported in this year was from Bāmora station and much of it therefore came from tracts outside the District. The exports from

Saugor station were 5,000 maunds. Cotton is mainly grown in the south in the Rehlī tahsīl. Other exports are hides and skins of which 15,000 maunds were exported in 1903 and valued at Rs. 3·68 lakhs. In 1902 the exports were 18,000 maunds valued at about Rs. 3½ lakhs. These exports mainly consist of the hides of cattle, but considerable quantities of sheep-skins are also sent away. These are used for making drums and book-binding and also for shoes. The skins and horns of antelope are also exported in small quantities for ornamental purposes. The exports of dried meat are not shown separately in the returns, but their value is probably substantial, as an important trade in jerked meat has sprung up with Burma and Madras. Slaughter-houses have been established at Saugor and Khurai, and numbers of cattle are also slaughtered at Garhākotā fair. Betelvine leaves are sent to Northern India as also timber and grass. Grass is now pressed and sent to Jhānsi. Herds of young male buffaloes are driven by road into Chhattīsgarh for sale, but no statistics of these are kept.

Imports—Yarn and piece-goods.

221. The principal imports are European and Indian yarn and piece-goods, sugar, salt, metals, grain and pulse, and kerosine oil. In 1903 the imports of European piece-goods were 15,000 maunds valued at Rs. 7 lakhs. This is a higher figure than has ever been recorded in the Karelī returns, the maximum shown there being 12,500 maunds in 1888. In 1891 the imports of Saugor station were 8,000 maunds only as against 15,000 maunds in 1903. Most of this cloth comes from Bombay. The imports of Indian piece-goods in 1903 were 6,000 maunds valued at Rs. 2½ lakhs. This is also the highest figure ever recorded. 2,000 maunds of English thread valued at Rs. 1·30 lakhs, and nearly 8,000 maunds of Indian thread valued at Rs. 2·34 lakhs were imported, the total imports of yarn and piece-goods thus amounting to Rs. 13 lakhs odd.

222. The imports of sugar in 1903 were 90,000 maunds valued at Rs. 6 lakhs, the figures for 1902 and 1901 being slightly lower. Out of this, 33,000 maunds valued at a little over Rs. 3 lakhs were sugar, and 57,000 maunds valued at Rs. 2·7 lakhs were *gur* or unrefined sugar. Sugar comes mainly from the Mauritius and also from Mirzāpur. *Gur* is obtained principally from the United Provinces. The produce of the sugarcane grown locally in the year of settlement (1891—93) was estimated by the Settlement Officer to be Rs. 1·41 lakhs, but at that time 1,900 acres were under this crop as against only 500 in 1902-03. The consumption of refined sugar is gradually increasing.

Sugar.

223. The imports of salt were 111,000 maunds valued at Rs. 3·89 lakhs in 1903 as against 106,000 maunds value Rs. 3·92 lakhs in 1902, and 106,000 maunds value 3·94 lakhs in 1901. The bulk of the salt consumed comes from the Pachbhadra marsh in Jodhpur. The imports are equivalent to 19 lbs. per head of population, a very high figure indeed; a proportion of the imports which come to Bāmora station may be consumed outside the District, but the figures show sufficiently that there is no class of the population which requires to stint itself in respect of this staple.

Salt.

224. The imports of metals were 14,000 maunds value Rs. 2·80 lakhs in 1903, as against 12,000 maunds value Rs. 2·12 lakhs in 1902 and 8.000 maunds value Rs. 1·28 lakhs in 1901. The last year thus shows a gratifying increase in imports under this head, from which it may perhaps be concluded that the people are now able to expend capital on replacing their stock of household utensils, depleted by forced sales during the bad years. The value of copper vessels imported increased largely in 1903. Brass vessels and brass sheets, iron, zinc and tin are the other metals imported.

Metals.

Other articles.

225. The imports of grain and pulse were 74,000 maunds in 1903 valued at Rs. 2·12 lakhs. This was less than a quarter of the quantity received in 1902, and may still be above normal, though the large decrease shows that the District had in this year replenished its stocks. Of the total imports 40,000 maunds valued at Rs. 1·33 lakhs consisted of husked rice. Rice is always imported as the quantity grown locally is insufficient for consumption. A small quantity of wheat was brought to Bīna for consumption in the Khurai tahsīl. The imports of kerosine oil were 27,000 maunds valued at Rs. 94,000. This has almost entirely supplanted the vegetable oils as a lighting agent. Four thousand maunds of tobacco valued at Rs. 32,000 were imported; tobacco comes principally from the United Provinces and Bengal. Gunny bags are largely imported for the carriage of grain, the figures for 1903 being 15,000 maunds valued at Rs. 1·35 lakhs. Plough-cattle are imported into Saugor from the adjoining States of Bhopāl and Gwalior. The bulk of the dyeing agents used are imported, alizarine and aniline dyes having supplanted the old vegetable products. Turmeric is imported for consumption, as very little is produced in the District. Cocoanuts and arecanuts come from Bombay and Calcutta, and almonds from Bombay and the Punjab. Assafœtida and other fruits and spices are sold by itinerant Afghān pedlars. Paper is imported from the Bombay and Lucknow mills. Woollen blankets are obtained from the adjoining Native States. Pearls and coral are sold by wandering Jogīs from Bombay. Scent is brought from Kanauj and Jaunpur, and balls of rough glass are obtained from Cawnpore to be worked up locally.

Value of rail-borne trade.

226. The following statement shows the quantity and value of the principal exports and imports in 1903 in tabular form :—

Articles.	Quantity in thousands of maunds.	Value in thousands of rupees.
Exports.		
Cotton—Raw	16	219
Fodder	16	20
Wheat	411	10,69
Other grains and pulses	393	814
Hides and skins	15	368
Horns	1	16
Oilseeds	187	736
Ghī	61	13,95
Others (Hemp and Jute)	4	32
Others (Value not known)	130	...
Total ...	1,234	46,69
Imports.		
Twist and Yarn	10	364
Cotton Piece-goods	21	955
Grains and pulses	74	212
Hemp and Jute	16	137
Metals	14	280
Kerosine oil	27	94
Salt	111	389
Sugar	90	586
Others (Tobacco)	4	32
Others (Value not known)	134	...
Total ...	501	30,49

The total value of the main articles exported from the four stations for which full returns are available, in 1903 was Rs. 46½ lakhs and of those imported Rs. 30½ lakhs, leaving a balance of Rs. 16 lakhs in favour of the District. This is the only normal year for which figures of value are available, and it would be unsafe, therefore, to draw any positive conclusions from them, but as they stand the results appear to show that the purchasing power of the people is larger at present than it has ever been before, though allowance must be made for the fact that since the opening of the Bīna-Katnī line, many such articles as thread, cloth, kerosine oil and sugar are imported for consumption in place of indigenous products which were formerly used. The total revenue of the District in 1902-03 was Rs. 7·75 lakhs, and the excess of exports over imports was double this figure, a satisfactory state of things for a purely agricultural District.

Classes engaged in trade.

227. The export trade is principally in the hands of Parwār and Gahoī Baniās who also import and retail cloth, groceries and spices. Stationery and small foreign goods are imported and sold by Muhammadan Manihārs and Bohrās. The caste of Jogīs who are also beggars bring pearls and coral from Bombay for sale. The hide merchants and butchers are Muhammadans, and are generally the representatives of firms in Cawnpore and Calcutta. A considerable quantity of merchandise is still carried by Baniās, Telis and Kalārs on buffaloes and pack-bullocks and by Dhobīs and Sunkars on donkeys.

COMMUNICATIONS.

Railways.

228. The main line of the Indian Midland Railway from Itārsi to Cawnpore passes through the north-west of the Khurai tahsīl, in two detached portions separated by a strip of the Kurwai State. The stations of Bāmora, Bīna, Agāsode and Karondā are in Saugor, the length of line within

the District being 23 miles. The Bīna-Katnī connection of the Indian Midland starts from Bīna and traverses the centre of the District in an easterly direction, having a length of 71 miles and the stations of Bīna, Khurai, Mundrā, Nariaolī, Saugor, Lidhorā-Khurd, and Ganeshganj within its limits. The Bīna-Goonā branch also passes for a few miles through Saugor but has no station in the District. The total length of railway line within the District is 108 miles.

Roads.

229. Owing to a large expenditure on road work during the famines the District is well provided with communications. The old trunk routes are the Saugor-Jhānsi, Saugor-Cawnpore, Saugor-Rāhatgarh, and Saugor-Damoh-Jubbulpore roads. The Saugor-Jhānsi road through Mālthone gave communication with Upper India by Lalitpur and Jhānsi; it was re-aligned in about 1880, and in 1888 was an excellent road, with bridges over most streams and passable in all seasons. From 1888 when the railway to Jhānsi was opened, the road was handed over to the District Council, but was taken back in 1901. It has lately been extensively renovated, and is a metalled road for the first five miles, while the remainder is gravelled. It does not carry much traffic, but is maintained as being an alternative trunk route to the railway. The Cawnpore road through Bandā remained scarcely more than a fair-weather track until 1888. It was re-aligned in 1890, and owing to the amount of work done in the famines has now been made a first-class road for 25 miles and a fairly smooth one passable in all weathers up to the border of the Pannā State in the 54th mile. This road is still of some importance as it carries a certain quantity of traffic between the Bandā tahsīl and Cawnpore. It enters the District in the extreme north-east near Hirāpur. The Saugor-Damoh road was important locally previous to the construction of the railway as it was the means of communication with Jubbulpore. It only began

to be metalled during the famines; 32 out of 35 miles in the District are now (1904) metalled, while the road is bridged throughout except at the Sonār and Gadherī rivers in the 28th and 29th and the Koprā in the 41st mile where ferries are maintained during the rainy season. The road has little through trade, but is useful along certain lengths and connects Saugor with Garhākotā.

Roads continued.

230. Immediately on the opening of the Great Indian Peninsula Railway, the Saugor-Karelī road, connecting Saugor with Karelī station in Narsinghpur, was projected and vigorously carried to completion. This road carried the bulk of the exports of the Saugor District and the adjoining States, and up to 1838 the traffic on it was almost the heaviest in the Central Provinces. It is bridged except at some eight or ten small rivers and the Nerbudda. Since the opening of the railway to Saugor it only serves the south of the Rehlī tahsīl. It passes through Surkhī, Gourjhāmar and Deorī and crosses the Nerbudda at Barmhān where a large annual fair is held. The Rāhatgarh road was formerly carefully maintained as a continuation of the Jhānsi road for travellers and caravans proceeding by road towards Bombay. It was afterwards allowed to fall to ruin but is now being renewed, and is at present one of the most important trade routes, connecting Saugor with the rich tracts of the Rāhatgarh pargana and the west of the Saugor tahsīl. A great deal of grain is also imported along this road from Gwalior and Bhopāl. It is metalled for half the distance of 28 miles to Rāhatgarh. There is a fine bridge over the Bina river at Rāhatgarh, another smaller one over the Dhasān near Sihorā, and culverts at all necessary places between Rāhatgarh and Saugor. The Saugor-Rehlī road is only of local use. It connects Saugor with Rehlī at a distance of 26 miles following the Karelī road for the first six and crossing the Bewas river 10 miles out. The first six miles which belong to the Karelī road are metalled and the remainder gravelled. A few local feeder roads connecting

producing tracts in the interior with the railway, are also of importance. Among these may be mentioned the Garhākotā-Patharia and Khurai-Khimlāsa roads. It is in contemplation to make the Garhākotā-Patharia road a first class one.

Course of trade.

231. The bulk of the trade of the District is now concentrated at Saugor station. The three southern parganas of the Rehlī tahsīl, Nāharmow, Gourjhāmar, and Deorī, still send their exports to Karelī; and from the Shāhgarh pargana in the north of Bandā there is a certain amount of traffic with Cawnpore by road. Garhākotā pargana sends its produce to Patharia station in Damoh, the Garhākotā-Patharia road being, as already mentioned, an important feeder. In the Khurai tahsīl, the produce of the Mālthone pargana goes partly to Lalitpur station along the Jhānsi road. Bīna is the station for the west of the tahsīl, and Khurai for the centre and south. The exports of the small pargana of Eran, which is cut off from the rest of the tahsīl by the Bīna river, go to Bāmora station along a village track. Excluding these tracts, Saugor city is the centre of trade for the rest of the District, that is the whole of the Saugor tahsīl, the east of Khurai, north of Rehlī and south of Bandā. The total bulk of exports and imports from the stations of Saugor, Bīna, Khurai and Bāmora in 1903 in maunds were:—Saugor exports 788,000, imports 289,000; Bīna exports 216,000, imports 124,000; Khurai exports 82,000, imports 33,000; Bāmora exports 148,000, imports 56,000. In 1902 the trade of two other stations in the District amounted to 10 per cent. of the total. Figures for 1903 for these stations are not available. A part of the rail-borne trade of the District goes to Patharia and Karelī stations, but on the other hand much of the trade of Bāmora belongs to the adjoining Native States.

Adequacy of road-communications.

232. There is still considerable scope for the construction of feeder roads before the communications of the District can be considered as complete. Such feeders are the

Bīna-Khimlāsa, Khimlāsa-Mālthone, Khurai-Rāhatgarh, and Sanai-Bāmora roads. Some connection is also needed between the Binaikā and Dhāmoni tracts and Saugor. The total length of metalled roads in the District is 117 and of unmetalled roads 162 miles. The annual expenditure on maintenance is about half a lakh. Of the 279 miles all except 39 miles of unmetalled roads under the District Council are managed by the Public Works Department. Seven hundred and eighteen miles of village tracks are repaired annually by the District Council at an average expenditure of Rs. 2 per mile.

Carts.

233. Carriage is principally by carts except in the hilly portions of the Rehlī and Bandā tahsīls, where bullocks, ponies and buffaloes are still used as pack-animals. Pack-bullocks carry about 3 maunds each. The ordinary country cart is used on the roads and has two bullocks in the yoke and frequently a third one in front. It carries from 8 to 10 bags or 20 to 25 maunds of grain, and the cart-hire is about 12 annas a day.

CHAPTER VI.

FORESTS AND MINERALS.

FORESTS.

Former system of management.

234. The Government[1] forests cover an area of over 750 square miles or about 19 per cent of that of the District. Over 50 square miles of forest in Saugor District were until recently included in Narsinghpur Forest division, but this arrangement has now been altered, and while 34 square miles in the south of the District have been transferred to Narsinghpur District, 22, including 4 square miles from that District, have been brought into Saugor Forest Division. The alteration took effect from 1902-03. Up till 1872 the forests were under the control of the Deputy Commissioner. They were then made over to the Forest Department, but up to 1892 license-holders were allowed to cut almost whatever timber they liked in their own fashion. The only exception made was in favour of teak grown on fire-protected areas, to cut which the sanction of the Forest Divisional Officer had to be obtained. The result of this was that high stools were left, and reproduction was bad. In 1893 all forests were closed to the cutting of green wood, except certain areas which were formed into provisional working circles.

Distribution of forests.

235. The distribution of the forests is as follows:—A series of five main blocks occupies the hills on the north and east; detached patches are scattered over the five ranges of parallel hills which run from north-east to south-west through the District; while another series of forests occupies the slopes of the hills overlooking the Nerbudda valley. This area is

---

[1] The description of forests is mainly based on a note kindly furnished by Mr. C. Somers Smith, Deputy Conservator.

that which has recently been re-transferred to the Saugor division.

236. Five main types of forest growth may be distinguished. The first is pure teak or teak mixed with a small proportion of inferior species. Pure teak forest is found principally about Jaisinghnagar and Rāhatgarh. The second type consists of teak mixed with large numbers of inferior species, principally *sāj* (*Terminalia tomentosa*), *tendū* (*Diospyros Melanoxylon*), *mahuā* (*Bassia latifolia*), *achār* (*Buchanania latifolia*), *bel* (*Aegle Marmelos*), and numerous other species. Such forests occur near Mundrā and Basiagaon. Sandal-wood is found in Jalandhar and Ramgarhā forests. The growth of the teak is not good, the trees being frequently distorted and unfit for timber. The forests mainly produce only poles, the bulk of the trees being from 12" to 24" in girth, while trees above 36" are found only in 3 or 4 blocks of the division. The density varies considerably, being good and complete on the slopes of the hills, and open on the plateaus and poorer soils. The origin of the crop is chiefly old coppice growth, the better poles, however, being reproduced from seedlings. Reproduction is fair especially in areas which have been closed to grazing. The third type or miscellaneous forest without teak, occurs principally on the poor sandstone soil of the southern hills. The principal trees are *dhaurā* (*Anogeissus latifolia*); *lendia* (*Lagerstroemia parviflora*), *ghont* (*Zizyphus xylopyrus*), *makoi* (*Zizyphus Aenoplia*), *aonlā* (*Phyllanthus Emblica*); *khair* (*Acacia Catechu*), *gunjā* (*Odina Wodier*), *jamrāsi* (*Elaeodendron Roxburghii*), with in some tracts, *sāleh* (*Boswellia serrata*), *kullū* (*Sterculia urens*), *harua* (*Erythrina suberosa*), and *haldū* (*Adina cordifolia*). The forests vary much in density but are usually very open; their condition is bad and reproduction by seed is wanting. The fourth type consists of bamboo forests, not usually pure but with bamboos predominating, and mixed with teak and other trees. Bamboo forest is fairly common in Rehli tahsil

Character of forests.

and round Mālthone and Bandā. Reproduction by seed is fair, though there has been no general seeding for many years. The forests are, however, full of dead bamboos, and are generally in somewhat poor condition. The growth is dense on the slopes of hills and in ravines, and generally open on plateaus or areas formerly cultivated. The fifth type consists of pure *chheolā* or *palās* (*Butea frondosa*) or chheolā mixed with *sāj*, *tendū*, and a few other trees. This forest is generally found on the rich black soil of the plateaus and at the foot of the hills. The forests are open and reproduction by seed is good, but the seedlings are killed by frost in the winter and by fires in the summer.

Products.

237. Teak is the timber principally used for building and other purposes, while *bījāsāl* (*Pterocarpus Marsupium*), *sāj* and *kohā* (*Terminalia Arjuna*), are those next in favour. Sāj timber is not much used unless cut in the rains. The poorer classes use lendia, dhaurā, tendū and tinsā for their huts. The revenue from sales of timber amounts to Rs. 5,000 or more in an ordinary year including exports to Gwalior and Bhopāl. Firewood is the only purpose for which most of the crop is fit, and it is produced in large quantities All species of trees are used, but deadwood and inferior soft timber are preferred. Charcoal is produced in small quantities mostly in the mālguzāri forests. The chief demand for it is from Tendūkhedā in the south and Hīrāpur in the north, where iron-smelting is carried on. Wood charcoal is used for smelting and bamboo charcoal for refining. Teak charcoal is generally used only by Lohārs and Dhobīs, and for ordinary purposes the inferior timbers are employed. The annual income from the sales of wood for charcoal is about Rs. 2,500. There is a good demand for bamboos for building purposes, and basket and mat-making, the revenue from sales being about Rs. 2,000. During the last few years, bamboos have begun to be exported to Cawnpore.

Grazing.

238. The forests are used for grazing both by cattle from the neighbouring villages and from Saugor city, and from adjoining Districts and Native States. Those coming from a distance generally stay in the forests from July to October, temporary shelters known as *khonrās* being erected at convenient centres. Some 150,000 animals enter the forests annually for grazing, and the revenue is twenty-five to thirty thousand rupees. Only a few square miles of forest are closed to grazing. The demand for grass found in the forests is small, the people generally deriving their supply from mālguzāri forest. The supply of grass is unlimited, and during the famine of 1899-1900 a total of 5,800 tons was cut, some of which was sent to Bombay. Though a fodder famine had been anticipated, however, there was no local demand.

Minor Products.

239. The chief minor products are mahuā, *achār* and *tendū*, the flowers of the former and the fruits of the two latter trees being collected in large quantities for food by the poorer classes. From the seeds of the *achār* tree the sweetmeat called *chironjī* is made. Gum is largely collected chiefly from the *dhaurā, khair, kullū, sāj* and *jamrāsi* trees; it is used chiefly for food and also for sale and export. Catechu is boiled from the wood of the *khair* tree (*Acacia Catechu*) by Gonds who come annually from Pannā State and are locally called Khaīrwās. They take a lease of the trees from February to June paying one rupee per *handī* or pot in which boiling is carried on. The industry is intermittent, and varies from year to year. Lac was formerly collected in large quantities and formed an important part of the revenue of the division, but the lac insect is said to have completely died out in the famine years. Efforts are now being made to reintroduce it. The hides and horns of animals dying in the forest are also collected by contractors, the revenue being derived chiefly from domestic animals. Other minor products are honey and wax, the honey being derived from four kinds of bees,

known as *bhonr mākhi, kāni mākhi, sāntia* and *kontia.* The income from minor forest produce is about Rs. 4,000.

Statistics of revenue and forest staff.

240. The annual income was Rs. 64,000 in 1881-82, Rs. 61,000 in 1891-92, and Rs. 43,000 in 1902-03. The bulk of the decrease has occurred under grazing dues which formerly realised Rs. 30,000 to 40,000, but have now sunk to Rs. 26,000. The expenditure has on the other hand risen from Rs. 28,000 in 1881-82 to Rs. 33,000 in 1891-92 and Rs. 47,000 in 1902-03. The bulk of the increase has been under the head of salaries, there having been no Divisional Officer in 1881. The establishment now includes a Deputy Conservator, 3 Rangers, 4 Deputy Rangers, 9 Foresters, and 122 permanent and 20 temporary Forest Guards. Practically the whole area is fire-protected at a cost varying between Rs. 3 and 4 per square mile.

Private forest.

241. Besides the Government forests the agricultural statistics show 360 square miles of tree-forest and 880 square miles of scrub jungle and grass in private hands or a total of 1,240 square miles. Including Government forest the total area of forest and grass land is therefore over 49 per cent of that of the District. Saugor is very well wooded and amply provided with grazing and waste lands.

Roadside Arboriculture.

242. Roadside avenues exist on the roads leading from Saugor to Karelī, Rehlī, Damoh, Jhānsi. Rāhatgarh and Cawnpore and are being planted on the Garhākotā-Patharia road, the operations on all the above roads being managed by the Public Works Department. The total length of avenues is over 150 miles, and it is gradually being increased, but the expenditure is almost nominal, and progress is slow. Of the total number of trees in the avenues about half are *babūl* (*Acacia arabica*) and next to this the commonest species is *reunjhā* (*Acacia leucophlœa*). Other species occurring in some numbers are *kanji* (*Pongamia glabra*), *palās* (*Butea frondosa*), *ber* (*Zizyphus Jujuba*), *kohā*

(*Terminalia Arjuna*), *khair* (*Acacia Catechu*) and teak. Babūl is the tree generally planted, but it is said not to be very long-lived. Experiments in growing mahuā trees have not been very successful. The avenues sustained much injury during the famine years. Avenues also exist for short distances on some roads under the management of the District Council, the principal one being the Saugor-Khurai road which is planted for 11 miles. The Etāwa-Khimlāsa road is the only one on which work is at present in progress. A special nursery was started for this road in 1902, but otherwise there are no nurseries.

Grass bīrs.

243. The District has no fuel and fodder reserves, but grass *bīrs* or fields for the cavalry regiment at Saugor are maintained at six villages.

MINERALS.

Iron.

244. No mines are worked by capital in Saugor. Deposits of iron ore are found in the north of the District in the villages of Tigorā, Hīrāpur, Baraithā and Amarmau, all of the Bandā tahsil. The mines near the latter village are in Government forest, and are controlled by the Forest Department, while the others are controlled by the Revenue Department. The Forest Department let their mines to a contractor for a small sum, and the iron-workers pay him; in the others any one is free to extract ore on payment of a royalty of 8 annas per year on each furnace maintained. The ore is red or yellow hæmatite and the proportion of iron to smelted ore appears to be from a seventh to a tenth. The mines are all surface workings, the ore occurring in lodes of from 6 in. to 2ft. 6 in, in thickness in the Vindhyan sandstone. The quarries are as a rule not more than 20 feet deep, but one of the old workings near Amarmau reaches to a depth of 60 feet. The number of furnaces has decreased in recent years. In 1899 there were 46 furnaces in Tigorā, Hīrāpur and Baraithā, and in 1896 there were 32 in Amarmau or a total of 78.

This number has decreased to 15 in the first three villages and 16 in Amarmau, or a total of 31 between 1900 and 1903. Each furnace employs 6 or 7 persons in smelting and working up the iron, and produces some 20 lbs. of iron a day. The iron is sold locally at 4 annas for 5 seers or Rs. 2 per maund. The earnings of a furnace do not appear to amount to more than Rs. 100 for the eight months during which work is carried on, so the business is a very poor one. The ore is smelted twice, and the furnaces stop working altogether in the rains.

Sandstone and other minerals.

245. The Vindhyan rocks yield a sandstone, which is well adapted for building purposes, and a number of quarries are worked. The best of these are at Rāhatgarh and Maswāsi near Saugor from which large slabs are obtained, the Maswāsi stone being of a reddish and that of Rāhatgarh of a whitish colour. The contracts of the quarries sell for Rs. 25 to Rs. 50 annually. The houses in several villages are built and roofed entirely with sandstone slabs. In Shāhgarh a soft stone is obtained which is made up into cups and vessels. Grinding stones are made in Narwān near Shāhgarh. The red clay found in Shāhgarh is worked up into earthenware of a good quality and superior strength. Mica exists at Baraithā, but is not worked.

CHAPTER VII.

FAMINE.

Early famines.

246. Nothing is known of the famine history of Saugor previous to the cession in 1818, and the only record of famines which occurred between that date and 1868 is contained in a letter written in 1867 by the Deputy Commissioner detailing such information as he had been able to gather on the subject by oral inquiry.[1] This is simply reproduced here. In 1819 the crops were destroyed by excessive rain in the cold weather, and scarcity was felt over the whole District, lasting for a year until the next cold weather. The prices of wheat and gram rose to 4 seers[2] per rupee from 17 seers in the previous year, while at the end of 1819 they again dropped to 40 seers. The poorer classes suffered much and some are said to have died of starvation. There is no record of any measures having been taken to relieve the distress. The next scarcity took place in 1834, and was caused by a failure of the rainfall affecting both the spring and autumn crops. Prices rose to 12 seers to the rupee from 20 seers in the preceding year, but distress was not severe, and no relief-measures appear to have been necessary. The next scarcity was in 1854. The spring crops were in a most promising condition at the commencement of the cold weather, but heavy rain set in with an east wind, and continued till the whole country was under water. The roots of the wheat and barley rotted in the fields, and the stalks and ears were destroyed by rust. Gram was attacked by thousands of the caterpillars called *illī*. Cattle were driven into the fields but refused to graze on the standing crops. The prices of wheat and gram rose to 12 seers to the rupee, and it is recorded that some of the

---

1 Letter No. 3729 from the Deputy Commissioner, Saugor, to the Commissioner, Jubbulpore, dated the 12th July 1867.

2 One seer = 2 lbs.

poorer classes died of want. No relief seems to have been given, but some Rs. 13,000 of revenue were remitted. A slight scarcity was again experienced in 1866 owing to a poor harvest and the export of grain to Bundelkhand. The price of grain rose to 9 seers a rupee, but the scarcity disappeared as soon as the autumn crops were ready. Collections were made in the towns for the relief of the poor and destitute.

The Bundelkhand Famine.

247. In 1868, the year of the Bundelkhand famine, the rains stopped in August and the rice crop was a complete failure. The spring crops also were apparently very poor. Scarcity was mainly felt in the Bandā tahsil adjoining Bundelkhand where the famine was more severe than in Saugor; an influx of starving wanderers from the adjoining Districts and States being responsible for most of the local distress. The grain-dealers held up their stocks, but there was a good harvest in Bhopāl, and Rs. 10,000 were spent in importing grain. Work was provided on the Saugor-Jubbulpore and Saugor-Hīrāpur roads, the expenditure being met, it is stated, from the collections of the Pāndhri tax. A poor house was opened at Saugor, and subscriptions amounting to Rs. 4,500 were collected; these were supplemented by a Government grant of Rs. 2,500 a month for five months. The mortality for the year appears to have been treble the normal.

Scarcity of 1877.

248. In 1877 a slight scarcity was caused by absence of rain in September and October. Only the autumn crops in the north of the District failed, but there was again a large amount of immigration from the adjoining Native States, 25,000 persons arriving in the District in a fortnight in search of work. Some work was provided on the Damoh road, while for those who were destitute a camp was opened near Saugor and maintained by private subscriptions with the assistance of a small Government grant. In the middle of October rain

fell and the flow of immigration subsided. The only local distress was in the Shāhgarh pargana, especially among the iron-workers. The spring crops of 1877-78 were poor, and there was also a poor spring crop in the next year. But there is no record of distress in this year.

The cycle of bad years from 1892.

249. In 1892 when the recent cycle of bad years commenced, the rainfall had been excessive in five out of the ten preceding years, though in the last three the wheat harvest had been good. In 1892-93 the crops were much damaged by frost and rust in the Khurai tahsīl, but the injury was too local to cause distress. The year 1893-94 was disastrous. Heavy rain in November induced an attack of rust, and the wheat crop was destroyed over the whole District. Old men said that the failure of 1854, still remembered as 'The Great Blight,' was not so severe as the present one. The attack commenced in the middle of December, and spread rapidly over all parts of the District; the damage at first varying from field to field, and village to village, but soon becoming universal. Rain and hail again fell early in February, and the final outturn of the wheat harvest, which in that year covered 61 per cent of the cropped area, was less than an anna. Much of the crop looked fairly good when standing in the fields, but on being cut it was found that the ears contained no grain. The other crops were not affected. The second instalment of revenue was suspended, and the forests were opened for the free collection of grass, fruits and roots, in June 1894. One relief work in each tahsīl was started in April and kept open till October. The highest number of persons on all the works was 11,593 in August, and the average for the whole period 5,102. The total expenditure was Rs. 67,000, the works all being roads. No gratuitous relief was given except from private sources. The mortality for 1894 was 43 per mille as against 29 in the preceding year, and the rate in November was nearly 6 per mille, so it is clear that the distress was considerable.

In the following year 1894-95, there was again excessive rain in the cold weather, and only a moderate harvest was obtained, the all-round outturn being 47 per cent of normal. The death-rate for 1895 was 53 per mille, showing that distress was still present, while the birth-rate also dropped to 21 from 41 in 1894, being affected, as usual, later than the death-rate. But the existence of distress was apparently not recognised. In 1895-96 the September rains were very partial and scanty, and there were practically no cold weather rains. The autumn crops were poor while the spring harvest was very bad in Khurai and fair elsewhere, the all-round outturn being 50 per cent of normal. The death-rate for 1896 was 78 per mille, and it has since been recognised that severe distress was prevalent for the whole of this year.

The Famine of 1897.

250. In 1896-97 the rains which up till then had been copious, stopped abruptly at the end of August, and practically no rain was received in September and October. The autumn crops failed completely, and owing to the dryness of the land the area sown with spring crops was greatly reduced; and though good rain was received in the cold weather, the harvest as a whole was only 42 per cent of normal. It was obvious in the autumn of 1896 that severe famine prevailed, and relief works were opened in December. Poor-houses had been established in Saugor and Khurai in the middle of the rains, and three more were opened in December. Village relief was started in the same month, and extended to the whole District in February. Subsequently the number of road works was increased, and tank works were also undertaken at Phular near Garhākotā, Jaisinghnagar, Khurai, Nariaolī, Binaikā, and Teorā in the Khurai tahsil. Loans aggregating Rs. 37,000 were given to mālguzārs for tank-work, and the embankment of fields. The earthwork of the Saugor-Katnī railway was also constructed as a famine relief-work. Forty-nine kitchens were opened, 33 being managed by the police and

16 by school-masters. Rs. 3·08 lakhs were expended in private charity mainly in grants for seed-grain and bullocks, the bulk of this sum coming from the Mansion House Fund. Agricultural loans were also given by Government to the extent of Rs. 55,000. Regular relief operations lasted from October 1896 to the end of December 1897; 3¼ per cent of the population were on relief in December 1896, and 6¼ per cent in January 1897. The numbers then rose gradually, and 58,000 persons or nearly 10 per cent were in receipt of assistance on the 31st May. The daily average for the fifteen months was 28,747 or 4·9 per cent of the population. The mortality was severe throughout, and rose greatly in the rains, reaching 11·6 per mille per mensem in August. The average monthly mortality for the whole famine period was 7·14. A severe epidemic of fever occurred in the autumn of 1897. Prices were at famine rates between October 1896 and October 1897, wheat ranging between 7·49 and 9·15 seers per rupee, and rice between 7·6 and 6·05, while juār was about 10 seers and gram 8 to 10 seers. The total expenditure on famine relief was Rs. 12·53 lakhs including loans.

The years 1898 and 1899.

251. The crops of 1897-98 were not more than fair as, though a good autumn harvest was obtained, the spring crops were damaged by frost and hail, and the whole outturn was only 61 per cent of normal. The autumn of 1898 saw a large area under juār, which was greatly injured by the abnormally heavy rainfall of that year, while the spring crops again suffered from frost and hail, and poor cold-weather rains. The whole outturn is given as only 33 per cent of normal, and early in 1899 village relief was started in the Khurai tahsīl, which with Saugor had suffered most. There was, however, practically no distress in this year, apparently because the harvests of the previous one had been fairly good. An abundant mahuā crop also assisted the people.

The famine of 1900.

252. The rains of 1899 failed from July, only 3 inches being received in August, 1½ inches in September, and half an inch in January, while the other months were rainless. Rice gave nothing, but moderate crops of juār, and fairly good ones of cotton and til were reaped, while the wheat harvest, though sown on a much reduced area, was 70 per cent of normal and gram 55 per cent. The combined outturn was, however, only 32 per cent of an ordinary harvest. The Khurai tahsīl was most severely affected throughout, and Saugor next, while Bandā was only moderately, and Rehlī slightly distressed. Regular relief operations began in September 1899 and lasted until December 1900. The highest number of persons on all forms of relief was 87,000, or nearly 15 per cent of the population in August 1900, while the average daily number throughout was 31,000 or 5·2 per cent. The total number of day units relieved was nearly 14 million, and the incidence per day unit Re. 0-1-3. Rs. 85,000 were spent on five road works and Rs. 1·44 lakhs on seven tank works under the Public Works Department, the tanks constructed or repaired being those of Dhīngar, Teorā, Khimlāsa, Chandrāpur, Binaikā, Rajwāns, and Barodia. While the work on some of the roads cost double or more the contract rates, that on the tanks varied as a rule from 25 to 50 per cent in excess of the contract value, and hence was considerably more economical Grass-cutting operations were also undertaken, both departmentally and through the Forest Department, and 6,898 tons were cut at a cost of Rs. 36,000. Of this about 600 tons were sent to Bombay, where there was a serious scarcity of fodder, and the remainder sold locally for Rs. 4,000. Rs. 11,000 were spent by the Forest Department on clearing boundary lines and other forest work. Ten village works were also undertaken, of which two were road works and the remainder, the construction or repair of tanks at Saugor, Eran, Kathelī, Pithoria, Mundrā, Dulchīpur, Hirāpur and Dhamoni, the total amount spent on village

works being Rs. 32,000. A poor-house was established at Saugor, and children's kitchens were opened all over the District. In August 1900 there were 165 of these, and 59,000 persons were receiving food at them. The mortality was normal up to April 1900, after which epidemics of cholera and small-pox broke out, and the rate rose. The deaths of starving wanderers, who arrived in the District in a moribund condition, also contributed to swell the mortality. The highest monthly mortality was 7·5 per mille in July 1900 and the average for fifteen months of famine only 3·5. Rs. 1·61 lakhs were spent from charitable funds, and Rs. 1·23 lakhs advanced in loans. The total expenditure incurred by Government was just under Rs. 11 lakhs The average price of wheat for 1900 was 9·9 seers per rupee, and it never rose above 9 seers. Gram was 10·4 seers and juār 12·4 seers with a maximum of 10 seers Prices were, therefore, substantially lower than in 1897, a factor which was of immense importance in mitigating the severity of the distress, and which may be attributed to the greater facilities for transport afforded by the new Saugor-Katnī railway.

General remarks on famine.

253. With the famine of 1900, the dismal record of failures of the harvest in Saugor comes to an end. Good crops were reaped in 1900-01, and though the autumn harvest of 1901-02 was only moderate, the outturn of the spring grains was fair, while in the two succeeding years both harvests have been excellent. The description of past famines shows that the administration of relief in Saugor is generally liable to be complicated by the influx of starving refugees from Native States for whom arrangements must be made. It is also clear that under ordinary circumstances, the people have at present great staying power. After a total failure of the wheat crop in 1893-94, there was only slight distress, which however gradually intensified through the two following years of poor harvests, while the famine of 1897 was really the accumulated result of four bad seasons. Again

a very poor crop in 1898-99 practically produced no distress, though only one fair harvest had been reaped since 1897. And the famine of 1900 was again due, not to one but to two consecutive bad years. Failures of crops have in the past resulted if anything more frequently from untimely rain in the winter months, sometimes accompanied by frost and hail, and effecting the destruction of the spring crops, than from shortness of the regular monsoon current. The spring crops and especially wheat have until recently been the more important, but, with the large increase in the cultivation of juār, the autumn harvest has now taken the first place.

CHAPTER VIII.

LAND REVENUE ADMINISTRATION.

Revenue system of the Marāthās.

254. The revenue system which the British Government found in operation in the tracts acquired from the Bhonslas and the Peshwā was one under which villages were farmed out to the highest bidder, and whatever rights or consideration the village headman may have enjoyed in the past, had been almost entirely effaced. The Marāthās were accustomed to keep as many villages as possible under their own management, collecting direct from the cultivators. Leases were, however, frequently given for short terms of from one to three years. The terms of the leases left but a very small margin of profit to the lessees, seldom more than a tenth of the rental assets, and very often the demand exceeded the estimated assets of the village. The profits left to village lessees were called 'Dupāsi,' a term which would appear to be a corruption of *do-bīswi* or two-twentieths (of an acre), one-tenth of the whole income constituting the lessees' profits, and nine-tenths being appropriated by the State. Similarly, in writing of the proceedings of the Bhonsla officials, the Settlement Officer of the adjoining District of Narsinghpur states that 'When extortion 'by main force failed, other means were not wanting. Patels 'were tempted by titles and dresses of honour to bid against 'each other, and were alternately coaxed and squeezed 'until they had nothing left to make them worth attention.' The procedure of Sindhia's subordinates was not materially different from that of the others. Under the Marāthās the ryots had no protection whatever. No cultivating rights of any kind were recognised. The lessee, who was being squeezed by the revenue officials, was compelled in self-defence to mete out similar treatment to his cultivators. If

he failed to get his revenue from them, he would infallibly have to make way for some one else.

Commencement of British Administration.

255. When the British first came into possession in 1818, they gave leases for a single year, followed by three settlements, each of which extended over a period of five years. During the earlier days of British rule, our attempts at revenue administration were far from successful. Colonel Maclean writes in his report that 'Our first assessments appear to have 'been based on the highest *kāmil-jamā* realised by the Marāthā 'rulers. Our officers just entering a ceded province appear to 'have had no other data to guide them, and they must have 'been very sanguine in their expectations of revenue, if they 'hoped to realise during a series of years the highest amount 'obtained by a native government with all its various imposts 'during one favourable year.' The demand fluctuated considerably, the figures shortly after cession being Rs. 5·88 lakhs; ten years subsequently this had been raised to Rs. 6·28 lakhs and in another ten years it had fallen to Rs. 6·10 lakhs. The total amount of remissions made during the period works out to an average of Rs. 75,400 per annum.[1]

Errors in over-assessment.

256. The attempt to work up to the figures of the Marāthās was therefore a failure, and there were several reasons which contributed to this result. In the first place, the Marāthā demand was, as has already been stated, only an estimate of what could be obtained under the most favourable circumstances, and realisations were adjusted from year to year in accordance with the character of the harvest. They seldom expected to recover their demands in full, but the system of the British was opposed to this method of procedure, and our officers considered themselves bound to recover the full amount on their roll, if this was by any means possible. In the next place the distribution of revenue in the later days of the

---

[1] See Mr. Fuller's note on the Land Revenue Settlements of the Central Provinces (1886).

Marāthā rule seems to have been very uneven. The ravages of the Pindāris rendered agriculture a most precarious means of subsistence. Their depredations were not confined to any particular season of the year, and the cultivators had to be constantly on the watch to protect their crops, their stock and their houses against these robbers. Much land was thrown out of cultivation and many villages deserted. Thus in the Jaisinghnagar pargana, 21 villages or nearly a third of the whole number were depopulated. Similarly the tract along the Bina river in the Khurai tahsil was practically abandoned, for the banks of the stream were a favourite robber route. The cultivators, who were thus driven out, either migrated or collected in the neighbourhood of fortified towns and villages, and the land situated under the walls of such protected places acquired an enhanced value. The Marāthās realised this fact, and naturally proceeded to make the most of it by raising the revenue demand, in order to counterbalance, if possible, the losses which they had to face in the plundered and abandoned tracts. The enhanced demand was too high to be paid over a series of years unless the outturn was exceptionally good, and as the constant cropping exhausted the land, the difficulty of raising the land-revenue increased. Thirdly, after the cession and subsequent pacification of the country, the local expenditure declined in consequence of the withdrawal of the troops which the Marāthās had entertained. The result was a considerable fall in the demand for the agricultural produce on which they had been supported, no new market being available in place of the old one thus closed. Thus in Betūl the price of a maund of wheat was 18 annas between 1800 and 1818, and had fallen to 7 annas in 1827, and although the figures are not available, a similar fall in prices appears to have taken place in Saugor. Lastly, the Marāthās granted the headmen every facility for realising the revenue by allowing them a free hand in the allotment of the demand among the cultivators and in squeezing them to the utmost. Our officers, on the other hand, appear to have habitually interposed themselves between the lessee and the ryot, with the idea of protecting the latter against the excessive demands of the farmers. The lessees consequently were deprived of the only chance which remained to them of maintaining their position. So long as they could make annual changes in the revenue payable by each ryot, the patels could provide for the realisation of the demand, heavy though it was. But with the discontinuance of the annual adjustment, inequality in individual assessments became inevitable; some ryots would pay comparatively lightly, and this would be at the expense of their fellows and of the patel.

Misguided interference of District Officers.

257. It is noticeable that the reductions and remissions which were constantly made were in the interests of the patels only. It was reported after a thorough examination of the system in 1833-34 that the existing system of remission was of advantage only to the farmers and the Kacheri officials, and that the cultivators obtained no relief. The District Officers constantly interfered between the cultivators and money-lenders. They were allowed, when the seasons appeared to be favourable, to estimate the productiveness of the crops, and then to fix the amount that should be collected; and this not once or at distant intervals on the occurrence of an overwhelming calamity, but as a regular practice. The result was that an extensive system of fraud and peculation was introduced, which by destroying all confidence drove away capital from the land. Instances were known of the stores of merchants having been opened, and grain forcibly taken out and given to the cultivators as seed, without any payment being made to the merchant or any assistance afforded him for the subsequent recovery of the property of which he had been despoiled. Capitalists having obtained decrees against agriculturists were not allowed to sell their

cattle or imprison their persons, because it was supposed that either of these measures would leave the land uncultivated.

The 20 years' Settlement.

258. The above state of things was disclosed in the report of Mr. Martin Bird, a high officer who was deputed to examine the revenue administration of the Saugor and Nerbudda territories in 1833-34. He recommended that a settlement should be made for a period of 20 years on lenient terms, and that all the unnecessary interference between headmen and tenants, to which Government officials had in the past been so prone, should be strictly prohibited. In accordance with his suggestions orders were issued for a twenty years' settlement at a reasonable assessment, on which no remissions would be allowed except in extraordinary circumstances. The headmen were to be left to fix the rents of tenants, and could alter them at their pleasure, provided that they filed annual rentrolls showing the changes made. The headmen were allowed to distrain the standing crops and personal property of the cultivators other than cattle, grain and implements of husbandry for arrears of rent, and in pursuance of unsatisfied decrees for arrears, to eject defaulters; and all interference with the internal management of the village on the part of Government officers was prohibited. The assessment operations were entrusted to Mr. Fraser, who submitted his report on them in May 1835. The result of the revision of revenue was to raise the payments of lessees from Rs. 6·10 to Rs. 6·28 lakhs. Reductions of revenue were effected in those parts which appeared to have been over-assessed by the Marāṭhās, but these were more than counterbalanced by the gain from the assessment of tracts which had been brought under the plough again on the restoration of order in the District. The people appear to have accepted the assessments cheerfully and to have started with a good heart to improve their lands; for the Settlement Officer was able to state by the

time he came to write his report, that in several tracts a number of new irrigation wells had been constructed since the new assessments were announced.

Currency of the 20 years' Settlement.

269. But, notwithstanding the fact that Mr. Fraser fully understood the reasons of the breakdown of our past administration, and made efforts to avoid the errors of his predecessors, the 20 years' settlement was not found to work well. In 1842 the disturbances caused by the rebellion of the Narhut and Chandrāpur land-owners did much damage to the agricultural community, and in 1845 it was found necessary to give a general reduction of 10 per cent on the revenue throughout the District, while the Rehlí villages got as much as 20 per cent, and the Garhākotā pargana 16 per cent.[1] On the expiry of the period of 20 years for which the settlement had been made, preparations were begun for a revision of the assessment. But the District at this time suffered from several misfortunes. In 1854 the spring crops entirely failed in the Bandā tahsil, and a similar fate befell the Saugor pargana in 1855. In 1856 the District suffered from drought, and in 1857 the Mutiny broke out. In 1859-60 there was a severe epidemic of fever of a fatal type, and a murrain among cattle in 1861. The demand of the 20 years' settlement, somewhat modified by subsequent reductions, was thus continued until 1864-65, when the 30 years' settlement was introduced.

The 30 years' Settlement.

260. This settlement lasted altogether from 1853 to 1867 and was under the charge of a number of different officers, being concluded by Colonel Maclean who wrote the existing report. This work, owing to a defective system of arrangement by which each pargana of the District is treated separately on all subjects, is of some-

---

[1] Settlement Commissioner's No. 989, dated 24th March 1867, para 22.

what moderate merit. The settlement was preceded by a regular survey and the construction of village *shajrās* or field-maps by the resident patwāris. The guide, which appears to have been most closely followed in fixing the revenue, was the figure designated as the 'soil rate rental,' half of which represented the 'soil rate revenue.' Villages were grouped into *chaks* or circles, for each of which a separate scale of rates was passed. The rates are said to have been brought out by calculation of averages from the rents actually paid for each class of soil. The Settlement Officer wrote of the rates adopted for pargana Saugor that 'Looking at the large breadth of fallow, not only in 'this pargana but throughout the District, I am of opinion that 'mālguzārs will not for years to come be able to raise rent-'rates, and as the rates adopted for assessment have been 'obtained by inquiry from the cultivators as to the rent paid 'for each description of soil, and tested by their leases and 'the rents realised in villages held under direct management 'and by holders of rent-free land, I think I am safe in 'adopting them as the revenue rates for the basis of my 'assessment. A moiety of their result is the declared value at 'deduced revenue rates.' But the revenue deduced from the rates was not in all cases closely followed. Thus in Bandā, the deduced revenue was Rs. 36,800 and that assessed Rs. 40,600, corresponding figures for Shāhgarh being Rs. 19,800 and Rs. 11,400 respectively. The wide departure from the revenue rates in Shāhgarh is explained by the great variation in the rent rates paid in villages in the same *chak*. The Settlement Officer wrote that it would have been possible to meet this difficulty by a sub-classification and by dividing each *chak* into classes, for each of which a different scale of rates might be adopted, but he considered that this course would not meet with the Settlement Commissioner's approval, apparently because it was held at the time that the *chaks* should be geographical.

Method of assessment.

261. The figures thus arrived at were partially checked by others called the 'produce jamā' and the 'plough jamā.' The 'produce jamā' was taken as a sixth of the value of the gross produce, but no details are given to show the method by which the gross produce was calculated. It is merely stated that the gross produce was arrived at by inquiry into the amount of seed-grain expended on certain portions of land, and the average produce and its market value during a series of years. This having been ascertained as nearly as possible, it was divided into three parts, one-third being considered as the value of the seed-grain and expenses of cultivation, one-third as the profit of the cultivator, and the remaining third as the rent payable to the mālguzār. A half of this or a sixth of the total was entered as the produce jamā. The produce jamā appears, however, to have received very little attention. The plough jamā was deduced from the number of ploughs in a village and the average rental value of a plough over the whole *chak* in which the village was included. Little regard either seems to have been paid to this guide, and the Settlement Officer seems to have generally followed the soil-rate jamā, except in cases where it fell considerably below the existing revenue, when he took a middle figure.

Reduction in the proportion of revenue taken.

262. At the previous 20 years' settlement of the Saugor and Nerbudda territories, the Government share had been nominally 66 per cent. But at the commencement of the 30 years' settlement the Government of the North-Western Provinces declared the 'Sahāranpur Settlement Rules' to be applicable, under which the demand of the State was to be limited to 50 per cent or one-half of the average net assets, with the caution, however, that 'it is not meant by this that 'the revenue of each estate is to be fixed at one-half of the 'net average assets, but that in taking these assets with other 'data into consideration, the Collector will bear in mind that

'about one-half, and not two-thirds as heretofore, of the net 'assets should be the Government demand.'

Results of the Settlement.

263. It was considered in Saugor that the existing demand was too high and that a substantial decrease was called for. The remissions and reductions on the demand of the 20 years' settlement had amounted on an average to close on Rs. 76,000 per annum. The revenue of Rs. 6·10 lakhs fixed at that settlement had been reduced at the commencement of revision to Rs. 5·27 lakhs.[1] The assets were found to be Rs. 8·19 lakhs, and the revised revenue fixed on them was Rs. 4·64 lakhs, or excluding Rs. 20,000 assigned, Rs. 4·44 lakhs. The gross revenue fixed was 11 per cent below the previously existing demand. Its percentage on the existing village assets was 56 and its incidence per acre in cultivation 11 annas 2 pies. The previously existing and revised revenue of the four tahsīls is shown in the margin.

	Before Settlement.	At 30 years' Settlement.
	Rs.	Rs.
Saugor ...	1,81,000	1,60,000
Khurai ...	1,34,000	1,04,000
Rehlī ...	1,46,000	1,48,000
Bandā ...	66,000	52,000

Adjustment of the rental.

264. A material difference between the procedure of the 30 years' settlement and that now followed, was that the Settlement Officer did not first deduce a rent-rate and then determine the percentage of it to be taken as revenue, but fixed the revenue in the first place, and only subsequently attempted such a readjustment of rents as seemed to be called for. The new assessment was announced to mālguzārs and tenants, and they were then directed to settle among themselves the rental enhancements which could fairly be made, and when they had come to a decision, it was recorded by the Settlement Officer. This

1 This figure is given in the Settlement Commissioner's review. A foot-note on page 94 of the Settlement Report states the demand before revision as Rs. 5·21 lakhs.

procedure in Saugor resulted in the increase of the total village assets, from Rs. 8·19 to Rs. 8·98 lakhs or by 9½ per cent of which *siwai* income accounted for only Rs. 11,000.

Creation of tenures.

265. This increase, coupled with the reduction of the revenue by 11 per cent, very substantially improved the position of the village headmen. The percentage of the revenue on the adjusted assets was 52. At the same time proprietary rights were granted to the village headmen, and different classes of tenant-right to the cultivators. The area in which proprietary right was reserved to Government, was 480,000 acres or 19 per cent of the total. Of the whole number of tenants, 8 per cent were made mālik-makbūzas, 17 per cent absolute occupancy, and 10 per cent occupancy tenants.

Currency of the 30 years' settlement.

266. During the currency of the 30 years' settlement, the District enjoyed a long succession of fairly prosperous seasons, which, coupled with a very light assessment and a largely increased export demand for grain, conferred such a degree of affluence on mālguzārs and tenants alike, as they had never before experienced. The cropped area increased from 670,000 to over a million acres, and the rise in the price of wheat during the period of settlement was estimated at 75 to 100 per cent.

The recent Settlement. Cadastral Survey.

267. As regards accuracy, the cadastral survey undertaken at the 30 years' settlement had been fairly satisfactory. But though much time and trouble had been expended on the original preparation of the village maps, unfortunately no steps were taken to correct and keep them up to date during the currency of the settlement. As the period for revision approached, it thus became necessary to undertake an entirely fresh survey. This was effected partly by professional survey parties and partly by patwāris. The professional surveyors made a preliminary traverse, and provided sheets

for each village on which they had laid down the position of survey marks placed as near the boundaries of the village as possible. The patwāris followed the professional surveyors, and with the help of the marks laid down by the latter, plotted the field boundaries and other details with the chain and cross-staff. Each man worked in his own circle, and the average outturn by each patwāri in the last year of working was over 6 square miles, the survey lasting from 1886 to 1891. The cost of the cadastral survey was Rs. 36-8 per square mile, and that of the traverse survey Rs. 33.

Procedure of the Settlement.

268. The 30 years' settlement expired in 1894-95 over the greater part of the District, and revision of settlement was commenced from 1891,[1] but owing to the delay caused by the years of distress and famine, was not completed until 1897. The settlement was begun by Mr. Cleveland, who subsequently relinquished it, and completed by Mr. De Brett who wrote the Settlement Report. Rai Bahādur Gajrāj Singh was the principal Assistant Settlement Officer. The method of assessment was that now prescribed for the Central Provinces, and included the elaborate classification and valuation of soils by relative factors, as explained in the chapter on agriculture, and the fixation of rents according to the soil-unit system. Reference may be made to Mr. De Brett's report (1902) for a detailed description of the methods followed.

Enhancements in the rental.

269. In addition to the revenue, the Settlement Officer fixed the rents of absolute occupancy and occupancy tenants. The payments of mālik-makbūzas were raised by 53 per cent on the figure of the previous settlement, their rental being 13 annas an acre as against 8 annas 11 pies. The large enhancement was mainly due to the very low

[1] The description of the last settlement is taken entirely from Mr. De Brett's report.

rates previously paid by this class, and its moderation is shown by the fact that their rental as now fixed was 30 per cent below that deduced from the sanctioned village rates, which amounted to Rs. 1-2-6 an acre. The rents of absolute occupancy tenants were raised by 14 per cent, the rate per acre being Rs. 1-2-9 as against Rs. 1-0-6 at the previous settlement. The revised rate for occupancy tenants was Rs. 1-1-0, the acreage rate being 7 per cent higher than that of the previous settlement, while the actual enhancement amounted to 12 per cent on the rental prior to revision. The rents of ordinary tenants were raised by 13 per cent above the rate of the previous settlement, the acreage rate payable by them being Rs. 1-2-1. Taking the payments of the three classes of tenants, and omitting those of mālik-makbūzas, the average incidence of the rental was raised from Rs. 1-0-1 at the previous settlement to Rs. 1-1-6, or by 9 per cent., while its total amount became Rs. 10·39 lakhs as against Rs. 6·93 lakhs at the previous settlement, an increase of 50 per cent. The bulk of this increase had been imposed by the mālguzārs themselves as the rental immediately before revision was Rs. 9·59 lakhs, and it was due in the main to expansion of cultivation, the area held by the three classes of tenants having increased by 35 per cent during the period of settlement. The net result of the action of the Settlement Officer was to impose an enhancement of 13 per cent on absolute occupancy, 12 per cent on occupancy and 4 per cent on ordinary tenants, giving an all round enhancement of 8 per cent. His action was thus largely limited to an equalisation of the pressure of rents already levied by the proprietors.

Valuation of sir and khudkasht lands.

270. The rental valuation adopted for sīr and khudkāsht lands was Rs. 2·73 lakhs, falling at Rs. 1-4-7 an acre. This was very nearly equivalent to the deduced rental value, and was in excess of the rate of Rs. 1-2-1 payable by ordinary tenants. It was justified by the rents paid for

the area sublet on cash rents. This amounted to over 19,000 acres and was sublet on a rental of Rs. 34,700 while the deduced rental of this land, and of 3,000 acres in addition sublet on grain rents, was Rs. 30,300 only.

Miscellaneous Income.

271. The miscellaneous or *siwai* income is mainly derived from mālguzāri forests and from the sale of grass and fruits or the leasing of tanks. The mālguzārs do not keep, or at any rate do not produce any accurate accounts of their miscellaneous income, and were generally averse from giving correct information about it. Efforts were made to ascertain the income as accurately as possible, and a substantial allowance was then made for fluctuations in the amount of receipts. The actual receipts at the time of resettlement amounted to Rs. 24,100 and the assumed average annual income was Rs. 16,900. The area under mālguzāri forest and scrub jungle is nearly 700,000 acres, and the assumed average income from miscellaneous sources fell at less than 5 pies per acre.

Figures of Assets.

272. The gross assets at the previous settlement as compared with those now arrived at were as follows :—

	At 30 years' settlement.	At new settlement.
	Rs.	Rs.
Malik-makbuzas' payments and tenants' rental	7,18,000	10,71,000
Rental value of sir, khudkasht and land held by privileged tenants	1,69,000	3,06,000
*Siwai income	11,000	17,000
Total ...	8,98,000	13,94,000

Some differences occurred between the figures sanctioned as given above and those actually announced, which were about Rs 20,000 less. The assets announced exceeded the assets of the old settlement by Rs. 4·77 lakhs or 53 per cent.

The revised revenue.

273. At the recent settlement mālik-makbūza lands were separately assessed. The mālguzārs entered into an agreement to collect and pay into the treasury the sums fixed on their plots,

and were allowed a drawback varying from 5 to 20 per cent of the payments. The revenue payable by the mālguzārs was calculated on the gross assets minus the mālik-makbūza payments. The revised revenue amounted to Rs. 6·96 lakhs which absorbed rather less than 51 per cent of the announced assets Excluding the payments of plot-proprietors the revenue absorbed only 49½ per cent. of the true mālguzāri assets. The percentages of revenue to assets in individual groups varied from 47 to 52. The revised revenue, as sanctioned, exceeded the revenue payable prior to revision by Rs. 2·26 lakhs or 48 per cent. Its incidence per acre in cultivation was 10 as. 3 pies, which was less than that of the previous settlement. The revenue demand absorbed only 5 per cent of the gross value of the produce of the District at a moderate valuation. Out of the gross revenue Rs. 24,000 was assigned and the net demand was therefore Rs. 6·72 lakhs.

Figures of incidence.

274. The rental incidence varied from Re. 0-10-10 in the Dhāmoni group of Bandā to Re. 1-7-0 in the Gourjhāmar group of Rehlī, while the least and greatest revenue incidences were Re 0-5-11 and Re. 0-13-7 in the same groups.

Duration of the settlement.

275. The settlement was made for a period varying from 10 to 13 years in different tracts, and was introduced between the years 1895 and 1897. It was due to expire in 1907 in Khurai and Bandā, 1908 in Saugor and 1909 in Rehlī. The cost of the settlement was Rs. 2·05 lakhs or Rs. 64 per square mile excluding the cost of the cadastral survey. The total cost of survey and settlement was Rs. 133-8 per square mile, this high figure being of course due to the protracted nature of the operations and the interruptions caused by famine. Under the subsequent orders of the Government of India the term of the settlement was extended to June 1913.

Modifications of the assessment.

276. The increase of revenue was made progressive, the instalments being spread over a period of five years before the full amount was reached. This measure was, however, found to be inadequate to the altered conditions of the District produced by the series of failures of crops which began in 1893. In the eight years from 1895 to 1902, the harvest was never more than 70 per cent of the normal yield on a normal area, and the average yield was only 49 per cent. Cultivation reached its lowest point in the famine year of 1899-00 when there was a decrease of 31 per cent in the area cropped prior to the revision of settlement, while the valuable wheat crop showed a still greater shrinkage of 66 per cent. The census of 1901 showed the very serious decrease of 20·4 per cent. in the population. Measures were taken to meet this deterioration not only by annual suspensions and remissions, but by the regular abatement of rents and revenue for a term of years. In cases where the rents or home-farm valuation were considerably in excess of the prevailing rates of the tract, a reduction was made for the whole term of settlement, the revenue being lowered to the same percentage of the reduced assets. The abatement of revenue so given amounted to Rs. 74,000 mainly in the worst affected tracts of Khurai and the Dhāmoni group of Bandā. In addition, temporary abatements of rents and revenue were given in all villages which showed deterioration by a decline in the cropped area. The rent and home-farm valuation of each holding was reduced in proportion to the decrease of cropping, and an abated revenue was fixed at the same percentage of the assets so reduced. This temporary abatement of revenue amounted to a further sum of Rs. 1·02 lakhs. It was first given for a period of five years from 1897-98 to 1901-02, and was further extended for a period of three years in the Saugor and Rehlī tahsīls. The revenue demand was thus

lowered from Rs. 6·72 lakhs, the nominal settlement figure, to Rs. 5·68 lakhs in 1897-98, Rs. 5·13 lakhs in 1898-99, and Rs. 4·97 lakhs in 1900-01. The collections for the six years up to 1903 averaged only Rs. 3·43 lakhs. At the end of 1904-05, when the period of the temporary abatements expires, the demand will be raised to Rs. 6·22 lakhs under normal circumstances. But the Government of India has directed that the villages in which abatements have been given, should then be examined, with a view to continuing the abatement for a further period of five years if their condition appears to require it.[1]

Cesses.

277. The demand on account of the road, school and postal cesses in 1902-03 was Rs.29,000, for additional rates Rs. 10,000[2] and for patwāri cess Rs 24,000. The patwāri cess is calculated at 5 per cent. of the land revenue, the education cess at 2 per cent., the road cess at 3 per cent., the postal cess at ½ per cent, and additional rates at 2 per cent. The tenants pay 3 pies in the rupee to the patwāri, and a sum varying from 3 to 12 pies to the kotwār.

Tenures. Sub-rents.

278. Of the total area of 11 lakhs of acres included in holdings in 1902-03, 131,000 acres or 12 per cent. were recorded as sīr land, 87,000 acres or 8 per cent. as khudkāsht land, 38,000 acres or 3½ per cent. as held by mālik-makbūzas, 162,000 acres or 14½ per cent. as held by absolute occupancy tenants, 229,000 acres or 21 per cent. by occupancy tenants, 421,000 acres or 38 per cent. by ordinary tenants, and 28,000 acres or 2½ per cent. as land held rent-free from the proprietors or in lieu of service. The area held by proprietors as sīr and khudkāsht forms about a fifth of the total. The sīr lands almost always include the best fields in the village. About 20,000 acres

---

[1] Letter No. 174C-305-2, dated 3rd November 1903, from the Revenue Secretary to the Government of India to the Chief Commissioner.

[2] This cess was abolished with effect from the 1st April 1905.

were sublet in 1902-03 at an average rate of over Re. 1-10-0 per acre. The area held by occupancy tenants increased very largely during the currency of the 30 years' settlement under the operation of the 12 years' rule, expanding from 108,000 to 297,000 acres. Since the settlement, the occupancy tenants have fared worse than any other class, the land held in this right having decreased to 229,000 acres.

Grain rents.

279. The practice of levying rent in kind is not very common in Saugor, but exists in the Shāhgarh pargana. Theoretically the system is not a bad one, as the mālguzār and tenant are supposed to suffer equally in the event of a failure of the crops. But the practice appeared to the Settlement Officer to be, not to divide the produce by measurement after it had been threshed out, but to make an estimate of the standing crop before it was cut, indeed in many cases before it was anything like ready to be cut. The persons who make this estimate are generally more afraid of incurring the displeasure of the mālguzār than of the tenants, and over-estimate the produce to the detriment of the latter. The commutation of grain rents for cash rents was appreciated by the tenants In Bandā tahsīl spring-crop land is sometimes let on a sub-rent of a sixth of the produce, and if the field contains a well for irrigation, of one-fourth. Land is also frequently given out on contract to labourers, who take a small plot and agree to do all the work of cultivation, the owner supplying the seed-grain and bullocks; when the crop is reaped the produce is divided equally, the seed-grain being first deducted. Juār, owing to the labour involved in its cultivation and the constant watching required to protect it from wild animals and birds, is often cultivated in this manner. Where the tenant has a large holding. he will give the outlying portions on contract and reserve the centre for himself, where the crop requires less protection.

Protected status.

280. The question of granting protected status to thekādārs or farmers of villages was most important in the case of the Etāwa group where all the mālguzāri villages were leased to thekādārs. Many of these had been in possession at the previous settlement, and had been given mālik-makbuza or tenant right in the areas which were then cultivated by them. They had usually taken up a considerable quantity of fresh land during the currency of settlement. The tālukdār objected strongly to the grant of protected status, and the question was finally compromised by awarding the thekādārs tenant-right in part or the whole of the area held by them as khudkāsht.

Ryotwāri villages and land alienated.

281. Six villages have been settled on ryotwārī tenure on land excised from Government forest. The area occupied in them was 2,500 acres, and the revenue assessed Rs. 900, in 1902-03. The villages are under the management of the Land Revenue Department. Nearly 16,000 acrès have been sold outright under the waste land rules.

Revenue-free and quit-rent tenures.

282. About 57,000 acres consisting of villages or shares of villages, and 9,000 acres included in holdings are held partially or wholly revenue-free, and the amount of revenue so assigned is Rs. 24,000. There are no very important muāfi estates. The temples of Pandharināth at Rehlī, and Khānde Rao at Deorī have one or two villages attached to them. Shāhgarh and two other villages belong to Mahādeo's temple at Saugor. A grant of six villages in the Bandā tahsil was made to a Marāthā Brāhman family of Gwalior for services in the Mutiny. Two villages are assigned to the tomb of the Muhammadan saint at Dhāmoni. The Bundelā family of Piprāsar, who were formerly rulers of Kanjia pargana, hold a grant of 5 villages. Garholā is held free of revenue by an old Dāngi family, formerly dominant in Eran and Khurai. Bamhorī Nawāb near Barodia is

held revenue-free by the Nawāb of Pathāri, Abdul Karīm Khān, the former ruler of Rahatgarh. Jagdīshpurā is held by the temple of Murlīdhar in Khurai, and the village called Madaiyā Muāfi is assigned to the temple of Rādha Kishen in that village. In Kanjia a number of grants of plots or holdings were made by the Gwalior Darbār and their continuance was agreed to when the tract was taken over. Many of these are in lieu of payment for worshipping in temples, and other service, and several are held by a class of persons called *Jimihās* who were process-servers or peons.

CHAPTER IX.

GENERAL ADMINISTRATION.

District Subdivisions and Staff.

283. For administrative purposes the District is divided into four tahsīls, Khurai lying to the north-west, Bandā north-east, Saugor in the centre and Rehli to the south. The old system of pargana subdivisions is not now maintained, but the Saugor tahsil comprises the former parganas of Saugor, Nariaoli, Rāhatgarh, and Jaisinghnagar; the Khurai tahsil, those of Khurai-Khimlāsa, Mālthone-Dugahā, Eran, Etawa and Kanjia; the Rehli tahsil, those of Garhākotā, Rehli, Gourjhamar, Nāharmow, and Deori; and the Bandā tahsil, those of Shāhgarh, Binaikā, Bherā and Dhāmoni. The head of the District is the Deputy Commissioner, who is also District Magistrate. He has three Executive Assistant or Extra Assistant Commissioners. The Saugor staff usually comprises at least one Assistant Commissioner or member of the Indian Civil Service, and very frequently a second in training. In 1904, the subdivisional system was introduced, one subdivision comprising the Saugor and Khurai tahsils, and another, the Rehli and Bandā tahsīls. Each of the four tahsils has a tahsildār and naib-tahsildār, except Bandā which has only a tahsildār. The civil staff consists of a District and a Subordinate Judge and a munsiff at each tahsil. The tahsīldārs and naib-tahsīldārs also usually have civil powers. A Cantonment Magistrate with 3rd class powers, exercises jurisdiction within the cantonment. There are two benches of honorary magistrates, one at Saugor and one at Deori. Another bench formerly existed at Rehli, but is at present in abeyance Saugor is included in the Jubbulpore Division, and the Divisional and Sessions Judge of Jubbulpore has superior civil and criminal jurisdic-

tion. The District usually has Commissioned Medical and Forest Officers and an Executive Engineer for the Saugor Public Works Division comprising the Saugor and Damoh Districts.

Land Record Staff.

284. The Land Record Staff, working under the District Superintendent of Land Records, comprises an Assistant Superintendent, 13 Revenue Inspectors, and 385 patwāris. The headquarters of the Revenue Inspectors are at Surkhī, Pāmākherī, Nariaolī, and Rāhatgarh in the Saugor tahsīl; Garhākotā, Chāndpur, Deorī and Keslī in the Rehlī tahsīl; Barodia Kalān, Garholā and Etāwa in the Khurai tahsil; and Kandari and Rurāwan in the Bandā tahsīl. The average number of villages in a patwāri's circle is between 5 and 6. The number of patwāri's circles was reduced at Mr. De Brett's settlement from 420 to 387, and has been further reduced by two, owing to the transfer of territory in 1902; 229 of the old circles remained untouched, while 40 were absorbed and 7 new ones opened. The minimum pay of a patwāri is Rs. 100 and the maximum Rs. 120 per annum. In some cases the patwāris hold service land free of rental, and the amount of the rental is then deducted from the mālguzār's contribution. The mālguzārs have now to pay 5 per cent on the land revenue as patwāri cess, while the tenants, including malik-makbuzas, pay 3 pies per rupee of rental. The demand on account of patwari cess is Rs. 24,400, from which Rs. 1,980, the rental value of service land, is deducted. The estimated receipts from the payments of tenants, after allowing a margin for possible short collections, amount to Rs. 4,100. The mālguzārs' payments are made into the treasury with the second instalment of the land revenue, while the patwāris continue to collect the fees due from tenants direct, as this tends to keep the two classes in touch, and to ensure that the receipt-books of the tenants are regularly written up. A certain sum has been set apart from which deserving patwāris may be given local allow-

ances as a reward for good work. The patwāris are mainly Kāyasths while there are a few Muhammadans. As a class they are intelligent and worked hard and well during the settlement operations.

Litigation and Crime.

285. The people of the District are not particularly litigious. The bulk of the litigation is brought on bonds for money and grain, and exorbitant interest is usually charged. Mortgages by conditional sale are a common class of cases affecting immovable property. In the early years of the decade 1890-1900, the number of civil suits averaged between 6,000 and 7,000 a year. At the end of the decade, the total number fell below 5,000, and in 1902 it was only 3,700. Litigation between landlord and tenant on the other hand has somewhat increased since 1897, the number of suits rising from under 800 in that year to nearly 900 in 1900, 1,400 in 1901, and 1,050 in 1902. The number of title suits has not materially changed, and while the number of suits for money or movable property has considerably decreased, the total value of suits has risen substantially in the last few years. The crime of the District is somewhat heavy as compared with other parts of the Central Provinces. Robberies and dacoities are comparatively frequent, 30 cases of this class having occurred annually during the decade ending 1901. Cattle-stealing and simple theft are also common classes of crimes. Opium-smuggling is prevalent especially from Bhopāl, and offences are detected with difficulty. The lower price at which opium is sold in the adjoining District of Jhānsi also leads to a considerable amount of petty smuggling. In the case of organised opium-running from Bhopāl, the usual method is to give the opium to a coolie made up into an ordinary parcel, so that if caught the coolie can disavow all knowledge of its contents. Defamation cases are common enough and generally centre round an accusation which has put the complainant out of his caste. Forest offences are somewhat numerous in the Rehli tahsīl.

Statistics of revenue.

286. The following statement shows the realisations of revenue in the District under the principal heads of receipt, at the end of the last three decades and during the years 1902-03 and 1903-04.

Year.		Land Revenue.	Cesses.	Forests.	Stamps.	Excise.	Income-tax.	Registration.	Other receipts.	Total.
1880-81	...	3,84,271	58,690	55,862	56,377	72,585	...	2,327	34,025	6,64,137
1890-91	...	4,51,946	56,799	49,367	85,267	70,349	16,385	5,115	32,121	7,67,349
1900-01	...	4,91,218	33,202	39,953	71,627	53,979	11,968	3,583	28,650	7,34,180
1902-03	...	5,06,871	57,332	43,259	70,655	57,067	11,678	4,274	23,406	7,74,542
1903-04	...	4,97,578	63,539	46,956	63,766	54,075	8,726	3,862	12,933	7,51,435

Excise. Country Liquor.

287. Up to 1905 the system for the supply of country liquor consisted of a *sadar* distillery at Saugor which included the bulk of the Saugor tahsīl, and outstills for the remainder of the District. In that year the new Central Distillery system was introduced. The consumption of liquor is comparatively small in Saugor, the number of shops for the sale of country liquor having hitherto been fewer, both in respect to area and population, than in nearly all other Districts. The excise revenue of the District in 1902-03, amounting to Rs. 55,000, was the lowest but two in the Province, the incidence of revenue being 1 anna 2 pies per head of population as against the Provincial figure of 2 annas 4 pies. Tāri is scarcely consumed in the District, and the demand for foreign liquor is very small.

Opium and Gānja.

288. The revenue per head derived from opium and gānja is similarly only about half the Provincial average. In 1902-03, the opium revenue amounted to Rs. 19,000, and that from

gānja to Rs. 6,000. Both heads of revenue have greatly declined since 1892-93, and especially opium, which at that time realised from Rs. 25,000 to Rs. 30,000 41 shops are licensed for the sale of opium and 50 for gānja. Owing to the proximity of Native States, the smuggling of exciseable articles, and especially of opium, is very prevalent.[1] *Bhāng* is imported from Central India. There is very little consumption of *mājum*.

Registration.

289. The District has seven registration offices, including that of the District Registrar at head-quarters, sub-registration offices at each tahsil, and two other offices at Sihorā in Saugor tahsil and Deorī in Rehlī. Each office has now a special salaried sub-registrar. The last two offices were opened in 1889. The receipts from registration were about Rs. 5,000 at the commencement of the decade 1891-1901, and rose to Rs. 8,000 in 1895-96, from which figure they declined to between Rs. 3,000 and Rs. 4,000 at the end of the decade. The decline in the receipts may be attributed to the effect of the restrictions imposed on the transfer of immovable property by the new Tenancy Act. Loans and mortgages of immovable property are the most numerous classes of documents registered.

District Council and Local Boards.

290. The management of schools, dispensaries, pounds, and minor roads with ferries on them, outside municipal areas, is entrusted to a District Council with 15 elected and 16 nominated members. The average income of the District Council for the decade ending 1901 was Rs. 53,000. The principal heads of receipt are road cess, Rs. 8,400; education cess, Rs. 6,500; receipts under the Cattle Trespass Act, Rs. 13,000; and contributions from Provincial revenues, Rs. 12,000. The average annual expenditure for the decade ending 1901 was Rs. 54,000, the principal heads being educa-

[1] See under Crime.

tion, Rs. 15,000; civil works, Rs. 17,000; medical charges, Rs. 3,000; and cattle-pound charges, Rs. 5,000. Under the District Council are four Local Boards, each having jurisdiction over one tahsīl. The Saugor Board has 3 nominated and 12 elected members, the Khurai Board 3 nominated and 11 elected, the Rehlī Board 3 nominated and 14 elected, and the Bandā Board 3 nominated and 7 elected. The Local Boards have no independent income but perform inspection duty and supervise minor improvements.

Municipalities.

291. There are at present (1904) three municipal towns Saugor, Deorī, and Khurai. The municipalities of Rehlī and Garhākotā were abolished in 1901. The Saugor municipality contains 6 nominated and 11 elected members, Khurai 3 nominated and 5 elected, and Deorī 2 nominated and 5 elected. The average income of the Saugor municipality for the decade ending 1901 was Rs. 78,000, that of Khurai Rs. 15,000, and that of Deorī Rs. 4,000. The income of the Saugor municipality is mainly derived from octroi and that of Khurai from fees on the registration of cattle and on markets and slaughter-houses. The chief source of income in Deorī is a tax on houses and lands. The total population within municipal limits is now 42,404, and the average municipal income per head Rs. 2-1-0, the figure for Saugor being Rs. 2-6-5. General administration, conservancy, and education are the principal heads of expenditure.

Village Sanitation.

292. The Village Sanitation Act is in force in Etāwa, Garhākotā, Hirdenagar, Patnā and Rehlī. Of these, the adjoining villages of Garhākotā and Hirdenagar formerly constituted the Garhākotā municipality, and those of Patnā and Rehlī the Rehlī municipality. These two municipalities were abolished in 1901 and the Village Sanitation Act was introduced in all the villages from the same year. In Etāwa, the receipts of the sanitation committee are derived mainly from weighmen's fees, and in the years 1901—03 they amounted

to Rs. 2,000. The receipts of the Rehli committee during the years 1901—04 averaged Rs. 750 and those of the Patnā committee Rs. 150 only; the average income of the Garhākotā committee for the same period was Rs. 350, and that of the Hirdenagar committee Rs. 1,200. The receipts of these committees are derived from a tax on the residents graduated according to incomes. The Etāwa committee has spent Rs. 1,000 on the improvement of roads, while the funds of the others have been expended on sanitation in the ordinary manner. In Rāhatgarh, a town fund has been established, the receipts of which are about Rs. 300 a year. Proceedings for the improvement of the sanitation and water-supply of villages were initiated in the District in 1892-93; from that date until 1904-05 a sum of Rs. 9,000 was spent from Provincial and District funds, while the amount raised by private subscription and the value of free labour given came to Rs. 16,000. For this sum 18 new wells were constructed, and 114 provided with parapets or otherwise improved.

Public Works.

293. The total cost of buildings borne on the books of the Public Works Department is Rs. 3·83 lakhs. This total does not include the cost of any military buildings except a Volunteer Sergeant's quarters at Bīna. The principal buildings are the jail constructed in 1845 at a cost of Rs. 80,000 including subsequent additions, the District Court-House built in 1818 and costing Rs. 25,000, the new Circuit-House built in 1894 and enlarged in 1904 at a total cost of Rs. 23,000. The total number of buildings in charge of the Public Works Department in 1901-02 was 100, and their maintenance charges amount to Rs. 5,000 per annum.

Police.

294. The total sanctioned strength of the Police force is 660 officers and men, this number including 92 officers and 7 mounted constables. A special trained reserve of 32 men is maintained for dealing with serious crime in Saugor and the

adjoining Districts. A force of 5 officers and 20 men is stationed in the cantonment and paid for from cantonment funds. The District has usually a District and Assistant Superintendent, 2 Inspectors and 14 Sub-Inspectors. A small body of railway police is maintained at Saugor and Bina stations. They are considered as on deputation and are under the orders of the District Superintendent. Owing to the proximity of a number of Native States great difficulty is experienced in dealing effectually with crime in the border villages, and the District is subject to the inroads of dacoits from the States. To cope with these a force of one Sub-Inspector, 4 head-constables and 28 constables has been deputed in addition to the special reserve. The strength of the police force is stronger in Saugor than in any other District, the figures being one police official to every 7 square miles of country and every 1,000 persons, as against one to every 10½ square miles and 1,700 persons for the Province as a whole. The native police force is mainly recruited from Saugor and the adjoining Districts, and Brāhmans and Muhammadans predominate in its ranks. The total annual cost of the police is Rs. 95,000. The District has 16 Station-houses and 26 outposts. The Station-houses are located at Saugor city and cantonment, Rāhatgarh, Gopālganj, Ṣurkhī, and Jaisinghnagar in the Saugor tahsīl; Khurai, Etāwa, Khimlāsa, and Barodia in the Khurai tahsil; Rehlī, Deorī, Garhākotā, and Keslī in the Rehlī tahsīl; and Bandā and Shāhgarh in the Bandā tahsil.

Kotwārs.

295. At Mr. De Brett's Settlement 1,523 kotwārs were appointed for 1,924 inhabited villages, and their remuneration was fixed at an average of Rs 36-5-0 per annum, the total amount recoverable for pay of kotwārs being Rs. 55,000. The tenants pay a contribution of 3 to 12 pies per rupee of rental. The kotwārs are usually Khangars or Chadārs, the Khangārs having formerly had criminal propensities. Both castes rank above the impure Koris and Chamars.

Jail.

296. Saugor has a 3rd class District Jail with accommodation for 181 male and 22 female prisoners, exclusive of hospital and observation cells. The average daily number of convicts in 1901, 1902 and 1903, was 137, 124, and 101 respectively. The industries carried on in the jail are aloe-pounding and oil-pressing. The leaves of the agave, of which there is a considerable plantation round the jail, are pounded to separate the fibrous parts from the softer material. The fibre is sometimes sold raw and sometimes made up into rope, both articles finding a ready market within the town. The oilseeds pressed are jagnī and ramtilli and the oil produced is of superior quality to that obtainable from the local Telis.

Education.

297. The founder of education in Saugor was Captain James Paton of the Bengal Artillery, who opened 9 schools when in charge of the District in 1827. Previous to this, the only instruction available was given by wandering Hindu pandits who held classes for the training of boys as village priests and astrologers, or by Muhammadan maulvis who taught their pupils to recite verses of the Korān in Arabic and Persian, the meanings of the words being unexplained. In Captain Paton's schools the boys were rewarded by sweetmeats and money prizes, no fees were taken, and books, slates and paper were given without payment. A native gentleman Rao Krishna Rao opened a private school at Saugor at the same time, and in 1833 this was inspected by Lord William Bentinck when Governor-General. A grant of Rs. 100 a month was made towards the support of the school by the Government of India, and this was subsequently increased to Rs. 300 a month. Lord William Bentinck was so pleased with Krishna Rao's work that he conferred an estate of the annual value of Rs. 600 on him, and presented him with a medal specially struck in his honour. In 1836 the Saugor school was raised to the status of a high school

and in 1860 it was affiliated to the Calcutta University. In 1873 the high school classes were transferred to Jubbulpore and became the present Jubbulpore College, leaving the Saugor institution as a middle school. But the want of a local high school was severely felt, and it was re-established in 1885. The imposition of the education cess and the formation of inspection circles for rural schools took place in 1854 under the Government of the North-Western Provinces. In 1871, 95 schools were in existence, 74 of which were Government schools and the remainder private. 4,316 boys were in receipt of instruction and there were also 19 girls' schools with 892 pupils. During the next twenty years no very great advance was made, and in 1891 the numbers of schools and scholars showed little improvement since 1871. After 1891 a period of expansion set in owing to the special grants made by Government and the introduction of the combined system, by which the masters received a small fixed salary in addition to grants depending on the results of examinations. Efforts were made to educate the depressed castes and a Chamār school was opened at Khurai. A special school for Gonds was also started but subsequently had to be closed. The progress of education was checked by the famines but since 1900 has made rapid strides. The high school was affiliated to the Allahābād University in 1891. In 1902-03 it contained 64 pupils in the high school and 235 in the middle school classes with an average attendance of 88 per cent. Besides the high school and its branches the District had in 1902-03, 110 boys' schools and 28 girls' schools with 6,032 boys scholars and 1,290 girls; 116 girls were learning in boys' schools. Statistics of the total number of pupils under instruction in past years have been as follows—1880-81, 5,255; 1890-91, 5,959; 1900-01, 6,339; 1902-03, 8,147. Out of the 138 schools, 109 are maintained by the District Council and 11 by the municipalities; the remaining 18 are private schools, but all except one of them receive fixed grants from Government. Next to the high school the most important institution is the English middle school at Khurai, which with its branch school contains about 250 pupils. There are first grade vernacular middle schools at Garhākotā, Rehli and Deorī, containing 596 scholars and 2nd grade vernacular middle schools at Shāhgarh, Pithoria, Mālthone, Khimlāsa, Etāwa, Jaisinghnagar, Gourjhāmar and Rāhatgarh with a total of 766 scholars both in the primary and middle school classes. Two private institutions, the Swedish Mission and Marāthī schools at Saugor, also rank as middle schools and contain 126 pupils. Saugor is probably the leading District in the Province in respect of the popularity of primary female education. The best girls' schools are those of Khurai, Deorī and Garhākotā. The school at Khurai is a 2nd grade middle school and contains 65 pupils. The Swedish Mission girls' school for orphans also ranks as a middle school and was for a long time the largest in the District. For inspection purposes, the District has two Deputy Inspectors of Schools, the head-quarters of one being at Saugor and of the other at Rehlī. The school masters of Saugor are a noticeably well-educated and intelligent class as compared with other Districts. The expenditure on education in 1902-03 was Rs. 38,000, of which Rs. 24,000 were spent on primary and Rs. 14,000 on secondary education. The proportion of children under instruction in the same year to those of school-going age was 13½ per cent. in the case of boys and over 2 per cent. in that of girls. These are the best results ever achieved. At the census of 1901 Saugor stood sixth among the Districts of the Central Provinces in respect of literacy, 77 per 1,000 of males being able to read and write. Only 919 women were returned as literate in 1901, but this is probably an understatement as some castes object to admitting that their adult women can read and write.

Dispensaries.

298. The District has seven dispensaries maintained from dispensary funds, two of which, the Main and Victoria City branch dispensaries are located at Saugor, and the others at Garhākotā, Khurai, Rehlī, Deorī and Bandā. There are also jail and cantonment dispensaries and a police hospital at Saugor, and a dispensary maintained by missionaries at Etāwa. A dispensary which formerly existed at Shāhgarh was closed in 1900. The Saugor Main dispensary has accommodation for 50 in-patients, and those of Garhākotā, Khurai and Deorī, for 16, 10 and 4 respectively. The average daily number of indoor patients in the dispensaries maintained from dispensary funds during the decade ending 1901, was 37 and that of outdoor patients 556. The average annual number of operations was 2,434. The major operations are mainly for cataract. The average annual income of the dispensaries for the same period was Rs. 16,000, of which Rs. 5,500 were contributed by Government, Rs. 8,500 by local funds and Rs. 2,000 were realised from subscriptions. A hospital for women under the Countess of Dufferin's fund has been established at Saugor, and is in charge of a female hospital assistant.

Vaccination.

299. Vaccination is compulsory only in the municipal towns of Saugor, Khurai, and Deorī, but is carried on all over the District in the open season. The staff consists of a native superintendent and 14 vaccinators. The hospital assistants at outlying dispensaries also vaccinate persons in the town or village where the dispensary is situated, and in the case of Rehlī and Bandā, of other villages within a radius of two miles. The proportion of persons vaccinated per mille of population has varied during the last decade from 27 in 1898 to 40 in 1903, this last being the best result ever achieved. The annual cost of the operations is something over Rs. 2,000.

Veterinary Dispensaries.

300. A veterinary dispensary was opened at Saugor in 1903 and 1,400 animals were treated at it in that year. The expenditure was Rs. 1,100, the dispensary being supported by grants from Government and from local and municipal funds. Another dispensary was opened at Khurai in 1904.

APPENDIX.

GAZETTEER OF TAHSILS, TOWNS, IMPORTANT VILLAGES, RIVERS AND HILLS.

APPENDIX.

GAZETTEER OF TAHSILS, TOWNS, IMPORTANT VILLAGES, RIVERS AND HILLS.

Baleh.—A large village 36 miles south-east of Saugor, and 11 miles from Rehli with which it is connected by a village road. Its area is 4,457 acres, and the population in 1901 was 1,300 persons as against 1,900 in 1891. The Baleh Tappā of 53 villages was granted to the Gond family of Pitehrā[1] by the Marāthās in 1747. Baleh has some old tanks and betel-vine gardens producing a leaf of some reputation. It has a primary school for boys, a girls' school, and a forest post.

Bamora.—A railway station on the Indian Midland line from Bīna to Itārsi being the second station from Bīna. It is 57 miles from Saugor by rail. Bāmora receives the produce of the Eran pargana. The village has an area of 1,400 acres and the population numbered 700 persons in 1901, showing an increase of 150 during the previous decade. The village contains an old temple built of stones without mortar in the mediæval Brahmanic style like the one at Jānjgir in Bilāspur. It is now in ruins. Bāmora has a primary school and a post office.

Banda tahsil.—The north-eastern tahsīl of the District, lying north of Saugor tahsīl, and east of Khurai. On the east, the tahsīl adjoins Damoh District, and on the north the Native States of Pannā and Bijāwar. On the north-west, the Dhasān river divides Bandā from the Lalitpur subdivision of Jhānsi District. Its area is 704 square miles or a little over a sixth of that of the District. Bandā is the smallest and poorest of the four tahsīls. The

Natural features.

[1] See Gazetteer article Pitehra and section on Leading Families.

northern part consists almost entirely of rocky and hilly land generally covered with jungle. To the south the hills alternate with some open plains, but these are of limited extent. The rivers Dhasān and Bewas flow through the tahsīl but exercise no fertilising action and do not assist cultivation. 190 square miles or 27 per cent of the total area are occupied by Government forest.

Population.

The population in 1901 was 72,829 persons or 15 per cent. of that of the District. In 1891 the population was 87,193, and in 1881, 82,333. Between 1881 and 1891 the rate of increase was a little higher than that for the District as a whole, Bandā having probably afforded more scope for development. During the last decade the decrease was 16½ per cent. as against the District figure of 20·4. Bandā fared better than the rest of the District during the famines, as it has a large proportion of autumn crops, which were generally more successful than the spring crops. The density of population is 104 persons per square mile, which is larger than that of Khurai, while the rural population is nearly the same as in Saugor. The tahsīl contains 269 inhabited and 38 uninhabited villages.[1] The villages containing over 1,000 persons in 1901 were Amarmau, Baraithā, Bara, Bandā, Chhāpri, Dalpatpur, Dhabolí, Khatorā Kalān, Narwān and Shāhgarh.

Agriculture.

The soils resemble those of Saugor, but there is a much smaller proportion of good land, and a large area of shallow and stony soil. The harder and more impervious nature of the soil in some parts of the tahsīl is favourable to the construction of tanks, and these are more often to be found here than in other parts of the District, and are used to irrigate both rice and wheat land. The area so irrigated is, however, not large. Excluding Government forest, 53 per cent. of the available area is occupied for cultivation. The proportion of occupied

---

1 These figures are taken from the village lists and differ from those arrived at in the census, when uninhabited villages were not counted.

area at settlement was 55 per cent as against 57 in Khuraī, 62 in Saugor and 63 in Rehlī. The Dhāmoni group was the most sparsely cultivated tract in the District at settlement, little more than a third of the total area being occupied. The cropped area of the tahsīl at settlement was 148,000 acres, which decreased to 119,000 in 1900-01, and 134,000 in 1903-04. The decrease in the cropped area since settlement in 1903-04 was 9 per cent. and was considerably smaller than in any other tahsīl; Bandā as a whole has thus fared distinctly better than the rest of the District during the series of bad years. The following statement shows the area under the principal crops at settlement (1893-94) and during the years 1900—1904.

Year.	Rice	Juār.	Kodon and Kutki	Til.	Sugarcane.	Wheat.	Gram.	Linseed.	Total cropped area (a)
At Last Settlement.	4,690	12,760	19,501	12,904	178	57,384	8,516	8,890	1,47,551
1900-01 ...	3,350	31,005	14,827	6,370	35	20,558	14,199	3,276	1,19,467
1901-02 ...	3,972	18,240	16,165	7,323	58	28,202	23,359	3,116	1,28,556
1902-03 ...	3,722	31,762	15,629	9,827	42	27,581	13,195	3,494	1,37,154
1903-04 ...	3,267	20,143	15,014	7,861	21	40,552	9,884	6,045	1,34,062
Percentage on total cropped-area in 1903-04.	2½	15	11	6	...	30	7½	4½	

The proportion of kodon-kutki is the highest in the District and that of juār is also large. Til and jagnī are important crops. The area under wheat and gram on the other hand forms a smaller proportion of the total than in other tahsīls. During the currency of the 30 years' settlement a very large development of agriculture took place in Bandā, the cropped area increasing by no less than

(a) Includes double-cropped area.

84 per cent. This was, however, partly only a return to normal conditions, as much land had been thrown out of cultivation during the Mutiny.

Land-revenue.

The revenue at the 30 years' settlement was Rs. 53,000, and fell at 54 per cent of the assets. At last settlement the revenue was raised to Rs. 82,000 giving an increase of Rs. 29,000 or 55 per cent. The new revenue absorbed only 48 per cent of the assets as against 50 in the other tahsīls. The rent-rate per occupied area was Re. 0-14-8 as against Re. 1-1-6 for the District as a whole, the corresponding revenue-rates being 8 annas and Re. 0-10-3 respectively. Since the settlement, in order to meet the deterioration in agriculture, permanent abatements of revenue have been made in the Dhāmoni group, and temporary ones over the rest of the tahsīl. The land-revenue demand in 1902-03 was Rs. 66,000, giving a decrease of 19 per cent. on the settlement figure. The demand for cesses in the same year was Rs. 8,000. For the purpose of assessment the tahsīl was divided into the following four groups, the number of villages contained by each being shown in brackets against it – Dhāmoni (35), Binaikā (82), Shāhgarh (116), Bherā (67). Of these the Bherā group was the most heavily assessed and next to this Binaikā, while Shāhgarh and Dhāmoni had the lightest assessment in the District with a revenue-rate of only 5 annas 1 pie per occupied acre.

Miscellaneous.

Under the old pargana system the tahsīl was divided into the following four parganas—Shāhgarh containing 116 villages, Dhāmoni 35, Binaikā 82, and Bherā 67. The parganas thus corresponded in name and number, and fairly closely in area, with the assessment groups now adopted. The tahsīl has 2 Revenue Inspector's circles with head-quarters at Kandari and Rurāwan, and 56 patwāri's circles It has 2 police Station-houses at Banda and Shāhgarh, and 5 outposts.

Banda village.—The headquarters of the Bandā tahsīl, situated 20 miles south-east of Saugor on the Cawnpore road. The river Bewas passes about two miles from the village. Its area is 2,500 acres, and the population in 1901 was 1,406 having decreased by about 100 during the decade. The village contains some Jain temples. There is a small tank to the east of the village and a Government encamping ground. The headquarters of the tahsīl were moved to Bandā from Binaikā in 1861 on account of its more central position on the Cawnpore road. Bandā has no trade. Some moneylenders reside here. The village is divided between Brāhman, Baniā, and Lodhi mālguzārs. A weekly market is held on Wednesdays. Bandā has primary schools for boys and girls, a police Station-house, post-office, dispensary, forest post and sarai. A room for European officers is located on the roof of the tahsīl building.

Baraitha.—A village in Bandā tahsīl 37 miles north-east of Saugor. Its area is 2,370 acres and the population in 1901 was 1,130, showing a decrease of 70 during the previous decade. The village is surrounded by jungle. The mālguzār is a Bundelā Rājput. The village has an old fort on a hillock. A mica quarry was formerly worked here, and iron vessels were manufactured, but this industry has now greatly declined. Baraithā has a primary school, a police outpost, and a forest post.

Barodia Kalan.—A village in the Khurai tahsīl 30 miles north of Saugor on the Jhānsi road Its area is 5,700 acres, and the population in 1901 was 950 as against 1,100 in 1891. The village contains a ruined fort. Rai Sāhib Seth Mohan Lāl, Parwār Baniā, is the mālguzār. Barodia has a police Station-house, primary school and post office.

Betwa River.—A river which rises in Bhopal State close to the large tank at Bhopāl. It flows in a northerly direction through the Bhopāl and Gwalior States, and forms the boundary between Saugor District and Gwalior State for about 30 miles on the north-west of the Khurai tahsīl. It is crossed by a railway bridge at Hinnode. It finally falls into the Jumna near Hamīrpur after a course of 360 miles. The Bina, the Dhasān and the Narain river which drains the central portion of the Khurai tahsil are tributaries of the Betwā.

Bewas (Bias) River.—A river which rises in the Sīrmau hills of Bhopāl State close to the south-western boundary of Saugor. Passing into Saugor, it flows from south-west to north-east draining the east of Saugor and the south-east of Bandā tahsīl. It passes close to Jaisinghnagar and within ten miles of Saugor, where it is crossed on the Damoh road by an iron suspension bridge constructed in 1832, by Colonel Presgrave, Mint-master at Saugor. The bridge, which is of 200 feet span, was constructed entirely by native workmen with Tendūkhedā iron at a cost of Rs. 48,000. The river is also crossed by the Saugor-Damoh railway at Lidhorā. A little north of Bandā, it turns east through a gorge into the Damoh District, and passing Panchamnagar joins the Sonār about 3 miles from Narsinghgarh. Its length is about 92 miles.

Bhapel.—A large village 9 miles from Saugor on the Rāhatgarh road. Its area is nearly 4,000 acres and the population in 1901 was 850 persons as against 1,150 in 1891. Bhāpel was the site of an engagement between a detachment of the British garrison from Saugor and the rebels in 1857. The village is also called Phuler, as it contains a temple of Phūlnāth, a local name of Mahādeo. An annual fair is held at the end of Kārtik or in November which lasts for one day only, the average attendance aggregating some 12,000 persons. The pilgrims bathe in the tank, and make offerings at the temple. Barren women believe that they will get children by worshipping here

Bhera.—A small village 28 miles north-east of Saugor in the Bandā tahsil. Its area is about 1,200 acres and it had a population of 500 persons in 1901. Bherā was formerly the headquarters of the pargana of that name, which contained 67 villages.

Bilehra.—A village in the Saugor tahsīl 17 miles south of Saugor. Its area is 4,000 acres and the population in 1901 was 1,400 persons as against 1,800 in 1891. Bilehrā with other villages was assigned as a grant for the maintenance of the old Dāngi rulers of Saugor, and their descendants still hold it, the present representative being Rājā Ratan Singh Dāngi. The village was founded about 1650 A.D. by a Rājput chief named Pargal Shā, brother of Udan Sha, the founder of Saugor, who built the small fort which still stands. It has a primary school, and a market is held on Tuesdays.

Bina.—A village in the Rehlī tahsīl four miles from Deorī. Its area is 2,700 acres, and the population in 1901 was 614 persons. The mālguzār is a Gond. A large Jain temple stands here and a fair is held on Aghan Sudi 5th (November—December) at which some 2,000 to 3,000 persons assemble, the fair lasting for 8 days. The fair is called 'Jaljātrā.' The temple is over two hundred years old.

Bina.—A railway junction in the Khurai tahsīl 47 miles from Saugor by rail and two miles from the town of Etāwā. The main line of the Indian Midland Railway from Itarsī to Cawnpore and Agra, passes Bīna, and is connected here with Katnī junction on the East Indian Railway by a branch line through Saugor and Damoh. Another branch line has been constructed from Bīna to Goonā and Baran. Bīna is 607 miles from Bombay and 806 miles from Calcutta. The village is rapidly increasing in size, its population in 1901 having been 1,826 as against 714 in 1891. Bīna is practically a part of the town of Etāwa, the station having been named after the Bīna river instead of the town owing to the existence of another Etāwa in Northern India. A number of railway officials reside here and form a company of Volunteers. There are three schools, a mission school for European children, and another for native children, and a primary school. A dispensary is maintained by the railway. There is a station of the American Mission known as the Disciples of Christ.

Bina River.—A river which rises in Bhopāl State and enters Saugor District from the south-west. It flows almost due north past Rāhatgarh where it is crossed by a large stone bridge of fourteen arches. It then forms the boundary between Saugor and Pathārī State for about twenty-five miles, when it again enters the District and cuts off the small Eran pargana from the rest of Saugor. In this part of its course there are no fords easily practicable for carts, and as a consequence the trade of the Eran pargana goes to Bāmora station. Leaving Eran, the Bīna again forms the boundary between Saugor and the Kurwai State for a few miles and finally falls into the Betwā. It is crossed by the railway at Kaithorā. The length of its course in Saugor is about 62 miles. Near Rāhatgarh it flows in a deep bed between rocks of polished sandstone and affords some picturesque pieces of scenery. The jungles on the banks of the Bina near Eran were formerly a favourite route of the Pindārīs. A project is under consideration to construct a large reservoir by damming up the Bina at a point about 7½ miles below the Rāhātgarh bridge and 3 miles above Jhilā.

Binaika.—A village in the Bandā tahsīl 24 miles north of Saugor. Its area is 2,200 acres and the population in 1901 was about 800 as against nearly 1,100 in 1891. Binaikā was the headquarters of the pargana of Binaikā Pātān, and the tahsīl headquarters was located here until 1861 when it was removed to Bandā. Binaikā is supposed to have been founded in the 15th century and was held by the Mandlā Gond dynasty, from whom it was taken by Rājā Birsingh Deo, the Bundela chief of Orchhā; it was ceded to the Marāthās in 1730 by Chhatar Sal of Panna. The Marāthā Governor Vināyak Rao built a small fort here. The village belongs to the Tiwāri family of Dhāna. It has a large tank which was improved in the famines of 1897 and

1900 by Government at a cost of Rs. 65,000 Binaikā has a primary school. A weekly market is held on Thursdays.

Deori.—A town in the Rehlī tahsil on the Karelī road 40 miles from Saugor and 35 from Karelī. The town stands on the Sukchain river. It contains an old fort enclosed by the river on three sides. Deorī was founded about three and a half centuries ago by a Chandel Rājā who built the fort. The place was formerly called Rāmgarh or Ujargarh, but when the temple was built the Brāhmans changed it to Deorī or 'The abode of God' In the 18th century Deorī was the capital of the tract known as the Panch Mahāls of Deorī, Nāharmow, Gourjhāmar, Chānwarpātha and Tendukhedā, and was in the possession of Durga Singh, the Gond ruler of Gourjhāmar, who built the fort. In 1767 Deorī and the Panch Mahāls were bestowed rent-free by the Peshwā on one Dhondū Dattātreya, a Marāthā Brāhman. This man's son placed himself under Sindhia's protection, and hence at the cession in 1818 Sindhia put forward a claim to the Panch Mahāls and they were assigned to him, the descendant of the Marāthā *mūafidār* being given Pithoria. Deorī was subsequently transferred to the British Government in exchange for other territory in 1825. It was at first the headquarters of a tahsil and was subsequently included in the Hattā subdivision. During the Mutiny the fort was held by a rebel named Durjan Singh, the Gond landowner of Singhpur, but was captured by Safdar Husain, a local police officer. The population in 1901 was 4,980 persons as against 6,306 in 1891, and 7,414 in 1881. At the period when the produce of the Saugor District was taken by road to Karelī, Deorī was a place of some commercial importance, but this is no longer the case, and it is now little more than an ordinary agricultural village. It was created a municipality in 1867, and the average receipts for the decade ending 1901 were Rs. 4,200. The bulk of the receipts are derived from a house-tax and realisations from pounds. The expenditure is mainly on education and conservancy. The municipality includes the three villages of Deorī, Berdhāna, and Jhunkī, and there are only a few plots of nazūl land. The Municipal Committee consists of five elected and two nominated members. The municipality maintains a dispensary, a vernacular middle school for boys, and a primary school for girls. There is also a police station, post office, and a registration office. An inspection bungalow has been constructed and there is a Government encamping ground. A weekly market for grain and cattle is held on Fridays. The mālguzār is a Kāyasth and an Honorary Magistrate. There is a bench of Honorary Magistrates with three members. Deorī has a temple of Khandobā which is locally famous, built by the Dhondū Dattātreya already mentioned. On Aghan Sudī 6 (November-December) a fire-walking ceremony is held here. An *agnikund* or fire-pit is prepared, 4½ feet long, about 2 feet broad and 1½ feet deep, and is filled with hot coals, and people who have made vows to Mahādeo walk over it. The proceedings last for about five days. On Janamashtamī in August a ceremony is held in honour of Krishna. A boy is dressed up as Krishna, and a representation is given of his playing with the milkmaids. A bowl full of curds is also suspended in the air and broken, and as the curds fall, people catch them and rub them on their heads. The broken pieces of the bowl are taken away and placed in cattle-stalls.

Dhamoni.—A village in the Bandā tahsīl 29 miles north of Saugor. The population is now only 79 persons. The village belongs to Rājā Gokul Dās of Jubbulpore. A police outpost is located here. Dhāmoni has an old and very extensive fort which is now in ruins. The fort stands on an eminence at a short distance from the summit of the passes leading to Bundelkhand, and commands the valley of the Dhasān river. It is of a triangular ground plan and encloses a space of 52 acres, the ramparts having been generally 50 feet high and 15 feet thick with enormous round towers. There are also interior works strengthening the eastern defences, where the magazine and officers' quarters were probably situated. Dhāmoni was a very important town under Muhammadan rule and the ruins of numerous mosques and tombs are still visible. It is said that a market was held here for the sale of elephants. There is a large tank a mile from the fort, from which water was supplied to it by underground pipes. The whole place is now covered by jungle, with a number of custard-apple trees, and is a favourite haunt of tigers. The fort is said to have been built by one Sūrat Shā, a scion of the Mandlā Gond dynasty, at the end of the 15th century. It was taken by Rājā Birsingh Deo, the chief of Orchhā, who rebuilt it, and subsequently passed into the hands of the Muhammadans. In 1700 it belonged to Chhatar Sāl of Panna, and was afterwards taken by the Bhonslas. In 1818 after the flight of Appa Sāhib, it was invested and taken by a British force under General Marshall. It is locally said that Abul Fazl, the well-known minister of Akbar, was born in Dhāmoni, but there seems to be no authority for this statement. Prominent objects are the tombs of two Muhammadan saints. The most important is that of Bāljati Shā, said to be the gurū of Abul Fazl. The villages of Sesai and Ishākpurā are held revenue-free for the support of this tomb, and there is a managing committee with the tahsīldār as president. There is a hereditary guardian of the tomb who has some old title-deeds including grants from Chhatar Sāl of Pannā and the Chanderī Rājā of Gwalior. Until recent years the tomb was visited and worshipped by one of the responsible officers of the Nizām of Hyderābād. The other tomb is supposed to be that of one Ainthā Sha Walī, a Muhammadan saint, who is said to have cursed Dhāmoni and the surrounding country because he could not get water there; and his curse is believed still to lie on the country and prevent its being brought under cultivation. Various legends are current about the tombs of these saints.

Dhana.—A village of fairly large size 11 miles south-east of Saugor on the Rehli road. Its area is over 2,000 acres and the population in 1901 was 1,800 persons as against 2,200 in 1891. It has a primary school, a post office and a police outpost. An inspection-hut has been built here. Dhāna is the headquarters of the Tiwāri family, who rendered good service in the Mutiny.[1] A Hazāri family are also shareholders, whose ancestors were military officers under the Marathās, Hazāri meaning the master of 1,000 horse.

Dhasan River.—A river which rises in the Sirmau hills of Bhopāl State and enters Saugor District on the south-west close to the Betwā. It flows north, draining the centre of Saugor tahsil and the centre and north of Bandā. For the last twenty miles of its course in the District, it forms the boundary between Saugor and Jhānsi, and passing into Jhānsi joins the Betwā after a course of about 220 miles of which 94 are within Saugor District. It is crossed by a stone bridge on the road from Saugor to Rāhatgarh, and by a railway bridge at Nariaoli.

Dugaha.—A village in the Khurai tahsil 9 miles from Khurai. Its area is 1,200 acres and the population in 1901 was 400 persons as against nearly 800 in 1891. There is a small fort here, now in ruins, and the village contains a primary school. Dugaha formerly gave its name to the pargana called Mālthone-Dugāha which contained 175 villages.

Eran.[2]—A village on the south bank of the Bina river, 6 miles from Bamora station on the Indian Midland Railway, and 46 miles north-west of Saugor. Its area is 1,400 acres, and the population in 1901 was 170 persons. Eran is one of the oldest places in the District. Its old name was Erākainā, possibly derived from *erāka*, a kind of grass. It was formerly held by the Dāngis who built a fort, of which

---

[1] See 'Leading Families.'

[2] See also Cunningham's Archæological Reports, vols. X (pp. 76—90), VII (pp. 88—90), Cousen's Lists of Monumental Antiquities and Inscriptions in C. P. and Berar (pp. 34—35) and Fleet's Gupta Inscriptions (Introduction 80, Text 20, 88, 91 and 158).

the ruins remain. Eran was the centre of the pargana to which it gave its name, and which contained 27 villages and an area of 26 square miles. The Eran pargana is cut off from the rest of the District by the Bīna river, which has no fords practicable for carts. and its trade goes to Bāmora station. The present interest of Eran is mainly archæological, as it contains a most interesting collection of remains upon some high ground on the bank of the river about half a mile from the village. There were here at one time a number of small Vaishnava temples, but nothing now remains of them except some of the lower courses of masonry, four standing columns with their architraves, and some beams and parts of doorways. The other remains are a colossal *Varāh* or figure of a boar, a gigantic image of Vishnu, a broken one of Narsingh, and a great stone column. The pillar is 47 feet high and is placed on a pedestal 13 feet square. The shaft is 2 feet 10 inches square up to a height of 20 feet, and is then octagonal for 8 feet, to the bottom of the capital. The lower portion of the capital is formed of a reeded bell, above which is an abacus surmounted by a square block. The lower half of this is plain, but the upper half presents two lions on each face sitting back to back. On the top of the column stands a two-armed male figure about 5 feet high which faces both ways, and has a radiated halo round the head. There is an inscription of nine lines a few feet above the plinth on the side facing the temples. The figure of the boar measures nearly 16 feet from snout to tail, and is nearly 11 feet high. The neck is surrounded by a garland of small human figures sculptured on a band, while the body is covered by small circular ornaments. It has the earth represented as a woman hanging on, in accordance with the legend, to its right tusk, and over its shoulders there is a small four-sided shrine with a sitting figure in each face of it. On the under side of the neck is an inscription. The boar is surrounded by the remains of a temple to Vishnu. This is the oldest known Brahmanical statue in this part of India. The statue of Vishnu is a colossal figure facing east, dressed in a *dhotī* or loin cloth and wearing a *janeo* or sacrificial thread; he holds a sword in one hand and a *gadā* in the other, and has an immense round shield on his back, and bangles on his wrists. Another relic is a shaft, octagonal throughout, the lower octagonal portion above ground measuring nearly 8 feet in perimeter and being over 9 feet high. While above this a smaller shaft rises, leaving all round an offset or step of 9 inches. This shaft is locally known as Bhīm's mother's churning stick. Another large *Varāh* stands in the courtyard of a house in the village, with an old inscription of one line. The inscriptions show that these remains belong to the period of the Gupta dynasty in the 5th century. The oldest of them has been removed to the Imperial Museum, Calcutta. It is a fragmentary inscription, but is very important, having been engraved by the great king Samudragupta. The other inscription on the column is also of great interest as it contributed to fix the era of the Gupta dynasty. Its own date is 484-85 A. D. and records the erection of the column, which is called the flagstaff of the God Vishnu, by two brothers Mātri Vishnu and Dhanya Vishnu, the latter of whom built the temple in which the colossal boar was enshrined, on the death of his elder brother Mātri Vishnu. The inscription on the boar relates to a king Toramāna. Another inscription on a small pillar standing under some tall trees near the bank of the river, records the burning of the wife of Goparāja, a chieftain who came to Eran with the powerful king Bhānu Gupta in 510 A.D., and was killed there in a battle, his wife cremating herself on his funeral pyre. This is perhaps the oldest record of a *satī* immolation in India.

Etawa.—A town in the Khurai tahsīl two miles from Bina railway junction and 48 miles from Saugor. Its area is 3,296 acres and the population in 1901 was 6,418 persons as against 3,268 in 1891. The above figure includes the residents at Bīna Railway station numbering 1,826, and without them the population of Etāwa amounts to 4,592 persons. Etāwa was the headquarters of the Etāwa pargana or zamīndāri, which contained 44 villages with an area of 61 square miles. This tract was assigned after the cession to a Marāthā Brāhman Rām Bhao in lieu of Kanjia and Malhārgarh.[1] Musammāt Jānki Bai, who was until recently the proprietress, belonged to this family, but owing to the indebtedness of the estate a half of it has been sold outright and the remaining half mortgaged with possession to Nathūrām Singhai of Etāwa and Rai Sāhib Seth Mohan Lāl of Khurai for 18 years from 1901. Some temples in and near the town contain fine specimens of carved stone-work. Bardorā, near Etāwa, has four temples of Krishna, which also contain fine carvings. Etāwa has now a very considerable trade in grain and other produce, and owing to its favourable position as an exporting station is rapidly rising in importance. Corn and ghī are exported, and sugar and spices imported. A market is held on Fridays. The town has a sanitation committee whose sole income is derived from weighmen's fees and amounted to Rs. 2,300 in 1902-03. It contains a police Station-house, and post and telegraph office, and a dispensary supported by the mission known as 'The Disciples of Christ' which has a station in Bīna. An inspection bungalow has been constructed here. The educational institutions comprise a vernacular middle school with 140 pupils enrolled in 1902-03, and a girls' school. Substantial school buildings were presented by Nathūrām Singhai, at a cost of Rs. 5,000.

Garhakota.—A town in the Rehlī tahsīl 28 miles east of Saugor on the Damoh road. Its area is 2,700 acres and the population in 1901 was 8,500 persons as against 9,500 in 1891, and 11,400 in 1881. The town lies at the junction of the Sonār and Gadherī rivers, on both banks of the Sonār. It is said to have been founded by the Gonds, but in the 17th century it passed into the possession of a Rājput chief called

[1] See under 'Leading Families' in Chapter on Population.

Chander Shā, who began to build the fort which is now standing. Before the building of the fort, the place was called Kotah, but its name was then changed to Garhākotā from *garh* a fort. In 1703. Hirde Sā, the son of the famous Bundelā Chief Chhatar Sāl of Pannā, captured the fort, giving the Rājput owner the single village of Naigaon which is still held on quit-rent by his descendants. Hirde Sā built a town on the east of the Sonār and called it after his own name Hirdenagar. In 1810 when Mardan Singh, a descendant of Hirde Sā, was in possession, the Rājā of Nāgpur invested the fort. Mardan Singh was killed in its defence, and his son Arjun Singh, applied for assistance to Sindhia, promising to cede a half of his territories as the condition of relief. Sindhia despatched an army under Colonel Jean Baptiste who defeated the Nāgpur troops, and according to the agreement took possession of Mālthone and Garhākotā, leaving to Arjun Singh Shāhgarh with other territory. It is said that when the division was being made, Arjun Singh asked for Shāhgarh thinking that this would induce Sindhia to consider it the best part of the territory and to take it himself. But instead of this he was held to his bargain, and lost the most valuable portion of his possessions. It was a descendant of this Arjun Singh, who, as Rājā of Shahgarh, rebelled in the Mutiny and whose estate was confiscated. Baptiste remained at Garhākotā for some time as governor. In 1819, Arjun Singh seized the fort again by treachery, but after holding it for six months was ejected by Colonel Watson with a British force. The place was managed on behalf of Sindhia until 1861, when it was acquired by exchange. In 1857 it was seized and held for some months by the rebels, but when Sir Hugh Rose's army appeared before the fort the garrison evacuated it by night. The fort stands on a commanding eminence in the fork of the Sonār and Gadheri in a position of great natural strength, and was very substantially built. It was breached by Sir Hugh Rose and is now partly in ruins. The inner wall encloses a space of 11 acres and is covered with the remains of buildings and palaces. At a distance of two miles from the town in the forest, are the remains of what appears to have been a large summer palace attributed to Rājā Mardan Singh. The most remarkable part of the ruins is a lofty tower, the ground plan of which is square, each side measuring about 15 feet. It is about 100 feet high and a winding stone staircase runs round it. The tower is said to have been built by Rajā Mardan Singh in compliance with a whim of his wife who wished to see the lights of Saugor and Damoh from its summit. The situation of Garhākotā is very picturesque, and it contains a number of groves, temples, and stone terraces leading down to the river. A considerable part of the town is now, however, abandoned, and many ruined houses are to be seen. In 1867, Garhākotā is stated to have been one of the most flourishing places in the District and its chief cotton mart. but as is shown by the figures of population its prosperity has long been declining, the development of trade between Saugor and Karel, having probably deprived Garhākotā of its importance, while being now comparatively remote from the Saugor-Damoh line, it is unlikely to regain its former trade. The town was a municipality until 1901-02, when its municipal constitution was abolished, and separate committees formed under the Village Sanitation Act for Garhākotā and Hirdenagar. The receipts of the Garhākotā Committee amounted in 1901-02 only to Rs. 300 odd, and those of the Hirdenagar Committee to Rs. 1,200. Garhākotā is now best known as the site of a large annual cattle fair which is one of the most important in the Province. It lasts for 40 days from Basant Panchamī to Holī between January and March, and is attended by some twenty to twenty-five thousand persons. The figures of the three years 1902-04 show that 15,000 head of cattle were sold annually on an average, their total value being Rs. 1·60 lakhs. A brisk trade is also carried on in cloth, metal wares, provisions, sweetmeats and other articles. The average realisations from dues and registration fees at the fair exceed Rs. 2,000, while the expenses are under Rs. 1,000. Prizes were formerly given by Government for the best cattle, and the system after being in abeyance for some years was revived in 1904. A large proportion of the cattle brought to the fair, however, are worn out animals, which are sold to the butchers and slaughtered on the spot, and the only really valuable animals are the plough bullocks brought from Gwalior, Bhopāl and the surrounding States. This fair is said to have been started by Rājā Mardan Singh, mainly as an occasion for a state performance of the *rahas* or commemoration of Krishna's dances with the milkmaids, which is celebrated at the Holī, and of which Mardan Singh was very fond. In order to inaugurate the fair successfully, he is said to have issued a proclamation that any one who came to the fair, and was robbed on the way, would be reimbursed by the State, and if any one did not sell his cattle they would be bought by the State. The fair is still called *rahas* by the people, though the dance is no longer performed. Another small fair is held in the month of Asārh (June-July), when the image of *Jagdīsh* (Vishnu) is taken from his temple and carried on a car to the temple of Jānki, where he remains for two days and is fed, together with all the Bairāgis who have assembled. Some 10,000 persons are collected on the principal day, of whom about 1,000 are fed. Several industries are carried on in Garhākotā. There are a number of weavers and dyers, and the red and blue cloths with white lines, which they produced for women's skirts, were formerly held in considerable estimation. Glass bangles are also made. These industries are, however, no longer prosperous. Garhākotā was the headquarters of the pargana of the same name which contained 109 villages and an area of 193 square miles. It has a vernacular middle school with 180 pupils enrolled, a police Station-house and post office. There is an encamping ground, and an inspection bungalow has been constructed. A weekly market is held on Fridays. The present proprietor is Har Prasād Naik, a Baniā.

Garhola.—A village in the Khurai tahsīl about 22 miles from Saugor. Its area is 5,500 acres and the population in 1901 was about 600 persons as against nearly 1,200 in 1891. The village is surrounded by a stone wall and contains a small fort. To the east of it is a tank covering 76 acres. Garholā is held revenue-free by an old Dāngi family, who formerly owned an extensive tract in Khurai. The soil of the village is fertile and much rice is grown close to the tank. The plantains of Garholā are also well-known locally. Garholā has a primary school.

Garhpahra.—A village in Saugor tahsīl 6 miles north of Saugor on the Jhānsi road. Its area is 923 acres and the population in 1901 was 54 persons. Garhpahrā is otherwise known as old Saugor, and was formerly the capital of the Dāngi chiefs of Saugor, who built the fort there. The capital was removed to Saugor by the Marāthās after the Dāngis had been ousted. On a hill by the village is a temple of Mahābīr or Hanumān in whose honour a fair is held every year on each Tuesday in Asārh (June-July). The third Tuesday is the most important day when some 2,000 persons assemble from Saugor and the surrounding villages. Below the hill to the north is a small lake called the Moti Tal. There are also the remains of a summer residence of the Dāngi chiefs called the 'Shīsh-mahal' or glass palace. This is a small square two-storied building like a Muhammadan tomb, with pieces of glass of various colours stuck into the masonry. Close to the hill is another one, and the story is, that once a very agile Natnī or female acrobat so pleased the king that he told her that if she could walk from one hill to the other he would give her half his kingdom. So a rope was stretched between them, but when she had nearly walked across successfully, the queen who was jealous, cut the rope and she fell and was killed. Her tomb is still pointed out and is an object of worship, but it may be noted that this story is told in various other places where two adjoining hills are found.

Gourjhamar.—A large village in the Rehlī tahsīl situated on the Karelī road 28 miles south of Saugor. Its area is 1,400 acres and the population in 1901 was 2,264 persons, as against 2,413 in 1891. The village is an old one and was founded by the Gond rulers of Deorī. It contains a small fort, and was the capital of the pargana of the same name comprising 31 villages. Gourjhāmar has a vernacular middle school for boys, and a primary school for girls, a police outpost, forest post and post office. There is an encamping ground and an inspecting officer's room in the outpost. The proprietor is a Parwār Baniā. A bazar is held on Sundays.

Hirapur.—A village in the Bandā tahsīl 47 miles north of Saugor on the Cawnpore road. Its area is over 6,000 acres and the population in 1901 was 924 persons as against 1,293 in 1891. It has a small fort in fairly good repair, and a tank which was improved in the famine of 1900 by Government at a cost of Rs. 7,000. Iron ore deposits occur in the neighbourhood, and there is an iron-smelting industry which is not prosperous. The reserved forest of Tigorā lies to the north-east of the village. A police outpost is located in the fort, and the village has a primary school. A weekly market is held here, and there is an encamping ground. The proprietor is a Baniā.

Jaisinghnagar.—A large village in the Saugor tahsīl 21 miles south-west of Saugor. Its area is 2,600 acres and the population in 1901 was 2,131 persons as against 2,181 in 1891. Jaisinghnagar was founded about 1670 A.D. by Rājā Jai Singh the ruler of Garhpahrā, who gave it his name and built a fort which is now in ruins. After the cession, Jaisinghnagar was assigned in 1826 as an appanage to Rukmā Bai, the widow of Abba Sāhib, who appointed one Ganpat Rao Bhauji to manage the estate for her. Three years later, however, she relinquished the estate for a cash payment and it was subsequently given in farm to Ganpat Rao, whose descendants are the Tālukdārs of Jaisinghnagar. They are Karhāda Brāhmans. Jaisinghnagar was the capital of the pargana comprising 51 villages to which it gave its name. It is a flourishing village and has a vernacular middle school and girls' school, a post office, police Station-house and forest post. Ornaments of bell-metal are made here, and a market is held on Mondays and Fridays. The village contains a large tank which was improved by Government at a cost of Rs. 30,000 in the famine of 1896-97.

Jaitpur.—A small village in the Rehlī tahsīl 12 miles from Deorī, with an area of 800 acres and a population of 800 persons in 1901 as against 1,200 in 1891. A fair is held on the last two days of the Naodurgā in the months of Chait and Kunwār (March and September approximately), lasting for two days on each occasion. About 4,000 persons assemble at the fair. It is held in honour of one Kalyān Bāba, a holy man of Barmhān, who died here. The people bathe in the Koprā river which flows past the village. There is a primary school and a weekly market is held. The proprietor is a Dāngi.

Jalandhar.—A large village in the Saugor tahsīl about 20 miles west of Saugor. Its area is 5,792 acres and the population in 1901 was over 1,000 persons. The village has a primary school and forest post. A sandal-wood plantation has been started in the adjoining Government forest. The proprietor is a Jāt.

Jhagri.—A small village in the Bandā tahsīl about 5 miles from Bandā on the river Bewas. Its area is 1,100 acres and the population in 1901 was 600 persons. The proprietor is a Lodhī. A small fair is held here in January on Makar Sankrānt, at which between one and two thousand persons assemble. The fair is held in honour of Mahādeo, who is said to have appeared to a Brāhman in a dream, and declared that he was incarnate in a stone lying here. The stone is now held sacred and a temple has been built over it.

Kanjia.—A village in the Khurai tahsīl 69 miles north-west of Saugor. Its area is 3,100 acres and the population in 1901 was 900 as against 1,100 in 1891. Kanjia is said to be some hundreds of years old. Its founder was a Bundelā chief, whose son Shāhju built the fort which is still standing on an eminence to the south of the village. It is a square erection with a tower at each corner, and encloses a space of about two acres covered with ruined buildings. The Bundelā chiefs held the Kanjia tract from the Emperors of Delhi. In 1725 A.D., one of them by name Vikramājit was expelled by the Nawāb of Kurwai, who was himself ousted by the Peshwā. On the cession of Saugor in 1818, the Kanjia pargana was made over to Sindhia, with whom it remained until 1860, when it became British territory by exchange. During the Mutiny of 1857, a party of Bundelās came down from the adjoining Native States, expelled Sindhia's officer and set up a descendant of Vikramājīt as ruler. They decamped on the approach of Sir Hugh Rose. The village contains an old Idgāh constructed in 1631 A. D. according to an inscription on a stone inside it. A great battle is said to have taken place here in the time of Chhatar Sāl, and the graves of the dead are pointed out in a place called 'Ganj Shahīd' which is now held sacred. Kanjia was the headquarters of the pargana to which it gave its name, comprising 105 villages with an area of 187 square miles. Kanjia has a primary school and a police outpost. A weekly market is held on Tuesdays. The present proprietor is a Baniā.

Karnelgarh.—Also called Atā, a small village in the Khurai tahsīl on the Jhānsi road near the border, with an area of 350 acres and a population of 150 persons in 1901. Karnelgarh is so called because it was once the residence of Colonel Jean Baptiste of Sindhia's army. It has an old fort now in ruins. Stone of good quality is obtained from a quarry in the village. The present proprietor is a Rajput.

Khamaria.—An old village in the Rehlī tahsīl, one mile from Rehlī. Its area is 2,200 acres and the population in 1901 was 1,300 persons as against 1,750 in 1891. Khamaria is said to have been the headquarters of the pastoral Ahīrs or

Baladeos, who were formerly dominant in Saugor. There is a local legend to the effect that Khamaria contains buried treasure, and from time to time the descendants of these Ahīrs come in the night and remove it. The proprietor is Bhaiyā Lāl Naik of Rehlī.

Khimlasa.—A village in the Khurai tahsīl 41 miles north-west of Saugor. Its area is 2,700 acres and the population in 1901 was 1,700 as against 2,500 in 1891. The proprietor is a Parwār Baniā. The town is said to have been founded by a Muhammadan under the Mughal Empire, and was afterwards held by Anūp Singh, Rājā of Pannā. It is surrounded by a stone wall about 20 feet high, and contains a fort. The whole town is built of stone obtained from a quarry in the vicinity, and owing to the decline in the importance of Khimlāsa, many houses are now standing empty. Inside the fort is a Muhammadan tomb constructed of slabs of stone about 1½ inches thick, and cut with beautifully perforated screen-work. There are also an old mosque and an Idgāh, dated 1025 Hijrī (1616 A.D.), and several Muhammadan tombs, the inscriptions from which in Persian characters have been collected in the mosque. Another building is a 'Shīsh-mahal' or glass palace, the upper story of which was said to be formerly filled up with mirrors. In the neighbourhood of the town are some inscribed *satī* pillars. Khimlāsa had formerly a local reputation for the learning of its Sanskrit scholars. It was the headquarters of the Khurai tahsīl up till 1834, and of the Khurai-Khimlāsa pargana, which contained 175 villages with an area of 286 square miles. It has a vernacular middle school and girls' school, a police Station-house containing a room for inspecting officers, and a post office. A market is held here on Sundays.

Khurai tahsil.—The north-western tahsīl of the District, adjoining Bandā tahsīl on the north-east, Saugor on the east and south-east, Gwalior State on the west, and Lalitpur on the north.

Natural features.

Its area is 940 square miles or rather more than a quarter of that of the District. The tahsīl consists generally of an open undulating plain with a stretch of stony and hilly land in the north, and belts of forest on the borders of the rivers Binā, Betwā, Narain and some less important streams. A long ridge of hills on the south-eastern border divides Khurai from the Nariaolī pargana of Saugor. 128 square miles or 14 per cent. of the total area consist of Government forest.

Population.

The population in 1901 was 93,788 persons or 19 per cent. of that of the District. In 1891 it was 126,000, and in 1881, 117,000. The increase between 1881 and 1891 was nearly 8 per cent. as against the District figure of 4·7. The opening of the Indian Midland Railway during the decade, is sufficent to account for the higher rate of increase in Khurai. During the last decade the population decreased by nearly 27 per cent., the rate for the District being 20·4. Khurai was more severely affected than any other part of the District during the famine years. The density of population is 100 persons per square mile. The tahsīl has two towns Khurai and Etāwa, and 470 inhabited and 95 uninhabited villages.[1] The following villages contained over 1,000 persons in 1901—Agāsode, Basāhrī, Binā Station, Khimlasā, Mālthone and Pithoria.

Agriculture.

The soil of the tahsīl is stiffer and more clayey than in Saugor and Rehlī. The best soil, *mār*, is found in the Jharai, Khurai, Etāwa Eran, and Khimlāsa groups in fields which are quite level, or of which the edges are higher than the centre. This soil is considered to be somewhat more fertile than the *kabār* of Saugor and Rehlī. The soil of Khurai is, however, peculiarly liable to attacks of *kāns* grass (*Saccharum spontaneum*), which rapidly infests any field exhausted by cultivation or allowed to remain fallow, and cannot be eradicated by the ordinary coun-

---

[1] These figures are taken from the village lists and differ from those arrived at in the census when uninhabited villages were not counted.

try plough. This soil is also more difficult to cultivate, and bullocks get worn out more rapidly. A considerable amount of damage is done to the crops by the large herds of antelope, which wander over the open country. Excluding Government forest, 44 per cent. of the available area is occupied for cultivation. At last settlement, the percentage of area occupied was 57 as against 62 per cent in Saugor and 63 in Rehli. Even at settlement a considerable quantity of culturable land was left fallow, and the amount has since substantially increased. The people, with the exception of a few rich moneylenders, are indebted, and lack capital to develope the land. In the Kanjia group only 49 per cent. of the available land was occupied at settlement, and a large area was overgrown with *kāns*. In the Pithoria group the percentage of area occupied was only 47. The cropped area at settlement was 229,000 acres, and decreased to 123,000 acres in 1900-01, and to 141,000 in 1903-04. The decrease in 1903-04 was 38 per cent. on the area cropped at settlement. The following statement shows the area under the principal crops at settlement and during the years 1900—04 :—

YEAR.	Rice.	Juar.	Kodon and Kutki.	Til.	Sugar-cane.	Wheat.	Gram.	Linseed.	Total cropped area (a).
At last Settlement.	4,578	18,083	16,563	15,615	133	106,562	39,210	4,217	228,640
1900-01 ...	3,857	45,045	10,222	2,443	12	13,947	23,650	499	122,651
1901-02 ...	4,530	32,093	12,404	1,782	17	16,387	33,102	428	127,611
1902-03 ...	4,173	53,830	9,245	2,423	14	12,274	26,364	336	139,814
1903-04 ...	3,884	43,581	5,948	3,118	9	22,300	33,457	870	141,223
Percentage on total cropped area in 1903-04.	3	31	4	2	...	16	24	...	...

The cultivation of wheat shrank to absolute insignificance in the famine years, and, in place of the large exports of former years, this grain was imported into Khurai for food. The area under it is still very small, compared with the District

(a Includes also double cropped area.

proportion. The area of kodon fell off greatly in 1903-04. Before that year it was larger than in any tahsil except Bandā. The proportion of juār and gram grown, is at present very high in Khurai. This tahsīl has two-fifths of the District acreage of juār, and three-sevenths of that of gram.

Land-revenue.

The revenue at the 30 years' settlement (1867) was Rs. 1·06 lakhs, which fell at less than 52 per cent. of the assets. At last settlement the revenue was raised to Rs. 1·49 lakhs giving an increase of Rs. 43,000 or 41 per cent. on the previous figure, and falling at 50 per cent of the assets. The rental incidence per acre was Rs. 1-0-8 as against Rs. 1-1-6 for the District as a whole, the corresponding figures of revenue incidence being Re. 0-9-5 and Re. 0-10-3 respectively. The incidence of revenue was lower than in any tahsīl except Bandā. Since the settlement, both permanent and temporary abatements have been made to meet the great deterioration in cropping, and the demand in 1902-03 was Rs. 76,000, showing a reduction of 49 per cent on the settlement figure. The demand for cesses in the same year was Rs. 9,700. For the purposes of assessment, the tahsil was divided into the following nine groups, the number of villages contained by each being shown in brackets against it—Kanjia (99), Etāwa (44), Eran (27), Jharai (46), Khurai (56), Khimlāsa (75), Barodia (96), Chandrapur (76), Pithoria (28). The revenue rate was highest in the Khurai group, and next to this came Etāwa, Eran and Jharai. Kanjia, Khimlāsa and Barodia ranked next, and the poorest groups were Chandrāpur and Pithoria.

Miscellaneous.

Under the old pargana system, the following five parganas made up the tahsīl—Kanjia containing 98 villages, Etāwa 44, Eran 27, Mālthone-Dugāha 175, and Khurai-Khimlāsa 179. The tahsil has three Revenue Inspector's circles with head-quarters at Barodia, Garholā, and Etāwa, and 100 patwāri's circles. It has four police station-houses at Barodia, Etāwa, Khimlāsa, and Khurai, and five outposts.

Khurai town.—The headquarters town of the Khurai tahsīl. It is a railway station 33 miles from Saugor on the line towards Bīna. The town is half a mile from the station. Its area is 2,600 acres, and the population in 1901 was 6,000 persons as against 6,200 in 1891, and 5,400 in 1881. Khurai is supposed to have been founded by Aurangzeb, who selected the site, because when he was hunting there a hare turned and pursued the dogs. He considered therefore that a place in which an animal, ordinarily timid, displayed such courage must also produce brave men, and determined to found a city. Khurai was formerly held by one Khemchand Dāngi who built the fort, and whose descendants hold Garholā revenue-fee. Govind Rao Pandit enlarged the fort, excavated the tank which washes its southern wall, and built the little temple of Radhā Kishen inside the fort, which stands in a masonry tank surrounded by water. The fort has eight large towers and a fine gateway, and a good view of the surrounding country can be obtained from it. The older part of the building is constructed without mortar. The large tank to the south of the fort is bordered for the greater part of its circuit, with stone *ghāts* or flights of steps. It was improved at a cost of Rs. 30,000 in the famine of 1896-97. The town also contains some fine Jain temples, one of which has carved stonework. Khurai is one of the centres of the Jain religion, and a large number of Parwār Baniās reside here, including some leading money-lenders. Khurai was created a municipality in 1867, and the average annual municipal receipts for the decade ending 1901 were Rs. 15,300. The bulk of the receipts are obtained from fees on the registration of cattle, and next to this the most important head is octroi. The Municipal Committee contains three nominated and five elected members. A very important weekly cattle market is held here on Mondays, to which cattle are brought from the surrounding Native States. During the three years 1901—1903, 40,000 head of cattle were sold annually on an average of the aggregate value of

Rs. 4 lakhs. Khurai has also a fair amount of trade. A large cattle-slaughtering industry has now sprung up, as many as 25,000 head of cattle being killed annually. The tahsīl headquarters were removed to Khurai from Khimlāsa in 1834, and Khurai at the same time became the headquarters of the Khurai-Khimlāsa pargana, which contained 175 villages with an area of 286 square miles. The proprietor of the village is Shrīmant Seth Mohan Lāl, Parwār Baniā. The tahsīl offices are located in the fort. Khurai has a police Station-house, dispensary, post office and forest post. The educational institutions comprise an English middle school, and two branch schools and a vernacular middle and another mission school for girls. The Swedish Lutheran mission carries on work here. An inspection bungalow has been built near the station.

Malthone.—A village in the Khurai tahsīl in the extreme north of the District, 40 miles from Saugor on the Jhānsi road. The village is built on the slopes of the Vindhyās leading down to Bundelkhand on the pass called the Narhut Ghāt. Its area is 2,000 acres and the population in 1901 was 1,500 persons as against 2,100 in 1891. Mālthone is supposed to have been founded by one of Akbar's officers in about 1600 A.D. It subsequently passed into the possession of the Gonds, and then into the hands of the Rājā of Orchhā. He was in turn ousted by Prithwī Singh from Garhākotā, who belonged to the Pannā house. It was ceded in 1809 by Arjun Singh of Garhākotā to Sindhia, and was acquired by the British in 1820 in exchange for other territory. During the Mutiny, Mālthone was held by the rebel Rājā of Shāhgarh, Arjun Singh's descendant, for several months, and was abandoned by him in January 1858 on the advance of Sir Hugh Rose. An old Idgāh to the east of the village on the bank of a tank, contains an inscription which is supposed to indicate the existence of buried treasure. There are also the ruins of a fort, one massive tower of which is still intact, and is called 'Kamal-durg' or the lotus-tower. Inside the tower the spirit of a very holy Muhammadan saint is supposed to reside, of whom various miracles are related. There are several shallow wells in the rock inside the fort, which always contain water, and never dry up owing to the benignant influence of the saint. Women are not allowed to draw water from the principal well, as this would offend his spirit. Near the tank are several inscribed *satī* pillars erected between 1732 and 1778 A.D. Mālthone gave its name to the Mālthone-Dugāha pargana comprising 197 villages with an area of 361 square miles. It has a vernacular middle school with 83 pupils enrolled in 1902-03, a girls' school, a police outpost and a forest post. An inspection bungalow has been erected, and there is an encamping ground. A weekly market is held on Saturdays. Rājā Gokul Dās is proprietor of the village.

Naharmow.—A small village in the Rehlī tahsīl, 8 miles west of Gourjhamar. Its area is 2,251 acres and the population in 1901 was 500 persons as against 800 in 1891. Nāharmow has an elevation of 2,240 feet and is one of the highest places in the District. A temple of Mahādeo stands on an island in the tank, and small fairs are held here on the days of Makar Sankrānt in January and on Shivrātri in March, and are attended by some 500 persons. Nāharmow was formerly the headquarters of a pargana containing 46 villages with an area of 72 square miles. A forest post is located here. The proprietor is a Kāyasth.

Naigaon.—A small village in the Rehlī tahsīl held on quit-rent by the descendant of the Rājput chief who formerly owned Garhākotā, and was dispossessed by the Pannā family.

Nariaoli.—A village in the Saugor tahsīl, 12 miles from Saugor on the Khurai road and the first railway station from Saugor on the line towards Bīna. Its area is 2,900 acres and the population in 1901 was 975 persons as against 1,424 in 1891. Nariaolī was the headquarters of the pargana to which it gave its name, containing 95 villages. It has a small fort perched on a high hill, and was the site of an engagement between the Saugor garrison and the rebels during the Mutiny. A large tank in the village was improved by Government in the famine of 1896-97 at a cost of Rs. 22,000. Nariaolī contains primary schools for boys and girls, a post office and a police outpost. A weekly market is held on Sundays. The village has recently had an unenviable notoriety as the residence of a number of bad characters. The proprietor is a Khedāwāl Brāhman.

Pitehra.—The headquarters of an estate known as the Pitehrā jāgīr held by an old Gond family. Pitehrā has recently (1902) been transferred to the Narsinghpur District. The village is 57 miles from Saugor on the banks of the Nerbudda.

Pithoria.—A village in the Khurai tahsīl 12 miles north-west of Saugor with an area of 3,000 acres and a population of 1,200 persons in 1901 as against 2,100 in 1891. The village contains an old fort, and some temples built without mortar. Pithoria was the headquarters of an estate known as the Pithoria jāgīr, comprising 26 villages with an area of 51 square miles. This estate was awarded to Rao Rāmchandra Rao of Deorī, when the latter place was transferred to Sindhia immediately after the cession. The estate is still held by his descendants. Glass bangles are made in Pithoria. The tank here was improved in the famine at a cost of Rs. 2,000. The village has a vernacular middle school for boys, a girls' school and a forest post.

Rahatgarh.—A large village in the Saugor tahsīl 25 miles west of Saugor on the Bhopāl road and situated on the Bīna river. Its area is 1,000 acres and the population in 1901 was 3,600 persons as against 3,500 in 1891. A fragmentary inscription found in the fort and dated 1255 A.D., shows that Rahatgarh was in the possession of the Pramara Rājās of Dhār as early as that date. It subsequently belonged to the Gond dynasty of Garhā-Mandlā, was ceded to the Mughal Empire, and was conferred by Aurangzeb on a Muhammadan family. Later still, it came into the possession of the Nāwabs of Garhī-Amāpāni in Bhopāl, who held it until 1807 when the fort and town were taken and annexed by Sindhia. It came under British management in 1826, to defray the expenses of a contingent of troops, and was finally ceded in 1861. In 1857 the descendants of the old rulers, the Nawābs of Garhī-Amapāni came and took possession of the fort with a band of insurgents. They held it until 1858 when the fort was invested and captured by Sir Hugh Rose and the rebels subsequently defeated at Barodia Naonagar with great slaughter, one of the Nawābs being taken and hanged. The fort is situated on a lofty eminence to the south-west of the town. The outer walls consist of twenty-six enormous towers, some of which were used as dwellings, connected by curtain walls, and enclosing a space of 66 acres. This space was covered with buildings of all descriptions, and contained a bazar and numerous temples and palaces. One of these was called the Bādal Mahal or 'Cloud Palace' from its great height and elevated situation. It is attributed to one of the Rāj-Gond chiefs of Garhā-Mandlā. Another high tower is called the Jogan Burj or 'Executioner's Tower' as culprits were hurled down from it on to the smooth rocks of the Bīna below. Most of the buildings are now in ruins as are also the outer walls of the fort. The east wall was breached for a distance of nearly a hundred yards in 1858 by Sir Hugh Rose's siege guns. Rāhatgarh is picturesquely situated on the banks of the Bīna which has many beautifully wooded reaches in the vicinity, while two or three miles from Rāhatgarh is a water-fall of nearly 50 feet. The river flows here in a deep bed between banks of polished sandstone. A large bridge of fourteen arches, over which the Bhopāl road passes, was completed in 1863 at a cost of Rs. 56,000. Good building-stone is found in the vicinity, and all the houses are constructed of stone.

Rāhatgarh is not under the Village Sanitation Act, but a local committee makes some provision for sanitation. A considerable trade in grain is carried on, and large numbers of cattle are also slaughtered here, and many traders visit the place to purchase hides and horns. Native shoes are made here and sent all over the District, and there are also a number of glass and bell-metal workers. Iron plough-shares and other implements are also made. A weekly market is held on Saturdays. The bulk of the village is nazul property and is let out in plots for vegetable cultivation. The remainder consists of malik-mākbūza and revenue-free holdings. Rāhatgarh was the headquarters of the pargana to which it gave its name, comprising 134 villages with an area of 206 square miles. Rahatgarh has a vernacular middle school for boys, and a girls' school, a police Station-house, post office and forest post. There is an encamping ground and an inspection bungalow has been constructed.

Rajwans.—A small village in the Khurai tahsīl 27 miles north of Saugor on the Jhānsi road. Its area is 2,400 acres and the population in 1901 was 300 persons as against nearly 600 in 1891. The village contains a small fort, and a tank, which was improved by Government in the famine of 1900 at a cost of Rs. 12,000.

Rangir.—A small village in the Rehlī tahsīl about 10 miles from Rehlī and 21 miles from Saugor. The village is situated on the bank of the Dehār river and is surrounded by forest. The population is only about 100 persons. On a hill adjoining Rāngir is a temple of Devī, known as the Harsiddhī or 'Ever Victorious.' Fairs are held in honour of the goddess in Kunwār (September-October) and Chait (March-April). The Chait fair is the important one and some 20,000 persons then visit the temple. The image of the goddess is said to change its form daily and to be at dawn a child, at midday a young woman, and in the evening an old woman. Various miracles are related of the temple, for the support of which a large estate was formerly assigned by Sindhia.

Rehli tahsil.—The southern tahsīl of the District lying south of Saugor tahsīl and north of Narsinghpur District, from which it is separated by the escarpment of the Vindhyan Hills and the Nerbudda river flowing beneath them. It adjoins Bhopāl State on the west, and Damoh District on the east. The tahsīl consists of an undulating stretch of country with large breadths of table-land round Deorī, Rehlī and Garhākotā, bordered and often intersected by ranges of tree-covered hills. Dense belts of forest occur on the south and east, and a tract of poor hilly country forms the western border. The surface slopes gradually from south-west to north-east and most of the rivers flow in this direction. The south-eastern corner of the tahsīl is drained by the Beārma river, which forms the boundary with Damoh District during part of its course. West of this, the Koprā drains the north-eastern portion of the tahsīl. The Sonār traverses its centre passing Gourjhāmar, Rehlī and Garhākotā, and is joined during its course by the Dehār, the Kaitu and the Gadherī. In the south, two small streams the Biranj and Sindhor rise in the Deorī pargana, and flow south to the Nerbudda. The total area is 1,254 square miles or a little less than a third of that of the District. Of the whole area 275 square miles or 22 per cent are occupied by Government forest.

Natural features.

The population in 1901 was 138,030 persons or 28 per cent. of that of the District. In 1902, a small tract of 11 villages with some Government forest was transferred to Narsinghpur, and the adjusted figure of population is 136,463 persons. In 1891 the population was 171,090, and in 1881, 168,870. The increase between 1881 and 1891 was a little over 1 per cent as against the District figure of 4·7, and the decrease between 1891 and 1901, 19·3 as against 20·4 for the District as a whole. The tahsīl was probably already fairly closely cultivated and populated in 1881, and hence a certain amount of emigration would take place to the less developed

Population.

tracts in the north, accounting for the small development of population during that decade. The density of population is 109 persons per square mile. The tahsīl contains two towns, Garhākotā and Deorī, and 660 inhabited and 79 uninhabited villages.[1] The following villages contained over 1,000 persons in 1901—Baleh, Chhirāri, Chhullā, Nāharmow, Gunjorā, Gourjhāmar, Khamaria (Rehlī), Mahārājpur, Patnā, Rehlī, Sahajpur, and Tandā (Jāgīr).

Agriculture.

The soil except in the hilly country is of superior quality, the plain of the Havelī comprised in the Rehlī and Garhākotā parganas being perhaps the most fertile tract in the District. Excluding Government forest, 59 per cent of the available area is occupied for cultivation. At last settlement, the proportion of occupied area was the highest in the District, being 63 per cent of the village area. The cropped area at settlement was 321,000 acres, which decreased to 250,000 in 1900-01, and 261,000 in 1903-04. The decrease in 1903-04 was 19 per cent on the area cropped at settlement. The following statement shows the area under the principal crops at settlement (1893-94), and during the years 1900—04:—

YEAR.	Rice.	Juar.	Kodon and Kutki.	Til.	Sugar cane.	Wheat.	Gram.	Linseed.	Total cropped area [2].
At Last Settlement.	10,939	15,955	31,610	20,083	610	129,303	20,953	25,913	321,109
1900-01 ...	8,628	33,437	24,727	28,288	156	73,191	17,433	7,143	250,414
1901-02 ...	8,931	24,266	21,375	18,712	176	100,664	21,664	8,284	257,083
1902-03 ...	7,880	27,927	20,403	36,320	171	95,381	24,458	10,454	278,607
1903-04 ...	6,646	16,500	19,928	25,037	107	114,085	12,999	14,042	260,788
Percentage on total cropped area in 1903-04.	2½	6	8	10	...	44	5	5½	...

[1] These figures are taken from the village lists, and differ from those arrived at in the census, when uninhabited villages were not counted.

[2] Includes also double cropped area.

The tahsīl contains more than half the District acreage of til, and over a third of that of wheat. The area of gram was very small in 1903-04, and wheat is more commonly grown alone in Rehlī than elsewhere. The tahsīl has a comparatively large proportion of linseed.

Land-revenue.

The revenue at the 30 years' settlement (1867) was Rs. 1·48 lakhs which fell at less than 50 per cent of the assets. At last settlement this was raised to Rs. 2·18 lakhs, giving an increase of Rs. 70,000 or 45 per cent on the previous figure, and falling at 50 per cent of the assets, as against the same proportion in Saugor and Khurai, and 48 per cent in Bandā. The rent-rate per occupied acre was Rs. 1-1-8 as against the District figure of Rs. 1-1-6, the corresponding revenue-rates being Re. 0-10-4 and Re. 0-10-3 respectively. The incidence of revenue and rental was lower than in Saugor but higher than that of the other two tahsīls. Since the settlement, the revenue has been temporarily reduced in the manner described in the chapter on Land Revenue. The demand for land-revenue in 1902-03 was Rs. 1·71 lakhs or a reduction of 22 per cent on the settlement figure. The demand for cesses in the same year was Rs. 21,000. For assessment purposes the tahsīl was divided into the following eight groups, the number of villages contained in each being shown in brackets against it—Garhākotā (107), Rehlī (101), Chhirārī (93), Gourjhāmar (31), Nahārmow (46), Deorī (122), Keslī (136), Bharrai (59). The most highly assessed group was Gourjhāmar, next to this Rehlī and Garhākotā, then Chhirārī, Nahārmow and Deorī, while Keslī and Bharrai were the poorest.

Miscellaneous.

Under the old pargana system, the following five parganas made up the tahsīl—Garhākotā with an area of 193 square miles and 107 villages, Rehlī containing 376 square miles and 194 villages, Gourjhāmar 59 square miles and 31 villages, Nahārmow 72 square miles and 46 villages, and Deorī 571 square miles and

317 villages. The tahsīl has four Revenue Inspector's circles with headquarters at Garhākotā, Chāndpur, Deorī and Keslī, and 102 patwāri's circles. It has four police station-houses at Rehlī, Deorī, Garhākotā and Keslī, and five outposts.

Rehli village.—The headquarters village of the Rehli tahsil, 26 miles south-east of Saugor, with which it is connected by a partly metalled road and at the junction of the Sonār and Dehār rivers. Its area is 1,700 acres, and the population in 1901 was 3,665 persons as against 3,887 in 1891.[1] Rehlī is supposed to have been founded by the Faulādia Ahīrs, and was afterwards included in the dominions of Chhatar Sāl of Pannā who ceded it to the Peshwā. It became British territory in 1817. The village contains an old fort picturesquely situated above the Sonār river, which was built by the Marāthās, or as some say begun by the Ahirs and completed by the Marāthās. It is partially in ruins, and the space enclosed within it, nearly two acres in extent, is covered with the remains of Marāthā buildings. Rehlī itself has some fine temples, and in the suburb of Pandhalpur about a mile distant is a large temple of Pandharināth, an incarnation of Vishnu. The village of Chhirāri is assigned for the support of the temple, and the revenue is administered by the Rājā of Saugor. Small religious fairs are held in November and July at which some 3,000 persons assemble. A solid stone bridge has been constructed over the Sonār river opposite the village, the water flowing through passages in the stonework which can be closed by doors. The school has a curiously carved marble gateway said to have been brought from Garhākotā. The proprietor of Rehlī is Rao Gopāl Rao, Karhāda Brahman, and a large number of Brāhmans are resident in the town. A bench of honorary magistrates was formerly located here, but it is at present in abeyance. The village has little trade now. Cloth-weaving and dyeing industries are carried on, and a weekly market is held on

[1] These figures include the village of Patna.

Sundays. Rehlī has a vernacular middle school with 200 pupils enrolled in 1902-03 and a girls' school, a police Station-house, post office and dispensary. There is an encamping ground, and an inspection bungalow has been constructed. Rehlī was the headquarters of the pargana to which it gave its name, containing 209 villages with an area of 376 square miles. The town had formerly a municipal constitution which was abolished in 1901, while from the same date the provisions of the Village Sanitation Act were enforced. There are two sanitation committees—one for Rehlī, and one for Patnā, a village on the opposite side of the Sonār river whose population was included in Rehlī municipality. The average income of the Rehlī committee during the last three years was Rs. 750 and that of the Patnā committee Rs. 150.

Sahajpur.—A large village in the Rehlī tahsīl 46 miles from Saugor with an area of 1,200 acres, and a population of 1,500 persons in 1901 as against 1,750 in 1891. Sahajpur was formerly in the possession of one Balbhadra Singh who rebelled in 1857. In consequence of this, the village was confiscated and awarded with a taluk of 32 villages to Kanhyā Lāl Tiwari, of Dhāna, as a reward for his services. Sahajpur has a police outpost, boys' and girls' schools, and a post office.

Sanoda.—A village in the Saugor tahsīl 12 miles from Saugor on the Damoh road. It has an area of 4,800 acres, and its population was 1,500 in 1901 as against 1,850 in 1891. It has a small fort. Near the village is an iron suspension bridge built over the Bewas river by Colonel Presgrave, while he was assay-master of the Saugor Mint. The bridge was completed in 1830 at a cost of Rs. 50,000, and was constructed entirely with iron manufactured in the District. Sanodā has a primary school and a police outpost. Rao Venkat Rao Subhedār is the proprietor.

Saugor tahsil.—The central tahsīl of the District lying south of Khurai and Bandā, and north and west of Rehlī. To the west and south-west it adjoins the Bhopāl and Gwalior States.

Natural features.

The area of the tahsil is 1,064 square miles or rather more than a quarter of that of the District. The country comprised in it may be described as an elevated plain, broken in places by ridges of sandstone, and dotted all over with small trap hills of the most varied size and shape. The surface is irregular in almost every direction with a slight general slope from south to north. All over the tahsil there is a great deal of jungle which is mixed up with cultivation in the most remarkable manner. A large proportion of the best villages include hill and forest within their limits, and there are few large open plains. In almost every part of the tahsil prosperous villages with a large area of good deep soil are to be found side by side with small jungle villages where the cultivation is very poor indeed. Of the total area of the tahsil, 111 square miles or 10 per cent are occupied by Government forest, consisting of a number of small detached blocks scattered about in all directions. The Bewas and Dhasān rivers and the small Babnai Nullah flow through the tahsil.

Population.

The population in 1901 was 166,399 persons or 35 per cent of that of the District. In 1891, the population was 207,456, and in 1881, 196,980. The increase between 1881 and 1891 was 5·3 per cent as against the District figure of 4·7 per cent and the decrease between 1891 and 1901 was 19·8 per cent as against 20·4 per cent for the District. The tahsil has one town Saugor, and 488 inhabited and 65 uninhabited villages.[1] The density of population per square mile is 156 persons. The villages of Bilehrā, Dhāna, Jaisinghnagar, Jalandhar, Karrāpur, Pāmākherī, Padaria, Padrai, Rāhatgarh, Sanodā, Surkhī and Shāhpur contained over 1,000 persons in 1901.

Agriculture.

The prevalent soil is *mund*, generally of comparatively good fertility and easily workable. Owing to the numerous streams and

---

[1] These figures are taken from the village lists and differ from those arrived at in the census when uninhabited villages were not counted.

nullahs, and the uneven surface of the country, the soils change rapidly from field to field, and even in the same field. Excluding Government forest, 57 per cent of the available area was occupied for cultivation in 1902-03. At Mr. De Brett's settlement the occupied area was 62 per cent of the total available, and was exceeded only by the proportion of 63 per cent in Rehlī. The cropped area at settlement was 323,000 acres, which decreased to 249,000 in 1900-01, and 266,000 in 1903-04. The following statement shows the area under the principal crops at settlement and during the years 1900—04:—

YEAR.	Rice.	Juar.	Kodon and Kutki.	Til.	Sugarcane.	Wheat.	Gram.	Linseed.	Total cropped area. (a)
At last Settlement.	5,252	20,779	10,077	12,270	960	184,367	24,352	12,716	323,361
1900-01 ...	3,143	66,337	6,516	10,963	187	74,057	22,203	8,273	249,343
1901-02 ...	3,857	33,855	6,620	5,679	264	114,254	29,078	9,789	257,559
1902-03 ...	3,438	57,031	5,144	9,948	270	97,760	23,981	11,132	270,096
1903-04 ...	2,703	29,335	3,851	9,630	178	129,151	20,278	15,092	266,357
Percentage on total cropped area in 1903-04.	1	11	1½	4	...	48½	8	6	...

The cropping of Saugor is perhaps on the whole the most valuable of all the tahsīls. It has considerably more than a third of the District acreage of wheat, nearly half that of linseed, and not much under two-thirds of the whole quantity of sugarcane grown. On the other hand there is very little rice. The proportions of juār and gram are somewhat smaller than those of the District as a whole.

Land revenue.

The revenue at the 30 years' settlement (1867), was Rs. 1·60 lakhs falling at 51 per cent. of the assets. At Mr. De Brett's settle-

(a) Includes also double cropped area.

ment, this was raised to Rs. 2·46 lakhs giving an increase of Rs. 86,000 or 53 per cent. on the previous revenue, as compared with 48 per cent. for the District as a whole. The revised revenue fell at 50 per cent. of the assets, as against 50 per cent. in Rehlī and Khurai, and 48 per cent in Bandā. The rent-rate per occupied acre was Rs. 1-2-11 as compared with Rs. 1-1-6 for the District as a whole, the corresponding revenue-rates being Re. 0-11-10 and Re. 0-10-3 respectively. Since the settlement the revenue has been temporarily reduced in the manner described in the chapter on Land Revenue. The demand for land-revenue in 1902-03 was Rs. 1·84 lakhs or a reduction of 25 per cent on the settlement figure. The demand for cesses in the same year was Rs. 23,000. For the purposes of assessment, the tahsīl was divided into the following seven groups, the number of villages contained by each being shown in brackets against it—Nariaolī (93), Jhila (78), Sewan (56), Jaisinghnagar (51), Surkhī (82), Saugor (94), and Dhāna (84). Of these, Sewan, Saugor and Jhila had the highest revenue-rate, and next to these come Nariaolī, Surkhī and Dhāna, while Jaisinghnagar was the most lightly assessed group.

Miscellaneous.

The tahsīl has four Revenue Inspector's circles with their headquarters at Surkhī, Pāmākherī, Nariaolī and Rāhatgarh and 127 patwāri's circles. It has five police station-houses at Saugor city and cantonment, Jaisinghnagar, Surkhī and Gopālganj, and eight outposts. The tahsīl was formerly divided into the following four parganas, the number of villages contained by each being noted in brackets against it—Saugor (259), Rāhatgarh (134), Nariaolī (95), and Jaisinghnagar (51).

Statistics of population.

Saugor City.—The headquarters town of the District, situated at 23° 51′ N. and 78° 45′ E. Saugor is a station on the Bīna-Katnī connection of the Indian Midland Railway, 654 miles from Bombay, and 760 from Calcutta. It is 48 miles from Damoh and 114 from Jubbulpore by road. Its population in 1901 was

42,330 persons including the cantonment (population 10.918) and it is the third town in the Province in size. The population in 1872 was 45,655; in 1881, 44,461; and in 1891, 44,470. The population in 1901 included 32,038 Hindus, 8,286 Muhammadans, 1,027 Jains and 762 Christians, of whom 406 were Europeans and Eurasians. The garrison consists at present of one native cavalry and one native infantry regiment, a detachment of British infantry and a field battery. It is believed, however, that the reduction or removal of the garrison is in contemplation. The considerations which led to the maintenance of a substantial force at Saugor before the Mutiny, were the proximity of a number of Native States, at that time in an unsettled condition, and with forces of doubtful loyalty, as well as the turbulent character of many of the District land-holders, who were marauders and freebooters by descent and profession. Neither of these conditions is any longer operative. European troops were first stationed here after the Mutiny, the garrison up to that time having consisted solely of Native troops with details of European artillery.

Descriptive and historical.

Saugor is supposed to be the Sageda of Ptolemy.[1] The name is derived from *sāgar* a sea, and has been given to the town after the large lake, round which it is built. The legend of the lake is that it was constructed by one Lākha Banjārā who was told in a dream that no water would appear in it, until he sacrificed his daughter and a boy to whom she was betrothed. So he walled them up alive in a little shrine in the bed of the lake, which immediately overflowed with water. No Banjārā will drink the waters of the lake, and the people say that two lives have been lost in it every year since it was built, and that on the night of the Diwāli the ghosts of the murdered couple appear sitting in a swing above the lake. The history of Saugor is included

[1] But this seems impossible as until the 18th century it was a village of no importance.

in that of the District. The village of Parkotā, now a quarter of the town, was the first settlement made on the site by the Dāngis. Saugor was selected as the capital by Govind Rao Pandit, the Marāthā representative of the Peshwa, who greatly improved and beautified the town and built the fort. Saugor was three times sacked, twice by Amīr Khān Pindāri, and once by Sindhia after a long siege in 1814. During the Mutiny the fort and town were held by the British garrison, while the whole surrounding country was in the possession of the rebels. The town is very picturesquely situated on spurs of the Vindhyan Hills, and extending round the west, north, and east sides of the lake, the elevation of the hills being about 2,000 feet. The area of the lake is 395 acres, and its banks are adorned by numerous bathing-ghāts and temples, and surrounded by a circular road five miles in length. The lake was formerly much larger, and covered the ground on which the Mint, Town Hall and Gopālganj quarter now stand. The land to the south-east of the Town Hall was formerly a swamp which was drained in 1862-63 at a cost of Rs. 30,000. The lake ran very low in the famine of 1900 and was improved and deepened at a cost of Rs. 7,000. When the water reaches a high level it percolates under the fort into the town. The fort stands on an eminence to the north-west of the lake, and consists of 20 round towers from 20 to 40 feet in height and connected by curtain walls, in the shape of a quadrangle 400 yards long and 150 wide. It has hitherto been used as a magazine and store-house by the garrison, but is now to be given up to the civil department. A large castellated jail was built in 1846 at a cost of Rs. 50,000. The present Deputy Commissioner's Court, a large building situated on a hill overlooking the city, was constructed in 1820 as a residence for the Governor-General's Agent. In the same year, the Mint was built and coinage was carried on here for 10 or 12 years, after which the apparatus was removed to Calcutta. The Mint is now used as a Tahsīli and for the Forest and Public Works offices. A church built in the Gothic style stands in the cantonment. A fine Town Hall was constructed in 1873 at a cost of about Rs. 14,000. The principal Hindu temples are those of Rādha-Kishen, the temple of Brindāwan in Gopālganj, for the maintenance of which the village of Tili is assigned free of revenue, and a temple of Chitragupta, the god of the Kāyasths, which is one of the very few in existence. In the garden of the artillery mess-house are collections of old sculptures built up into small imitation kiosks. A few more sculptures lie in the house used as the District Council Office. There are two mosques, one with high minarets.

Municipal under-takings.

Saugor was created a municipality in 1867. The municipal area is about 4,700 acres, out of which about 1,000 acres are *nazūl* or Government property and the rest belongs to nine villages, which are partially or wholly included within municipal limits. The proprietor of Saugor is Har Prasād Dube, a Sanādhya Brāhman. The municipality is divided into 11 wards, and the committee consists of one elected member for each ward, and five nominated members. The average annual income of the municipality for the decade ending 1901 was Rs. 78,000. Four-fifths of the receipts are derived from octroi. The expenditure nearly balances the income and its main heads are conservancy, roads and education. The town has no water-works, the water-supply being derived from wells and the lake. The civil station and cantonment are situated on undulating ground to the east of the lake, many of the houses being on the tops and sides of hills, and have a pleasant appearance especially in the rains when the ground loses its parched and arid aspect. The average receipts of the cantonment for the decade ending 1901 were Rs. 25,000.

Trade.

Saugor is not a growing town and each census has shown it either stationary or slowly declining. At the time when a customs-line existed for the taxation of salt, Saugor had a large trade in the import of this staple from Rājputāna, and its distribution to the surrounding Districts of the Central Provinces. It also had a considerable trade in sugar, spices and fruits with Mirzāpur. The construction of the railways has deprived it of its importance as a central mart and has largely localised and restricted its trade. The agricultural depression of the District has no doubt also had an effect upon the town, but this last is, it may be hoped, only temporary. It formerly had substantial industries of weaving, brass-working, oil-pressing and the manufacture of gold and silver ornaments, but these have greatly declined in prosperity. The town has no factories, nor do there appear to be any circumstances which should induce the development of industries supported by capital. Notwithstanding this the leading citizens of Saugor are intelligent and proud of their town and of its history and associations, to a degree perhaps not equalled by those of any other in the Province. The most important weekly market is held on Wednesdays, when cattle, grain and other articles are sold. There are also bazars for the sale of thread on Thursdays and Fridays, and for grain on Sundays. A small religious gathering of Muhammadans is held on each Saturday in Jeth (May-June) at the tomb of a Muhammadan saint, situated on a hill three miles from the town, and a similar fair for Hindus is held at Garhpahrā at a distance of seven miles on the four Tuesdays of Asārh (June-July).

Educational and medical institutions.

Saugor has a Government high school affiliated to the Allahābād University, with about 60 pupils in its high school and over 200 in its middle school department. Attached to the high school are two vernacular middle and six primary branch schools with a total of over 700 pupils, these schools being under the direct supervision of the head-master of the high school. Urdū is taught in one of the primary schools and Hindī in the others. There are also seven other schools teaching up to the primary standard, and managed by private persons called *gurūs*. Instruction in these was formerly given on native methods, but they have now adopted the ordinary curriculum, submit to Government inspection and receive a fixed grant. Another private vernacular middle school teaches Marāthī, and one is also managed by the Swedish Mission, both of these receiving Government grants. There are five girls' schools, three of which are Government and two private schools ; one of the Government schools and a private school belonging to the Swedish Mission rank as middle schools. A Hindu Society, the Hit-Sabhā, manages two night schools where elementary instruction is given to adults. The Loretto Convent school teaches European and Eurasian children. The medical institutions comprise the Main and Victoria branch dispensaries, jail and cantonment dispensaries and a police hospital. The main dispensary has accommodation for 50 inpatients, 30 male and 20 female. 200 indoor and 10,000 outdoor patients were treated in the main dispensary in 1903, and 13,000 outdoor patients in the branch dispensary. Saugor has also a veterinary dispensary.

Shahgarh.—A village in the Bandā tahsīl, 43 miles from Saugor on the Cawnpore road, and on the right bank of the Lānch river. Shāhgarh stands at the foot of a lofty range of hills and is surrounded by dense forest. Its area is 3,700 acres and the population in 1901 was 1,650 as against 1,950 in 1891. The village has an old fort. Shāhgarh is supposed to have been founded by the Gonds nearly four centuries ago, and to have formed part of the Mandlā kingdom. In the 17th century the Bundelās took possession of it, and the forests of this tract became a regular shelter of these freebooters. In 1798 Mardan Singh of Garhākotā took Shāhgarh, to which his son Arjun Singh retired on being obliged to cede Garhākotā to Sindhia. In 1857, Arjun Singh's nephew Bakhat Bali rebelled and took possession of his old territories of Garhākotā and Mālthone. Before the Mutiny Bakhat Bali maintained a force of 150 cavalry and 800 infantry. He was defeated and his troops dispersed by Sir Hugh Rose, and soon afterwards he gave himself up, and was sent as a state prisoner to Lahore. His territories were confiscated and divided between Saugor, Damoh and Jhānsi. Shāhgarh was the headquarters of the pargana to which it gave its name, comprising 115 villages with an area of 300 square miles. Considerable deposits of iron ore occur in the vicinity, and iron is smelted by indigenous methods in Shāhgarh and the neighbouring villages. The industry is in a depressed condition. A good soft stone is also found from which cups and mortars are made, and the pottery manufactured here has a local reputation, and is sent all over the District. Shāhgarh has a vernacular middle school for boys, and a girls' school, a police Station-house and a post office. A dispensary, which formerly existed here, has been abolished. There is an encamping ground, and an inspection bungalow has been constructed. Weekly markets are held on Tuesdays and Saturdays. Shāhgarh is held revenue-free by a Marāthā Brāhman for the temple of Mahādeo, which is in the village.

Shahpur.—A village in the Saugor tahsīl, 19 miles from Saugor on the Damoh road. Its area is 4,400 acres and the population in 1901 was 2,400 persons as against 2,500 in 1891. The cotton grown at Shāhpur is considered to be the best in the District. Considerable quantities of sugarcane and vegetables are raised by irrigation by the Kāchhis who reside here. The village has primary schools for boys and girls, a post office and a police outpost. There is an encamping ground. A weekly market is held on Mondays. The village is held in shares by proprietors of different castes.

Singrawan.—A small village in the Bandā tahsīl, 28 miles from Saugor and on the Damoh border. Its area is 1,400 acres, and the population in 1901 was 450 persons. The village is on the Sujlī stream, and a small religious fair is held here in January on Makar Sankrānt at which some 2,000 persons assemble. The fair is held in honour of a distinguished devotee who has resided here for some years.

Sonār.

Sonar [1].—A river in the Central Provinces. The Sonār is the centre of the drainage system of the Vindhyan plateau comprising the Districts of Saugor and Damoh in the Central Provinces, and its course is north to the Jumna. This is the only tract of the Central Provinces whose waters are carried to the rivers of Hindustān. The Sonār rises in the low hills in the south-west of Saugor (23° 22′ N. and 78° 37′ E.), and, flowing in a north-easterly direction through that District and Damoh, joins the Ken river in Bundelkhand, a short distance beyond the boundary of the latter District. Of its total course of 116 miles, the first 112 are within the Central Provinces. The river does not attain to any great breadth, and flows in a deep channel, its bed being usually stony. It is not navigable and no use is made of its waters for irrigation. The valley of the Sonār lying in the south of Saugor and the centre of Damoh is composed of fertile black soil, formed from the detritus of volcanic rock. The principal tributaries of the Sonār are the Dehār joining it at Rehlī, the Gadherī at Garhākotā, the Bewas near Narsinghgarh, the Koprā near Sītānagar, and the Beārma just beyond the Damoh border. Rehlī, Garhākotā, Hattā and Narsinghgarh are the most important places situated on its banks. The Indian Midland Railway (Bīna-Katnī branch) crosses the river between the stations of Patharia and Aslāna.

Surkhi.—A large village in the Saugor tahsīl, 18 miles from Saugor on the Karelī road. Its area is over 5,000 acres, and the population in 1901 was 1,100 as against 1,400 in 1891. It has a police Station-house, primary school and post office. There is an encamping ground, and an inspection bungalow has been erected. A weekly market is held on Thursdays. The proprietor of the village is Balīchand Tiwāri of Dhāna.

Tinsua.—A small village in the Bandā tahsīl, 28 miles north-east of Saugor with an area of 800 acres and a popu-

[1] The article on the Sonār river is a reprint from the draft article for the Imperial Gazetteer.

lation of a hundred odd persons Near Tinsua is a high hill called Tinsmal, with an elevation of 2,139 feet, and on its summit is an old temple with carved stones ascribed by the people to the Chandels. A small fair is held in May on the last day of Baisākh. The tutelary deity of the hill is worshipped as Tinsmāl Bāba, and is believed to take compassion on thirsty travellers and to cause pools of limpid water to appear suddenly among the rocks for their delectation. The village has a fullers'-earth quarry.

Uldan.—A village in the Bandā tahsīl, two miles from Bahrol at the junction of the Dhasān and Bhānder rivers. Its area is 2,400 acres and the population in 1901 was 700 persons. A large religious fair is held here in January on Makar Sankrānt, which lasts for three or four days, and at which some 5,000 to 10,000 persons assemble from Saugor, Damoh and Jhānsi Districts. The fair is due to a local manifestation of Mahādeo, who appeared in a stone, and was recognised only by a Kāchhi who was accustomed daily to pour water on the stone, and was considered by the village as mad. On one occasion, however, a celebrated Mahant came to the village and gave a feast in honour of Mahādeo, and seeing the Kāchhi pouring water on the stone, asked him why he did it. The people said he was mad, but the Kāchhi taking five flowers of the *kachnār* tree (*Bauhinia variegata*) in his hand, changed them into five bottles of water, which he poured into a dry well, with the result that the well immediately overflowed with water. The Kāchhi said 'Let no one put his hand into the well, and it will go on flowing.' But some one must have put his hand in, because the well dried up and has never had any water since. A temple has, however, been constructed and the stone placed in it, and several blind persons and lepers are said to have been healed by it, and barren women to have obtained children. Clothes and vessels are sold at the fair. The proprietor of the village is a Gosain who lives in Saugor and is the Mahant of the Brindāwan temple.

Geographical extent and position.

Vindhya Hills[1].—(Ouindion of Ptolemy), a series of hills separating the Gangetic basin from the Deccan, and forming a well marked chain across the centre of India. The name was formerly used in an indefinite manner to include the Sātpurā hills south of the Nerbudda, but is now restricted to the ranges north of that river. The Vindhyās are not a range of hills in the proper geological sense of the term, that is, possessing a definite axis of elevation or lying along an anticlinal or synclinal ridge. The Vindhyan range to the north of the Nerbudda, and its eastern continuation, the Kaimur, to the north of the Son valley, are merely the southern scarps of the plateau comprising the country known as Mālwa and Bundelkhand. The range has been formed by sub-aerial denudation and is a dividing line left undenuded between different drainage areas. From a geographical point of view, the Vindhyan range may be regarded as extending from Jobat (22° 27′ N. and 74° 35′ E.) in Gujarāt on the west, to Sasseram (24° 57′ N. and 84° 2′ E.) in the south-western corner of Bihār on the east, with a total length of nearly 700 miles. Throughout the whole length of the range, as thus defined, it constitutes the southern escarpment of a plateau. The Rājmahāl hills extending from Sasseram to Rājmahāl, and forming the northern escarpment of the Hazāribāgh highlands, cannot be correctly considered as a part of the Vindhyan range.

Orographical features.

The range, commencing in Gujarāt, crosses the Central India Agency from Jhabua State in the west, and defines the southern boundary of the Saugor and Damoh Districts of the Central Provinces. From here, the Kaimur branch of the range begins and runs through Baghelkhand or Rewah into Bihar. The Kaimur hills rise like a wall to the north of the Son valley, and north of them a succession of short

[1] The article on the Vindhya Hills is a reprint from the draft article for the Imperial Gazetteer.

parallel ridges and deep ravines extends for about 50 miles. At Amarkantak the range touches the Sātpurā hills at the source of the Nerbudda. Westward from the Jubbulpore District the Vindhyan range forms the northern boundary of the valley of that river. Its appearance here is very distinctive, presenting an almost uninterrupted series of headlands with projecting promontories and receding bays like a weather-beaten coast line. In places the Nerbudda washes the base of the rocks for miles, while elsewhere they recede and are seen from the river only as a far-off outline, with the plains of Bhopāl or Indore spread out below them. The rocks are sandstone of a pinkish colour and lie in horizontal slabs, which commonly testify to their origin by curious ripple-marks, plainly formed by the lapping of water on a sandy shore. To the north of this escarpment lies the Bundelkhand or Mālwā plateau, with a length of about 250 miles and a width at its broadest part of about 225. The plateau is undulating and is traversed by small ranges of hills, all of which are considered to belong to the Vindhyan system.

Outlying ranges.

The most northerly of these minor ranges, called the Bindyāchal, cuts across the Jhānsi, Banda, Allahābād, and Mirzāpur Districts of the United Provinces, nowhere rising above 2,000 feet. The range presents the appearance of a series of plateaus, each sloping gently upwards from south to north, and ending abruptly in the steep scarp, which is characteristic of these hills. Many outlying isolated hills are found in these Districts standing out on the plains beyond the furthest scarp. One small hill, called Pabhosā, stands on the left bank of the Jumna, the only rock found in the Doāb. The Bhānrer or Pannā hills form the south-eastern face of the Vindhyan escarpment, and bound the south of the Saugor and Damoh Districts and the north of the Maihar State, in continuation of the Kaimur, thus being a part of the main range. They run from north-west to south-east for about 120 miles. Their highest peak is that of Kalumār, which has an elevation of 2,544 feet. Two other branches of the range lie in Mālwā, starting respectively near Bhilsā and Jhābua with a northerly direction, and bounding the plateau to the east and west.

Elevation and drainage.

The general elevation of the Vindhyan range is from 1,500 to 2,000 feet and it contains a few peaks above 3,000, none of which are of any special importance. The range forms, with the Sātpurās, the watershed of the centre of India, and among others, the Chambal, Betwā, Sonār, Dhasān and Ken rivers have their sources in these hills. The Son and Nerbudda rise at Amarkantak, where the Vindhyan and Sātpurā ranges join. The rivers generally rise near the southern escarpment and flow north and north-east.

Geological formation.

Geologically the range is formed principally of great massive sandstones of varying consistency, alternating with softer flags and shales, the whole formation covering an area 'not greatly inferior to that of England' (Mallet). The range has given its name to the Vindhyan system of Indian geological nomenclature. Over a great part of the Mālwā plateau the sandstone is covered by the overflowing Deccan trap, while from Ganurgarh fort in Bhopāl to near Jobat, the range itself is of basaltic formation, and the last sixty miles to the west from Jobat to near Jambughorā, consist of hills of metamorphic rocks. Economically the Vindhyan rocks are of considerable value, the sandstone being an excellent building material which has been extensively used for centuries; the Budhhist topes of Sānchi and Barhut, the eleventh century temples of Khajuraha, the fifteenth century palaces of Gwalior, and numerous large forts, at all important positions on the plateau, having been constructed of this material. At Nāgode and other places, limestone is found in some quantity, the pretty corraline variety, extracted from the Bāgh cretaceous beds, having been extensively employed in the palaces and tombs at Māndu; and at Pannā in the conglomerate, which underlies the shales, diamonds are met with, though none of any great value have been extracted. Manganese, iron and asbestos are also found in the various parts of the range. The lofty flat-topped hills and bold scarps which are such a marked feature of this range, were early recognised as ideal sites for fortresses, and besides the historical strongholds of Gwalior, Narwar, Chanderi, Mandu, Ajaigarh and Bandogarh, the hills are studded with the ruined castles of marauding Girasia and Bundelā chiefs.

Forests.

The hills are generally covered with a stunted forest growth of the species found in the dry forests of Central India. Teak only occurs in patches and of small size, and the forests are generally noticeable for their poverty of valuable timbers.

Mythological associations.

The term Vindhyā in Sanskrit signifies 'a hunter,' and the range occupies a considerable place in the mythology of India, as the great demarcating line between the Madhya-desha or 'middle land' of the Sanskrit invaders, and the non-Aryan Deccan. The Vindhyās are personified in Sanskrit literature, where they appear as a jealous monarch, the rival of king Himālāya, who called upon the sun to revolve round his throne, as he did round the peak Meru. When the sun refused, the mountain began to rear its head to obstruct that luminary, and to tower above Himālāya and Meru. The gods invoked the aid of Agastya, the spiritual guide of Vindhyā. This sage called upon the Vindhyā mountain to bow down before him, and afford him an easy passage to and from the south. It obeyed and Agastya passed over. But he never returned, and so the mountain remains in its humbled condition, far inferior to the Himālaya, to the present day. Another legend is that when Lakshman, the brother of Rama, was wounded in Ceylon, by the King of the Demons, he wished for the leaves of a plant which grew in the Himālayas to apply them to his wound. Hanumān, the monkey-god, was sent to get it, and not knowing which plant it was, he took up a part of the Himālayas and carried them to Ceylon. He happened to drop a portion of his load on the way, and from this the Vindhyan hills were formed.

Pioneer Press, No. 1492.—1-3-06.